Crimes of State Past and Present

T0316320

War Crimes and acts of genocide are as old as history itself, but particularly during the 20th century. Yet what are war crimes and acts of genocide? And why did it take the world so long to define these crimes and develop legal institutions to bring to justice individuals and nations responsible such crimes? Part of the answer lies in the nature of the major wars fought in the 20th century and in the changing nature of warfare itself.

This study, which begins with a discussion of the history of war crimes and international criminal law, also discusses war crimes committed during the Second World War in the USSR, Yugoslavia, Germany, and efforts to bring the perpetrators to justice. This led to successful postwar efforts to define and outlaw such crimes and, more recently, the creation of two international courts to bring war criminals to justice. This did not prevent the commitment of war crimes and acts of genocide throughout the world, particularly in Asia and Africa. And while efforts to bring war criminals to justice has been enhanced by the work of these courts, the problems associated with civil wars, command responsibility, and other issues have created new challenges for the international legal community in terms of the successful adjudication of such crimes.

This book was based on a special issue of *Nationalities Papers*.

David M. Crowe is a professor of History at Elon University and a Professor of Legal History at Elon University's School of Law. He is President Emeritus of the Association for the Study of Nationalities at Columbia where he has also served as a Visiting Scholar. He has taught at Central European University and has been a Fellow at the Center for Slavic, Eurasia, and East European Center at the University of North Carolina at Chapel Hill. He has also been a member of the Education Committee of the United States Holocaust Memorial Museum in Washington, D.C. and has served as chair of the North Carolina Council on the Holocaust. He has testified before the United States Congress' Commission on Security and Cooperation in Europe and the New York City Council's Subcommittee on Immigration. He currently serves on the Editorial Boards of *Nationalities Papers*, *Ethnopolitics*, and *First World War Studies*.

The Association for the Study of Nationalities
www.nationalities.org

Edited by
Karl Cordell, *University of Plymouth*
Florian Bieber, *University of Kent, Canterbury*
Stefan Wolff, *University of Nottingham*

The books in this series focus on the dynamics and interactions of significant
minority and majority nationalisms in the context of globalisation and their social,
political and economic causes and consequences. Each book is focused on an
important topic drawn from the rigorously peer-reviewed articles published in
Nationalities Papers and *Ethnopolitics*, and includes authoritative theoretical
reflection and empirical analysis by some of the most widely recognized experts in
the world.

Nationalities Papers

Conflict in South-Eastern Europe at the End of the Twentieth Century
A "Scholars' Initiative" assesses some of the controversies
Edited by *Thomas Emmert* and *Charles Ingrao*

Identities, Nations and Politics After Communism
Edited by *Roger E. Kanet*

Crimes of State Past and Present
Government-Sponsored Atrocities and International Legal Responses
Edited by *David M. Crowe*

Ethnopolitics

Gambling on Humanitarian Intervention
Edited by *Timothy W. Crawford* and *Alan J. Kuperman*

Ethnopolitics of Elections
Edited by *Florian Bieber* and *Stefan Wolff*

Internationalized State-building after Violent Conflict
Bosnia Ten Years after Dayton
Edited by *Marc Weller* and *Stefan Wolff*

Governance in Ethnically Mixed Cities
Edited by *Sherrill Stroschein*

Transnationalism in the Balkans
Edited by *Denisa Kostovicova* and *Vesna Bojicic-Dzelilovic*

Cultural Autonomy in Contemporary Europe
Edited by *David J. Smith* and *Karl Cordell*

EU Conflict Management
Edited by *James Hughes*

Crimes of State Past and Present

Government-Sponsored Atrocities and
International Legal Responses

Edited by David M. Crowe

Routledge
Taylor & Francis Group
LONDON AND NEW YORK

First published 2011
by Routledge
2 Park Square, Milton Park, Abingdon, Oxon, OX14 4RN

Simultaneously published in the USA and Canada
by Routledge
711 Third Avenue, New York, NY 10017

Routledge is an imprint of the Taylor & Francis Group, an informa business

First issued in paperback 2011

© 2011 Association for the Study of Nationalities

This book is a reproduction of *Nationalities Papers*, vol. 37, issue 6. The Publisher requests to those authors who may be citing this book to state, also, the bibliographical details of the special issue on which the book was based

Typeset in Times New Roman by Value Chain, India

All rights reserved. No part of this book may be reprinted or reproduced or utilised in any form or by any electronic, mechanical, or other means, now known or hereafter invented, including photocopying and recording, or in any information storage or retrieval system, without permission in writing from the publishers.

British Library Cataloguing in Publication Data
A catalogue record for this book is available from the British Library

ISBN13: 978-0-415-57788-5 (hbk)
ISBN13: 978-0-415-50900-8 (pbk)

CONTENTS

Introduction

David M. Crowe

Some of the most horrific war crimes and acts of genocide took place during the twentieth century. Though such crimes are as old as history itself, they were not defined legally until the nineteenth and twentieth centuries. The term genocide was coined and defined by a brilliant Polish Jewish legal scholar, Raphael Lemkin, who fled Poland during the early days of World War II. Lemkin, who had struggled for years to develop better legal definitions for some of history's worst war crimes, coined and defined genocide in his seminal work, *Axis Rule in Occupied Europe* (1944). He later played a key role in the creation of the 1948 Genocide Convention. This accord, in league with earlier conventions and the legal precedents established during the International Military Tribunal trials in Nürnberg and Tokyo after World War II, paved the way for the gradual emergence of a new body of international criminal and humanitarian laws that helps guide efforts by international judicial bodies such the International Court of Justice and the International Criminal Court to bring perpetrators of various international crimes to justice, whether they be states or individuals.

The essays in this collection bring to life many of the questions and issues surrounding not only some of the worst war crimes and acts of genocide in the twentieth century, but also the broader history of these crimes and legal responses historically. The introductory essay highlights the history of such crimes dating back to antiquity. While one would presume that crimes of war reflect a certain level (or lack thereof) of culture and societal sophistication, some of antiquity's greatest civilizations, whether in the Near East, Asia, or the West, committed horrible atrocities during and after military campaigns. Such practices continued well beyond this era, though there began to be hints, particularly in Europe, of efforts to curb such excesses.

Unfortunately, western powers failed to heed such restrictions when it came to the treatment of the indigenous peoples in the Americas and later Asia and Africa. On the other hand, by the nineteenth century, with the map of Europe almost settled, there were efforts to create a body of international law that tried to regulate the behavior of armies towards prisoners and noncombatants. But, as the twentieth century's two world wars showed, such laws were only as good as the willingness of individual countries to abide by them. It would take the atrocities of World War I, and particularly World War II, to convince the world of the need seriously to bring war criminals to justice. This ultimately led not only to the creation of a new body of international accords that better defined various crimes of war and genocide, but international bodies to adjudicate such crimes.

The nature of some of these crimes is the subject of essays by Michele Frucht Levy and Thomas Earl Porter. Levy's study looks in depth at efforts by Croatia's war time fascist government to mass murder the Serbs, Jews, Roma, and other minorities. Its particular foci are the Ustaša's brutal campaign against the Serbs, and the relationship between the Croatian government, Croatian Catholics, and the Vatican. Thomas Porter's essay discusses the fate of Soviet POWs in German prison camps during World War II. Given the deep racial hatred of the Nazis towards all things Soviet, it is no small wonder that death rates among Soviet captives was the highest among all POWs, whether Axis or Allied, during the war. Porter brings his analysis to life with detailed interviews with Russian survivors of the German camps.

But what about justice for the perpetrators of such crimes? Michael Bryant discusses US and West German efforts to bring to justice the architects and functionaries of Nazi Germany's vast euthanasia program which murdered hundreds of thousands of Germans and others whose only crime was that they were mentally disabled and, as such, a threat to Hitler's efforts to create an Aryan-pure Germany. Each country approached such trials differently. The US used the concept of conspiracy as the legal means to convict alleged criminals of crimes against humanity, while the West Germans used the German law of homicide to gain such convictions.

These trials and the evolving body of international criminal law, unfortunately, did little to still acts of genocide and war crimes globally. While the horrors of World War II and the Cold War's atomic age might have prevented the outbreak of major global wars, this era saw new conflicts, both international and domestic, where numerous crimes of war, crimes against humanity, and genocide took place with little regard for the value of human life or the new body of international standards created to prevent such crimes.

This was certainly the case of the crimes against humanity committed by Cambodia's Khmer Rouge between 1975-1979, and efforts to bring the perpetrators of such crimes to justice in Cambodia. As Wolfgang Form notes, such efforts, taking place as they did several decades after the crimes themselves, was a joint attempt by the international community and successive Cambodian governments to adjudicate such crimes, blending international and domestic law and traditions. This undertaking has tested not only the commitment of the international legal community to support such efforts, but also the political will of the Cambodian people to see justice realized domestically.

The last essay in this collection, William C. Peters' discussion of the question of command responsibility, particularly as it relates to charges of war crimes committed by American forces in various international conflicts since the 1960s, looks at the whole question of the role of superior officers in the commitment of such crimes, and the place, legally speaking, of such responsibility in the American military justice system. The issue, nationally and internationally, of command or superior responsibility, has become particularly important in the current discussion about the treatment of prisoners in US custody after 9/11, and in the various trials before international tribunals today. Consequently, this essay has importance beyond its value domestically to students of American military law.

War Crimes and Genocide in History, and the Evolution of Responsive International Law

David M. Crowe

War crimes and genocide are as old as history itself. So are regulations and laws that protect individuals during time of war, whether they be combatants or civilians. The Chinese philosopher Sun Tzu wrote in the fifth century BCE that it was important to treat "captured soldiers well in order to nurture them [for our use]. This is referred to as 'conquering the enemy and growing stronger.'"[1] Yet several centuries later, Qin Shi Huangdi, China's first emperor, committed horrible atrocities during his military campaigns to unite China.[2] Eric Yong-Joon Lee adds that it should be remembered that the Qin emperor also created that country's "first managed international legal order."[3] But, according to Robert Cryer, it was the West, not Asia, that created the world's first "international criminal law regime."[4] This "regime," R. P. Anand argues, was, in many ways, a form of *"Victor's Justice"* or "ruler's law," since it was forced on Asia and Africa by the West in the nineteenth century.[5]

Wartime atrocities, of course, abound in global history. The Bible is filled with accounts of military crimes against civilians during times of war. The book of Second Kings states that after King Menahem of Israel sacked the town of Tiphsah, "he massacred [its people] and ripped open all of its pregnant women" because it had refused to surrender to him.[6] In fact, as Rabbi Joseph Telushkin has noted,

> ancient documents from Mesopotamia to Egypt abound in joyous references to anni-hilating neighbors—frequently the very same peoples the Bible mentions. For example, in the Amarna letters, the Amorites [Babylonians] were said to be trouble-some foes of the house of Egypt's Pharaohs and deserved annihilation ... Officials writing these letters to [the Pharaoh] promised to bind all the Amorites: "a chain of bronze exceedingly heavy shall shackle their feet ... and we [shall] not leave one among them."[7]

Roman law, which was drawn from the ancient Greeks, usually forbade the wholesale slaughter of captives after a campaign, though Cato the Elder (234–149 BCE), a prominent Roman politician and general, reportedly ended each of his speeches in the Senate with the phrase, *Ceretum censeo delendam esse Carthanginem* (Besides, I think that Carthage must be destroyed).[8] His reference was to the century-old struggle (the Punic Wars) between Rome and Carthage over domination of the western Mediterranean world. But the spirit of Cato's words entered subsequent histories of the Punic Wars. Polybius, for example, claimed that Hannibal encouraged his troops, who were starving, to "eat [the] human flesh" of the local inhabitants as his army made its way from Spain to Italy during the Second Punic War (218–201 BCE).[9]

At the end of the Third Punic War (149–146 BCE), Roman forces totally destroyed Carthage, after Hasdrubal, Carthage's military leader, tortured Roman prisoners-of-war on the walls of the besieged city as Roman troops looked on. Once Carthage fell, the Romans plundered the city and enslaved its remaining population.[10] Two centuries later, the Roman Jewish historian Josephus, who wrote about Jewish rebels who fled to Masada with their families at the end of the Great Jewish Revolt (66–70 CE) to avoid the "miseries" they expected at the hands of the Romans if captured. Later, when it was apparent that the Romans would take Masada, the rebels committed mass suicide to avoid Roman "abuse" of their women and the enslavement of their children.[11]

The collapse of the western Roman Empire in the latter half of the fifth century had a dramatic effect on Europe. What followed were long centuries of decay amid European efforts to reconstitute itself along new nation-building lines. This effort was complicated by the emergence of a dynamic new faith in the eastern Mediterranean world—Islam.[12] It spread quickly after the death of the Prophet Mohammed in 632, and within a century Muslim leaders had created an empire that swept from the Middle East to most of Spain. What followed was a dramatic clash of civilizations that led to some of the worst brutality in medieval history.[13]

By the late tenth century, the once-besieged Byzantine Empire began to retake territories from the Muslims along their eastern borders. Within a century, though, a new Muslim power, the Seljuk Turks, began to challenge Byzantine power in Asia Minor. After successes at the battle of Manzikert in 1071, where Turkish forces captured the emperor, Romanos IV Diogenes, they moved into Asia Minor and played a role in restoring Sunni Muslim control over Jerusalem.[14] Western Europe responded with four major crusades designed to retake the Holy Lands from the Muslims. They pitted the best of Europe militarily against the Islamic world. With the exception of the First Crusade (1095–1099), which succeeded in retaking Jerusalem and a modest amount of territory around it, the Crusades were unsuccessful in achieving the complex goals envisioned by Pope Urban II, who issued the call for the First Crusade in 1095.[15]

What the Crusades did achieve was the introduction of a level of brutality to warfare not seen since Roman times, particularly towards Muslims. Driven by what David Nicolle calls the "sheer [religious] fanaticism" of the Crusaders, these Christian "holy warriors" committed untold atrocities against Muslim civilians. "Torture and mutilation became a feature of the early decades of Crusader warfare in the Middle East."[16] After the battle of Antioch, the Crusaders killed all of the men in the city and sold the women and children into slavery. They also killed all of the Muslims and Jews in Jerusalem because they "saw their God as a punisher" and their victims as infidels. Several myths arose after the First Crusade about Christian cannibalism. One centered on a Norman leader, Tafur, whose troops, according to one medieval writer, "'boiled the adults, placed the children on the spit and would eat them after roasting them'" after taking the city of Ma'arra. Another claimed that "our men would eat not only Turks and Saracens but also dogs.'"[17]

How could such behavior take place in the early part of this so-called age of chivalry? For one thing, this code of honor between knights was just that, "little more than an insurance policy for the fighting upper classes."[18] In fact, in some ways, the age of chivalry, which reached its peak at the height of the Middle Ages, was a reaction both to the violence of early medieval warfare and the Roman Catholic Church's efforts to temper the indiscriminate violence of war through its *Pax Ecclesie* (Peace of God) and *Treuga Dei* (Truce of God) efforts. Different wars dictated different codes of conduct for knights. The *guerre mortelle* (war to the death), meant either killing or enslaving the enemy. *Guerre mortelle* was waged "against Muslims and pagans."[19]

The atrocities committed by Christian knights during the Crusades stunned the Muslim world. They were driven not only by the idea that Muslims practiced a pagan faith but also by images from Byzantine sources that depicted the Muslims as extremely violent.[20] This deep hatred fed other stereotypes that fueled much of the Christian violence against the Muslims during the Crusades.[21]

The brutality of the First Crusade and the sacking of one of Islam's most holy sites, the Haram al-Sharif (Dome of the Rock), "has been etched deeply in the collective memory of Muslims." And when Salah al-Din (Saladin) retook Jerusalem in 1187, he was as magnanimous in victory towards the city's inhabitants as the Crusaders had been violent.[22] This is not to say that Muslim armies could not be just as brutal as their Christian counterparts. After the First Crusade, the Muslims adopted similar practices in some of their campaigns.[23]

Muslim armies operated with their own codes of war. Abu Bakr, Mohammed's father-in-law and successor, laid down a firm set of laws of war for his troops that were about to move into Byzantine territory:

> Stop, o people, that I may give you ten rules for your guidance in the battlefield. Do not commit treachery or deviate from the right path. You must not mutilate dead bodies. Neither kill a child, nor a woman, nor an aged man. Bring no harm to the trees, nor burn them with fire, especially those which are fruitful. Slay not the enemies flock, save for your food. You are likely to pass by people who have devoted their lives to monastic services; leave them alone.[24]

A century later, Islamic scholar Al-Shaybani wrote that soldiers in battle should "not cheat or commit treachery, nor should you mutilate anyone or kill children."[25] Such strictures, of course, did not insure civilized Muslim behavior on the battlefield. According to Javaid Rehman, "certainly wars and other societal conflicts of early Islamic experience by their very nature were destructive and bloody."[26]

Medieval European attitudes towards war were laid out in St. Thomas Aquinas' *Summa Theologiae* [Sum of Theology]. He drew many of his ideas from St. Augustine's early fifth-century classic *City of God*.[27] At a distance, Aquinas argued, war was "always sinful," though he did think there were three rationales for a "just war"—it had to be waged by one who held "supreme authority" in a state, it had to be waged to "avenge wrongs," and it had to "have a rightful intention."[28]

Such ideas did little to still the indiscriminate, inhumane violence of medieval warfare. Yet there were also emerging at this time new ideas about individual rights vis-à-vis those of the state, later an important issue in the development of international law. The *Magna Carta* (1215) gives some hints of this new shift as does Emperor Charles V's *Constitutio Criminalis Carolina* (1530/1532) or the "Carolina of 1532," whose criminal clauses identified a number of acts as severe crimes. In addition, its guidelines for the indiscriminate use of torture for those accused of witchcraft placed restrictions on such practices, thus providing indirect protections for individuals accused of such crimes. Regardless, the torture clause also spurred a dramatic rise in witchcraft trials throughout the empire over the next century[29]

This struggle between sovereign and individual rights continued in the midst of the dramatic political, intellectual, and religious upheavals that swept Europe in the sixteenth and seventeenth centuries. Martin Luther's emphasis on what Richard Marius calls his paradoxical concept of the "priesthood of all believers" vis-à-vis that of the Roman Catholic Church, gives a hint of the vibrant power of the idea of the individual in a spiritual context.[30] This subtle but powerful concept gained credibility over the next two centuries in the midst of the religious, political, social, and economic upheavals that swept Europe in the wake of the Reformation. Just as the Renaissance was the bridge to the Reformation, it could be argued that the Reformation provided a similar pathway to the Enlightenment.

That bridge was particularly strong during the seventeenth century, an era of devastating wars and religious-political upheavals that forever changed the face of Europe. This was certainly the case of the Thirty Years War (1618–1648). According to C. V. Wedgwood, the "individual peasant suffered atrociously during the war."[31] And though questions have been raised about the degree of death and destruction during the Thirty Years War, it remains one of the seminal events in post-Reformation German history.[32] What began as a rather obscure Catholic–Protestant brushup in Prague (the "defenestration of Prague") soon exploded into what would become a series of religious and political wars that ultimately pitted the vast Habsburg Empire against its greatest Continental rival, Bourbon France. Yet what was it about the Thirty Years War that made it such an important series of wars in European history, particularly when it came to development both of the laws of war and precedents for the later evolution of international humanitarian war? Part of the answer lies in the dramatic changes that had taken place in the nature of warfare during the previous century. This was now the era of the "new model army," meaning that the methods and tactics of fighting were now much more destructive and produced even greater suffering on the part of the combatants and civilians trapped in the midst of a battle or campaign.

One of the most innovative developments was the creation of large standing armies made up of local recruits. This was what led King Gustav II Adolf (Gustavus Adolphus; 1594–1632), Sweden's greatest monarch, to issue his *Krigsartiklar* (Articles of War), considered by some to be not only the basis of modern military law, particularly in the US, but also of modern international humanitarian law. A great deal is made of Articles 88–91 and 99–100 since they address questions of individual war crimes and violations of what we now call international humanitarian law. Unfortunately, the humanitarian strictures did little to keep his army from committing crimes against civilians in the German states, though their excesses were far less severe than those of other armies at the time.[33]

It was in this environment that Hugo Grotius wrote his monumental *De jure belli ac pacis libri tres* [On the Law of War and Peace; 1625]. Considered by some to be the father of international law, Grotius' ideas were a bridge between the medieval European laws of war and a new pre-Enlightenment insistence on a more civilized approach to warfare. He wrote, for example, that

> We must also know, that Kings, and those who are invested with a Power equal to that of Kings, have a Right to exact Punishments, not only for Injuries committed against themselves or their Subjects, but likewise, for those which do not peculiarly concern them, but which are, in any Persons whatsoever, grievous Violations of the Law of Nature or Nations . . . it is so much more honourable, to revenge others Peoples Injuries rather than their own.[34]

According to Theodor Meron, a member of the International Criminal Tribunals for the former Yugoslavia and Rwanda, Grotius' statement is "an important precursor to the recognition in modern international law of universal jurisdiction over such matters as genocide, war crimes and crimes against humanity."[35] Gustav II read *De jure belli* and considered it so important that he carried a copy of it with him in the field.[36]

To some extent, it could be argued that Grotius' work on law provided an important intellectual bridge to the development of Enlightenment legal ideas in the German states, particularly when it came to the concepts of *ius naturae et gentium* (natural law and the law of nations). The Enlightenment began with a revolution in scientific thought in the late seventeenth century, with two of the Enlightenment's three principal ideas coming from this "Scientific Revolution." The first was that natural law governs the universe, while the second emphasized that intelligence and scientific inquiry can lead to solutions and fundamental questions. John Locke developed the last important concept of the Enlightenment—that one's environment opened the door to unlimited human improvement. He argued in his *An Essay on Human Understanding* (1689) that human knowledge was acquired through education and life experiences.[37] He stated in his *Two Treatises of Civil Government* (1690), that, over time, governments, which theoretically existed as the collective will of the people, had occasionally abused their power. He proposed that when this abuse happened, people had the right to change it. Government, Locke said, never had any authority over people's lives, liberty, or property without their consent.[38] He added in his *Letter Concerning Toleration* that no one in a civil society should be deprived of their "civil enjoyments" because they belonged to another church or religion. In fact, "neither pagan, nor Mahometan [Mohammedan or Muslim], nor Jew, ought to be excluded from the civil rights of the commonwealth, because of his religion." Locke's ideas reflected the shift in thinking about the rights of individuals vis-à-vis that of governments.[39]

Such ideas would be given full birth during the French revolutions from 1789 to 1799. The French Assemblée nationale constituante's (National Constituent Assembly) *Déclaration des droits de l'Homme et du citroyen* (Declaration of the Rights of Man and Citizen) of 26 August 1789 stated that "men are born and remain free and equal in rights. Social distinctions may be founded only upon the general good." "Law," the *Déclaration* went on, "is the expression of the general will." Furthermore, all citizens were considered equal in the eyes of the law.[40]

The subsequent French and Napoleonic revolutions over the next quarter century had a dramatic impact on all dimensions of human, civil, and legal rights. It is important to remember that Napoleon Bonaparte was first and foremost a creature of the French revolutions of 1789–1799, and his armies carried the ideals of the revolution in their saddlebags throughout Europe. Tragically, these French "wars of the Revolution" also brought untold misery and devastation to much of Europe.[41] Consequently, David A. Bell has called the Napoleonic Wars, which resulted in the deaths of as many as 5,000,000 Europeans, Europe's first "total war."[42] The memory of the devastation and trauma of these wars was such that in 1919 the British government ordered a study of the British decision in 1815 to exile the former French dictator to St. Helena instead of executing him or trying him for his crimes. British Prime Minister David Lloyd George hoped the study would help his government decide how to deal with Kaiser Wilhelm II.[43]

The revolutions in France and the Napoleonic Wars cast a long shadow over Europe. The nineteenth century was a time of great social, political, and economic change and upheaval, caused in part not only by the ideas of the Enlightenment and the French revolutions, but also the Industrial Revolution. It was in this long century of dramatic transformation that a general body of international law evolved that addressed humanitarian issues during war. This was driven by a number of factors. It could be argued, for example, that the Enlightenment and its emphasis on human and civil rights, combined with the emergence of new, powerful nations in Europe, the rise of militant ethnic nationalism, the growing arms races triggered by new, impersonal industrial weapons of war and death, and growing conflicts between Europe's major powers, in Europe, Asia, and Africa, prompted a search for more civilized approaches to the conduct of war.

It should be remembered, though, that such conflicts, and their accompanying atrocities, had already taken place centuries earlier in the Americas when the Spanish, the Portuguese, the British, and the French began their push into the New World. What followed were policies that ravaged native populations. There is considerable controversy about the number of Indians in America on the eve of the European conquests. Some estimate that there were as many as 112.5 million indigenous peoples in the Americas at the end of the fifteenth century, while others suggest no more than 8.4 million. Russell Thornton cites a figure of over 72 million in his *American Holocaust and Survival*, though most scholars agree that trying to determine the exact number of native peoples in the Americas at this time is extremely difficult.[44] Despite these differences, most scholars accept the fact that within a century after the arrival of the Europeans, the native populations in the Americas had declined between 80% and 90%. Ward Churchill has called these declines "a vast genocide," while David E. Stannard sees the large number of indigenous deaths in the Americas as the "worst human holocaust the world has ever witnessed."[45]

Yet was what took place in the Americas between the fifteenth and nineteenth centuries really genocide? While statistics themselves seem to point to genocide, the fact remains that most Indian deaths were the result of interaction with Europeans who unconsciously introduced highly contagious diseases for which the native peoples had no immunity. While there is no question that the native peoples of the Americas suffered from horrible mistreatment at the hands of the European colonizers, most specialists do not think that native deaths were the result of genocide. On the other hand, there were certainly instances of extreme cruelty that gave birth to reports about genocide in Spanish America.

Bartolomé de las Casas, a young Spanish priest who was sickened by the murderous policies of his fellow Spaniards, became the "Defender of the Indians."[46] In 1515, he was granted an audience with King Ferdinand, and told him the tales of horror that he had seen in the New World. In 1542, he wrote *A Short Account of the Destruction of the Indies* to inform Spain's new king, Philip II, of the atrocities being committed by his countrymen in the New World.

> It was upon those gentle lambs . . . that from the very first day they clapped eyes on them the Spanish fell like ravenous wolves up on the fold, or like tigers and savage lions who have not eaten meat for days. The pattern established at the outset has remained unchanged to this day, and the Spaniards still do nothing save tear the natives to shreds, murder them and inflict upon them untold misery, suffering and distress, tormenting, harrying and persecuting them mercilessly.[47]

Las Casas' writings became the basis of the *Leyendra Negra* [Black Legend], the controversial indictment of Spanish policies in the New World linked not only to Spanish mistreatment of Indians but also the introduction of slavery into the Americas. Over time, slavery became an integral part of Spanish, Portuguese, and English colonial societies in the New World. Some even consider slavery, which still exists in the world today, to be genocidal. Michael Ignatieff disagrees, arguing that while slavery was "an infamy," it was first and foremost a system of exploitation and not one disguised "to exterminate the living."[48]

In some ways, of course, it could be argued that certain aspects of the *Leyendra Negra* could also apply to Dutch, English, French, and Portuguese treatment of Indians in the Americas. The same could be said for the fate of Indians in the new American states in the eighteenth and nineteenth centuries. According to anthropologists Wendell H. Oswalt and Sharlotte Neely, American settlers in the West thought that the "Indian impeded progress and was a form of vermin to be exterminated."[49]

Yet it was not exterminationist policies but disease that saw the Indian population in what later became the US drop from over 5 million in 1492 to 250,000 in 1900. Russell Thornton blames this decline on multiple factors all stemming from "European contract and colonization: introduced disease, including alcoholism; warfare and genocide; geographic removal and relocation; and destruction of ways of life."[50] He adds that while war and genocide were not the principal causes for the decline of the Indian population, these factors were extremely important in the destruction of certain tribes. He points to the 1890 massacre at Wounded Knee in South Dakota, which has been immortalized in Dee Brown's *Bury My Heart at Wounded Knee*, as an act of genocide against American Indians.[51]

Sadly, the sense of racial and cultural superiority that drove Europeans and Americans to brutalize Native Americans and African slaves gained new life during European conquests in Asia and Africa in the eighteenth and nineteenth centuries. In China, for example, the British, frustrated by China's refusal to open its ports significantly to more trade with the West, introduced opium as an addictive drug into Chinese ports. This led to two Opium Wars (1839–1842; 1856–1860). The first helped to trigger a civil war, the Taiping Rebellion, which saw 20 million Chinese die between 1850 and 1864. While most died from starvation and disease, there were also numerous atrocities committed by both sides during the rebellion.[52]

Over the next four decades, China's humiliation deepened as various European countries carved out autonomous enclaves along China's vast coastline. This collective sense of national humiliation helped trigger the Boxer Rebellion in 1900, which began with the murder of two German Catholic missionaries in June in Shandong.[53] What followed was the "'Great Powers' scramble for concessions, or the *guafen*, as the Chinese called it, the 'carving up of the melon.'"[54] The Chinese response to these new Western incursions was swift and brutal. Missionaries and Christians, long a symbol of Western culture and humiliation, were now increasingly subjected to a growing crescendo of violence. In late June 1900, hundreds of missionaries and over 18,000 Chinese Catholics were massacred in Taiyuan in Shanxi Province northwest of Shandong. The culminating episode of the rebellion was the siege of the foreign compound in Beijing (Peking) from 20 June to 14 August 1900. Spurred by horrible stories of atrocities against missionaries, Austria-Hungary, France,

Germany, Italy, Russia, the UK, and the US sent over 50,000 troops to lift the siege of Beijing. Once Western forces took control of the capital, they looted the Forbidden City and the city of Beijing of their most valuable treasures. As punishment, the Chinese government was forced to sign the Boxer Protocol a year later, which essentially insured the collapse of a severely weakened Qing dynasty, paving the way for further revolution and chaos.[55]

The opening of Japan in 1853 by the US was a far more peaceful affair, though the tension that rippled through Japanese society ultimately led to a civil war, the *Boshin Sensō* (War of the Year of the Dragon) or Boshin War, between Japan's traditional military caste, the Samurai, and the reform-minded Togukawa Shogunate, which ruled Japan. Though losses in the civil war were not excessive, there were a number of Samurai attacks against foreigners, who were associated with the "moral" corruption of Japan, particularly among Samurai. Over the next decade, the government gradually abolished the Samurai class, which led to another brief civil war, the Satsuma Rebellion. This was the last gasp of the Samurai, but not its warrior code, *Bushidō*, which lasted well into the twentieth century among the officer class of the Imperial Japanese military. *Bushidō* valued honor and loyalty above all else and governed conduct in battle. The Regulations of 1412, for example, "proscribed the wanton taking of life and called for humane, courteous and kind behavior."[56] In the 1930s, the Japanese military began to emphasize "brutal discipline" in its training and a deep hatred of Japan's enemies. *Bushidō* now emphasized loyalty to the emperor above all else. "Compassion for wounded enemies was discouraged, even forbidden ... Victories would no longer be sought within honorable rules of war but by any means, no matter how bestial or deceitful."[57]

India, which had been dominated by Great Britain's East India Company (EIC) since the mid-eighteenth century, also suffered from upheavals in reaction to what some perceived to be inequities of imperialistic domination. In 1857, a rebellion broke out that ultimately brought about a fundamental change in British rule in India, with the British monarchy assuming control over territory formerly under EIC domination. It was also a very violent revolt with wide-scale atrocities committed by the British and the rebellion's disparate Indian forces. Rebels butchered a large number of British captives after the siege of Cawnpore in June, and imprisoned the women and children in the home of the mistress of a British officer, the Bibighar, or "lady's house." Weeks later, all were brutally murdered and their bodies dumped into a nearby well. After the British retook Cawnpore, they searched for the missing women and children. One officer reported that "gore trailed and [was] smeared and spattered through the pillared rooms [of the Bibighar house] 'as if a hundred bullocks had been killed there.'" Another described the nearby well as "a mass of gory confusion."[58]

Afterwards, one British officer pledged that "I have spared many a man in fight ... but I will never spare another. I shall carry this with me in my holsters, and whenever I am inclined for mercy, the sight of it, and the recollection of this house, will be sufficient to incite me to revenge."[59] Many officers made similar pledges. The British retaliated with the cruel torture, humiliation, and execution of suspected Hindu and Muslim rebels. To Indian "onlookers," these "measures constituted a grotesque, nightmarish affirmation of the very fears that had incited them to rebellion in the first place: that the Feringhees [a derisive term for foreigners or Europeans] intended to destroy their caste and their religions."[60]

Similar hatred of the "Feringhees" drove Zulu warriors in distant Africa to butcher hundreds of British soldiers at the end of the battle of Isandlwana (22 January 1879) during the Anglo-Zulu War. "The Zulu, as was their custom, took no prisoners and spared no lives, despite pleas for mercy." Thought the Zulu later claimed that none of the British captives were tortured or mutilated before they were killed, evidence pointed to decapitation and scalping of some of the soldiers. The British were particularly horrified by "the cruel fate of the little drummer boys, who were hung and butchered."[61] But what troubled the British most were the Zulu rituals of disembowelment and multiple spear wounds.[62]

About 15 miles away, another British contingent at Rorke's Drift successfully fought off a Zulu army. After the battle, British troops, aided by a contingent of Black troops from the Natal Native Contingent (NNC), captured about 200 wounded or exhausted Zulus who had fled from the battle site. Driven partly by news of the Zulu atrocities at Isandlwana, and the NNC practice of killing any wounded they captured, the British bayoneted, beat, or speared the captured Zulu to death because they were so short on ammunition.[63] Several weeks later, the British *Annual Register* responded to the defeat at Isandlwana, calling it

> a shock for which this nation was totally unprepared. It was as complete and almost as horrifying a surprise as the Indian Mutiny [of 1857], and nothing had occurred since then to stir public feeling about imperial affairs so profoundly. It was not indeed felt that there was any danger of a province being lost to the Crown, but there were the same fears for the safety of English colonists, an unarmed population exposed to the fury of overwhelming numbers of savage enemies.[64]

But Great Britain was not the only colonial power involved in such tragedies in Africa.

That continent's most infamous colonial ruler was Belgium's King Leopold II, who ruled his Congo Free State as a personal fiefdom from 1885 to 1908 through his Association Internationale Africaine (AIA; International African Association). Set up with the help of his friend, British explorer Henry Morton Stanley, the Belgian monarch saw his holdings in the Congo through totally exploitative eyes—to use whatever means necessary to rob the Congo of its natural resources, whether it be rubber, ivory, or other natural treasures. In his lust for wealth, Leopold had his operatives create a quota system for rubber. His Force République used torture and other methods to exact these quotas from villages. The result was a man-made criminal disaster that ultimately resulted in the deaths of between 3 and 5 million Congolese from

1880 to 1920. While these deaths could not be termed genocidal, they were the direct result of Belgian colonial policies during this period.[65]

The atrocities in the Congo gained widespread attention internationally. Joseph Conrad, who visited the Congo in 1890, and later captured the essence of the brutality there in his *Heart of Darkness*, blamed all of Europe for creating his novel's protagonist, Kurtz, who argued that they must "Exterminate all the Brutes!"[66] Conrad was part of a larger British effort to bring international attention to the tragedy in the Congo. In 1903, Roger Casement, the British Consul to the Congo Free State, spent the second half of that year traveling through Leopold's African kingdom to investigate charges about Belgian treatment of the Congolese population. His detailed report was published by the British government in early 1904. This led to the creation of the Congo Reform Association, which, in league with considerable international pressure, prompted the Belgian parliament to force Leopold II to initiate his own investigation into the atrocities committed in the Congo. In 1908, the Belgian government forced the king to cede control of the Congo Free State to the government, in large part because of "raw, unedited" details in the king's Commission of Inquiry.[67]

Similar atrocities took place in Deutsch-Südwestafrika (DSWA; German Southwest Africa), today Namibia. Germany officially acquired this colony in 1884 and began immediately to exploit its human and natural resources. Most of the good land in DSWA was owned by the Deutsche Kolonialgesellschaft für Südwest-Afrika (German Colonial Society for Southwest Africa), which was funded by a group of German bankers and industrialists. From the outset, imperial efforts in DSWA were a losing proposition, since, according to some experts, the area was "unfit even for a penal colony."[68]

DSWA was inhabited by three tribes, the Ovambo and the Herero, who made up 80% of the population, and the Nama (the Germans called them the Hottentots). From the outset, there were conflicts between German colonists and these tribes because the Germans coveted tribal grazing lands, native cattle, and labor. Over time, the tension between these tribes and the small colony of Germans and other European settlers exploded into civil war. In early 1904, the Herero, led by Samuel Maherero, attacked German settlements throughout DSWA, killing "every German man who could bear arms." On the other hand, they "spared the lives of German missionaries and German women and children, as well as all Europeans of other nationalities." Some of those who were killed during the early days of the rebellion were "tortured in macabre rituals."[69]

German reservists quickly put down the rebellion, though Kaiser Wilhelm II decided to send General Lothar von Trotha to DSWA to "crush the revolt ... by fair means or foul."[70] Von Trotha, who had already gained a "reputation as a man of iron" during the Boxer Rebellion, arrived in DSWA in June and within a few months had driven the Herero to the edge of the Kalahari Desert. What followed would be "a great catastrophe" that some scholars call the first act of genocide in modern history. The Kalahari now became a deadly Herero "prison." Von Trotha ordered his troops to poison wells and erected guard posts along the Hereroland–Kalahari border. Any Herero who tried to enter German territory was shot. Herero who managed to survive were put into slave labor camps where they were forced to work for German businesses. Thomas Pakenham describes incarceration in such camps "a death sentence."[71]

On October 2, von Trotha issued what has been called his *Vernichtungsbefehl* (extermination order) to the Herero trapped in his vast desert prison.

> I, the Great General of the German soldiers, address this letter to the Herero people. The Herero are no longer considered German subjects. They have murdered, stolen, cut off ears and other parts from wounded soldiers, and now refuse to fight on, out of cowardice. I have this to say to them ... the Herero people will have to leave the country. Otherwise I shall force them to do so by means of guns. Within the German boundaries, every Herero, whether found armed or unarmed, with or without cattle, will be shot. I shall not accept any more women or children. I shall drive them back to their people— otherwise I shall order shots to be fired at them.[72]

The day after von Trotha issued his *Vernichtungsbefehl*, Hendrik Witbooi, a Witbooi Nama tribal leader, responded to an earlier request from Samuel Maherero to join in the rebellion against the hated Germans. Over time, the Nama rebellion evolved into a fruitless guerilla war that was almost over by the time that von Trotha left for Germany that fall, claiming full victory in DSWA. Estimates are that less that 20% of DSWA's Herero survived the conflict and about half of the Nama.[73] Isabel V. Hull concludes that Nazi Germany's "culture of violence" was unintentionally the "reification of practices and policies" at play in DSWA and other parts of Europe's colonial world.[74]

European colonial policy in Africa and Asia was driven by a new, potent force of white racism that centered on ideas that Rudyard Kipling called "The White Man's Burden"—the civilization of Kipling's "half devil/half child." Josiah Strong said that the Anglo-Saxon move into Asia and Africa was the prelude to the "*final competition of races for which the Anglo-Saxon is being schooled*." According to Peter Gay, Strong had blended together the Social Darwinism of Herbert Spencer, who coined the term "survival of the fittest," with new nineteenth-century concepts of racism. Carl Peters, the founder of the Gesellschaft für Deutsche Kolonisation (Company for German Colonization), and its German East Africa protectorate,[75] wrote in 1886 that colonial policy "is and remains the ruthless and determined enrichment of one's own people at the expense of other, weaker peoples."[76] Such attitudes, particularly when faced with what appeared to be the "insolence" of resistance by inferior peoples vis-à-vis the policies of superior white Europeans, was often met with various degrees of violence. Sir Leander Starr Jameson, a close friend of Cecil Rhodes, used such violence against South African natives, occasionally burning down their villages and "killing them wholesale." His explanation— "they had been 'impertinent and threatening.'"[77] According to Hull, imperialism itself "*was* war" that bred the "'economy of violence'" that centered not only on various racist and imperialistic ideas but most importantly on the idea of not appearing weak in the face of groups that Europeans saw as inferior.[78]

These colonial war crimes took place in the midst of the evolution of a new body of international humanitarian law that would, in time, come to define specifically crimes of war and genocide. In 1863, Francis Lieber wrote the *Instructions for the Government of the Armies of the United States in the Field* (General Orders No. 100), which declared that "all wanton violence committed against persons in the invaded country . . . all rape, wounding, maiming, or killing of such inhabitants, are prohibited under penalty of death, or such other severe punishment as may seem adequate for the gravity of the offense."[79]

Lieber, a gifted jurist, drew his ideas for Order No. 100 from a series of lectures he gave at Columbia University, *Lectures on the Law and Usages of War*, from 1861 to 1862. The Civil War, the most deadly war in American history, was quite personal for Lieber, since his three sons fought in it, two for the Union and one for the Confederacy. Lieber convinced his close friend, General Henry Wager Halleck, an outstanding legal scholar in his own right, and General-in-Chief of all Union armies from 1862 to 1864, to allow him to write what became Order No. 100.[80] Yet while Lieber's code should certainly be considered a cornerstone document in what Theodor Meron calls the "humanization of the law of war,"[81] he reminds us that Article 30 stated that war and "the law of war imposes many limitations and restrictions on principles of justice, faith, and honor."[82] This is certainly the case with Lieber's advocacy of "no quarter." Though Article 60 states that such acts are "against the usage in modern warfare," Lieber directly and indirectly supported use of "no quarter" in Articles 61, 62, and 66.[83]

The Prussian army adopted the Lieber Code in 1870 and four years later it became the basis of the Brussels Declaration on the Laws and Customs of War.[84] According to Egal Benvenisti, what most "fascinated the Europeans was not the ideas embedded in the [Lieber] Code, as these ideas were borrowed from Europe and had been discussed already by Halleck [*International Law*, 1861]. Rather, what was novel to them was the very system of a code, the possibility of a common text, potentially the basis of a treaty."[85]

The Lieber Code was also used to help develop the Institut de Droit International's 1880 "manual," *The Laws of War on Land*. Both European documents provided the legal framework for the 1899 and 1907 Hague Conventions on the Laws and Customs of War on Land, which established the basic modern concepts that regulate contemporary "laws and customs of war."[86] Of particular importance is the Martens Clause, which was in the introduction to both Hague Conventions. It declared that until "a more complete code of the laws of war is issued . . . populations and belligerents remain under the protection and empire of the principles of international law, as they result from the usages established between civilized nations, from the laws of humanity, and the requirements of the public conscience."[87] In its judgment against the 24 defendants at the Nuremberg International Military Tribunal (IMT) trial in

1946, the court alluded on a number of occasions to German violations of both Hague Conventions. Tragically, the existence of a relatively mature body of international humanitarian law by the mid-twentieth century did little to still the committing of war crimes and acts of genocide in that century's two world wars, certainly the deadliest conflicts in history.

If there was a turning point in all of this, it was World War I. Alan Kramer writes in his *Dynamic of Destruction: Culture and Mass Killing in the First World War*, that this conflict "produced the most extensive cultural devastation and mass killing in Europe since the Thirty Years War."[88] When coupled with the horror of World War II, the period between 1914 and 1945 saw four decades of human brutalization unparalleled in world history. World War I produced many human tragedies that went beyond the mass battlefield deaths on the eastern and western fronts. The Armenian genocide remains the single most horrible crime of that war. But World War I also bred the Russian Civil War which produced frightful civilian deaths. Few, though, were held responsible for these crimes.

While there is no doubt that Allied efforts to try alleged German and Ottoman war criminals was a case of "victor's justice," these efforts, particularly when it came to the question of German war crimes, should, according to Gerd Hankel, also be seen as "einer zivilisatorische Errungenschaft," a civilizing effort that would help prevent war crimes in the future.[89] The Allies addressed the question of war crimes in the Treaty of Versailles with Germany and in the Treaty of Sèvres with Turkey. Article 227 of the Versailles treaty accused Kaiser Wilhelm II of "a supreme offence against international morality and the sanctity of treaties" and created a special tribunal to try him for such crimes. Articles 228–230 required Germany to recognize the right of the Allies to try and sentence other German war criminals "before military tribunals," to turn over those accused of such crimes to these tribunals, and to supply them with all necessary documentation necessary to determine the nature of these crimes and the individuals who committed them. Finally, Article 231, the "war guilt" clause, forced Germany to accept responsibility for itself and its allies for "causing all of the loss and damage to which the Allies and Associated Governments and their nationals have been subjected as a consequence of the war."[90]

Allied outrage centered principally on the 6,500 civilian deaths and widespread property destruction caused by the German invasion of Belgium and France during the first year of the war, though each of the Allied nations would also point to later German war crimes.[91] Initially, the Allies hoped to extradite almost 1,600 alleged German war criminals for trial, but reduced the list to 862. It included the names of some of Germany's most prominent military and political leaders such as Feldmarschall Paul von Hindenberg, Generalquartiermeister Erich Ludendorff, and former Kanzler (chancellor) Theobald von Bethmann Hollweg. Conflicts between the British, French, and Belgians over the scope of the trials, coupled with strident German opposition to them, led to a compromise—the Germans would investigate and try their own war criminals before the Reichsgericht (Supreme Court) in

Leipzig. In 1921/1922, the Leipzig court heard 17 cases, convicted 10 defendants, and acquitted 7 of those accused of war crimes. While the British were satisfied with the outcome of the trials, the French and the Belgians were outraged and initiated their own national trials over the next few years. By 1924, French courts convicted over 1,200 Germans *in absentia* of war crimes, while the Reichsgericht continued its work, investigating over 1,700 cases between 1921 and 1927. The principal goal of the German court was "to exonerate" those Germans accused of war crimes.[92]

Gerd Hankel has concluded that the Leipzig trials helped spur extremist violence in Germany after the war, and left the impression, at least legally and morally, that war crimes would not be effectively dealt with in German courts. Hankel thinks this helped strengthen the legal and moral basis for Germany's barbarous conduct during World War II. John Horne and Alan Kramer also see the Leipzig trials as a failure, while Jürgen Matthäus notes that those convicted were viewed in Germany as war heroes, which "contributed as much to the prevailing German unwillingness to confront crimes committed during the Nazi era as did the continuity of German elites, including officers and jurists." As a result, it took the total conquest and occupation of Germany (and Japan) to create viable war crimes tribunals after World War II.[93]

The war crimes committed by the Germans during World War I paled compared to those committed by the Ottomans against the Armenians during this conflict. A subject of continuing debate, the basics of the Armenian tragedy are well known. According to Turkish scholar Taner Akçam, in the spring of 1915, the governing Committee of Union and Progress (CUP; İttihat ve Terakki Cemiyeti), made the decision to "deport" the country's Armenian population and rid it of a potential stumbling block to creating a united post-war Turkey.[94] Tension between the Ottoman Turks and its Christian Armenian population was longstanding. In the midst of the Turkish massacre of 20,000–300,000 Armenians in 1894–1896, the *New York Times* described the killings as "another Armenian Holocaust," possibly the first use of this term.[95] As many as 20,000 Armenians were murdered in a second wave of massacres in Cicilia in 1909.[96]

The war crimes that began six years later took place in the midst of growing Ottoman setbacks during the war. The CUP viewed the Armenians as a dangerous fifth column. What followed were deportations in name only. The CUP's Special Organization (SO) units oversaw most of the deportations and mass murders. Using the war to shield its actions, the government ordered the roundup and deportation of "population clusters on suspicion of espionage, treason, and military necessity."[97] SO killing squads or *chetes*, in league with military and police units, carried out what became death marches from Armenian communities throughout Turkey.[98] Death came in many forms—starvation, shootings, beatings, rape. Estimates are that 800,000 to 1 million Armenians died in 1915, with total figures for the 1915–1918 period ranging from 1 to 1.5 million.[99]

The international reaction to the deportation and massacres of the Armenians was harsh and swift. On 24 May 1915, Britain, France, and Russia released a memo that criticized the massacres as a "crime against humanity and civilization." They also warned Turkey that it would hold the officials who played a role in the massacres "personally responsible" for them.[100] At first, it seemed as though the Turkey would pay dearly after the war not only for its role on the losing side but also because of the Armenian tragedy. Article 88 of the Treaty of Sèvres (10 August 1920) between the Entente and Turkey stipulated that "Turkey, in accordance with the action already taken by the Allied Powers, hereby recognizes Armenia as a free and independent state."[101] Unfortunately, the realization of Armenian independence fell prey to the civil war that erupted in the midst of Turkish efforts to resist the Allied division of the Ottoman Empire. By late 1921, those parts of Armenia not under Turkish control were taken over by Bolshevik Russia and later integrated into a new Transcaucasian SFSR.[102]

The Allies compounded this tragedy by failing to bring to justice those Turks responsible for the mass murder of Armenians during World War I. During the early stages of the Paris Peace Conference, the Allies created the Commission of Responsibilities and Sanctions (CRS), which, through its First Subcommission or Committee of Fifteen, investigated, among other things, "offenses, 'barbarous and illegitimate methods of warfare,'" which included "'offenses against the laws and customs of war, and the principles of humanity.'" In March 1919, the CRS issued several reports listing more specific crimes against civilian populations, with specific references to the Turks' "barbarous or illegitimate methods in violation ... of the elementary laws of humanity." The report went on to say that "all persons belonging to enemy countries ... who have been guilty of offenses against the customs and laws of war or laws of humanity are liable to criminal prosecution."[103]

Other articles stipulated that Turkey had to recognize "the injustice of the law of 1917 in relation to Abandoned Properties," and to restore the homes and businesses of those forced to flee them "by fear of massacre or any other form of pressure" since 1 January 1914. Articles 226–230 required Turkey to recognize the right of the Allies to bring to trial before military tribunals individuals who committed violations of the "laws and customs of war," and turn over individuals as well as evidence about "the massacres committed on Turkish territory since August 1, 1914."[104]

In reality, Allied politics and the civil war in Turkey effectively neutralized efforts to bring the perpetrators of the Armenian genocide to justice. In early 1919, Turkish officials, prodded by Allied occupation authorities in Istanbul, began to arrest prominent Turkish politicians and military figures, with the idea that they would be investigated and tried by Turkish courts martial for their involvement in the Armenian massacres. Though these trials did convict some Turks of war crimes, the British, convinced that the Turks were dragging their feet on the matter, seized 67 of the accused and deported them to Malta, where they ultimately planned to try them, along with 51 other Turkish detainees. Politics, the uncooperativeness of Turkish authorities, and, most importantly, the lack of adequate evidence to charge not only the 118 Turkish prisoners on Malta plus another 1,000 Turks accused of roles in the massacres, sunk British efforts before they even started. In the end, "retributive justice gave way to the expediency of political accommodation."[105] On 23 October 1921, the British signed an accord with the new government of Mustafa Kemal that provided for an even exchange of British POWs for those Turkish prisoners on Malta who had somehow managed not to escape British custody. Thus ended Allied efforts to bring to justice those responsible for the mass murder of Armenians during World War I.[106] Telford Taylor, the chief American prosecutor at the Nuremberg trials, said that the best that could be said of Allied efforts to prosecute war criminals after World War I was that "the mountain labored and brought forth a mouse."[107]

The Allied failure adequately to deal with war crimes did not stop them from indirectly linking the Versailles settlement with a larger international disarmament initiative. The Covenant of the League of Nations, which pledged that its signatory powers would not "resort to war" to resolve international conflicts, also created a Permanent Court of International Justice to settle disputes.[108] This, in league with the Kellogg–Briand Pact of 1928, which outlawed war as a means of settling international disputes and pledged the signatory states to use peaceful means to resolve conflicts, "initiated a new approach ... with regard to the illegality of the use of force in international relations."[109] Yet the failure of the League of Nations, or more precisely, its great power members, to stand up to aggression severely crippled international efforts to make the Kellogg–Briand Pact anything more than an empty gesture.

These efforts did not stop war crimes and acts of genocide from being committed in the 1930s. Some scholars, for example, consider the famine in the Ukraine in 1932/ 1933 a genocide. Robert Conquest calls it a "terror famine" that centered on not only policies that led to the death of millions of Ukrainians but also an "attack on all Ukrainian cultural and intellectual centers and leaders, and on the Ukrainian churches."[110] The *Holodomor* (Ukrainian—death by starvation), as it is known to Ukrainians, was caused by Joseph Stalin's efforts to collectivize Soviet agriculture and became, according to Nikita Khrushchev, a time of "misery and brutality."[111] While it is questionable whether the 4–5 million Ukrainians who died were victims of genocide,[112] they were, as Bohdan Krawchenko has noted, "not merely incidental victims of the Stalinist terror that gripped the entire Soviet Union."[113] Regardless of the nature of the crime, Orest Subtelny says that Ukrainians consider this tragedy on the same plane as "the Holocaust was to the Jews and the Massacres of 1915 for the Armenians."[114] While some would question that comparison, George Liber considers the *Holodomor* "the most extensive state application of violence against its own civilians prior to the outbreak of the Second World War."[115]

The nature of the deaths in Ukraine contrasted significantly with those in Nazi Germany. But is should also be remembered that the first major war crimes of the World War II era took place not in Germany but in China, which was invaded by Japan in 1937. The Tokyo International Military Tribunal Trial estimated that the Japanese butchered over 200,000 Chinese civilians and POWs in the first six weeks of the occupation of Nanjing (Nanking), the nationalist capital, in 1937.[116]

Iris Chang claims that the Japanese killed 260,000–350,000 in Nanjing, while Peter Li estimates that they killed another 300,000 civilians en route to Nanjing.[117] R. J. Rummel thinks that over 19 million Chinese died during World War II. He suggests that almost 4 million Chinese "likely were killed in cold blood by the Japanese."[118] There was also widespread Japanese torture of civilians and POWs, biological warfare experiments, use of chemical weapons, mass rape, and the use of slave "Comfort Women" in Japanese military brothels. And at the end of the war, retreating Japanese troops butchered 100,000 Filipinos in what is known as the Manila Massacre. What took place in China and other parts of Japanese-occupied Asia between 1937 and 1945 made the whole question of war crimes and crimes against humanity truly a global tragedy during World War II.[119]

The question of war crimes and their prosecution became an integral part of Allied thinking during World War II. As Michele Levy, Thomas Porter, and Michael Bryant have noted in their essays in this collection, these crimes were far reaching and, in some instances, unique to modern warfare. The same could be said for post-World War II justice. Germany and Japan were warned time and again that they would be held responsible for such atrocities. The Allies were determined not to repeat the mistakes of World War I. As early as the fall of 1941, Winston Churchill and Franklin Roosevelt warned the Axis that one of the principal tasks of the Allies at war's end would be the prosecution of war criminals. In early 1942, the Allies created an Inter-Allied Commission on the Punishment of War Crimes and issued the Declaration of St. James, which stated that the Allied Powers opposed retribution "by acts of vengeance on the part of the general public" and stated that

> in order to satisfy the sense of justice of the civilized world required...Nine Powers place among their principal war aims the punishment, through the channel of organized justice, of those guilty of or responsible for these crimes, whether they have ordered them, perpetuated them or participated in them, [and] resolve to see to it in a spirit of international solidarity that (a) those guilty or responsible, whatever their nationalities, are sought out, handed over to justice and judged, (b) that the sentences produced are carried out.[120]

In October 1943, the Allies created the United Nations' War Crimes Commission (UNWCC) to gather materials and investigate possible war crimes. Its work paved the way for the post-war trials in Europe and Asia. Stalin refused to join the UNWCC, fearing Allied involvement in Soviet internal affairs, and instead created the Chrezvychainaia Gosudarstvennaaia Kommissiia (ChGK; Extraordinary State Commission for Ascertaining and Investigating Atrocities Perpetrated by the German Fascist Invaders and their Accomplices) to investigate war crimes in Soviet territory.[121]

The war in Europe officially ended on 7 May 1945, followed by Japan's capitulation on 14 August 1945. Six days earlier, the United States, Great Britain, France, and the Soviet Union put the final touches on the charter for the International Military Tribunal (IMT) as part of the London Agreement. The charter gave the IMT the right to try individuals for three crimes plus conspiracy to commit such crimes:

Crimes Against Peace: namely, planning, preparation, initiation, or waging of war of aggression, or a war in violation of international treaties, agreements or assurances, or participation in a common plan or conspiracy for the accomplishment of any of the foregoing.

War Crimes: namely, violations of the laws or customs of war. Such violations shall include, but not be limited to, murder, ill-treatment or deportation to slave labor or for any other purpose of civilian population of or in occupied territory, murder of or ill-treatment of prisoners of war or persons on the seas, killing of hostages, plunder of public or private property, wanton destruction of cities, towns or villages, or devastation not justified by military necessity.

Crimes Against Humanity: namely, murder, extermination, enslavement, deportation, and other inhumane acts committed against any civilian population, before or during the war; or persecution on political, racial or religious grounds in execution of or in connection with any crime within the jurisdiction of the Tribunal, whether or not in violation of domestic law of the country where perpetrated.

Leaders, organizers, instigators and accomplices participating in the formulation or execution of a common plan or conspiracy to commit any of the foregoing crimes are responsible for all acts performed by any persons in execution of such plan.[122]

The charter guaranteed that all of the defendants would get a fair trial based on rules agreed upon before the IMT trial began.

The IMT trial began on 18 October 1945 in Nuremberg, Germany, with the indictment of 24 Nazi war criminals. When the trial began, there were only 22 defendants in the dock. Martin Bormann was to be tried *in absentia*, while Gustav Krupp was declared too ill to stand trial. Robert H. Jackson, the US chief prosecutor, set the tone for the trial before it began when he stated that "you must put no man on trial before anything that is called a court ... under the forms of judicial proceedings if you are not willing to see him freed if not proven guilty."[123]

The accused were indicted for one or more of the crimes in the IMT charter. Count one, the charge of a "common plan for conspiracy," meant that membership in a number of organizations or groups deemed criminal by the court—the leadership of the Nazi Party, the SS, the SD, and the Gestapo—could, depending on the evidence, lead to the prosecution of individual members of these organizations. The charge of crimes against humanity was the most innovative of the charges, and most directly related to Holocaust deaths. Almost all of the IMT defendants were accused of this crime, and only two were acquitted of it.

In his opening statement to the court, Judge Jackson said that

The privilege of opening the first trial in history for crimes against the peace of the world imposes a grave responsibility. The wrongs we seek to condemn and punish have been so calculated, so malignant and so devastating, that civilization cannot tolerate their being ignored because it cannot survive their being repeated. That four great nations, flushed with victory and stung by injury stay the hand of vengeance and voluntarily submit their captive enemies to the judgement of the law is one of the most significant tributes that Power ever has paid to Reason.[124]

Nuremberg IMT Trial Defendants:

Hermann Göring (1893–1946). Reichsmarschall. Headed Luftwaffe, Four Year Plan. *Death*. Committed suicide before execution.

Fritz Sauckel (1894–1946). General Plenipotentiary for Labor Deployment. *Death*.

Alfred Jodl (1890–1946). Chief of the *Wehrmacht* Command Staff. *Death*.

Joachim von Ribbentrop (1893–1946). Foreign Minister. *Death*.

Wilhelm Keitel (1882–1946). Head of OKW (*Wehrmacht* High Command). *Death*.

Ernst Kaltenbrunner (1903–1946). Headed RSHA, Security Police, SD. *Death*.

Alfred Rosenberg (1893–1946). Head Party Foreign Office; Reichminister Ostland. *Death*.

Hans Frank (1900–1946). Governor General, General Government. *Death*.

Wilhelm Frick (1877–1946). Headed Interior Ministry. Reich Protector Bohemia and Moravia. *Death*.

Julius Streicher (1885–1946). Gauleiter of Franconia. Editor, *Der Stürmer*. *Death*.

Arthur Seyss-Inquart (1892–1946). Reich Governor, Austria. Reich Commissioner, Netherlands. *Death*.

Martin Bormann (1900–1945). Headed Reich Chancellery. Tried *in absentia*. *Death*.

Rudolf Hess (1894–1987). Deputy Party leader. Head of Party Chancellery. *Life*.

Walther Funk (1890–1960). Reich Economics Minister. *Life*.

Erich Raeder (1876–1960). Supreme Navy Commander to 1943. *Life*.

Baldur von Schirach (1907–1974). Youth Führer. Gauleiter and Reich Governor, Vienna. *20 years*.

Albert Speer (1905–1981). Reich Minister, Armaments and Munitions. *20 years*.

Konstantin von Neurath (1873–1956). Foreign Minister to 1938. *15 years*.

Karl Dönitz (1891–1980). Supreme Navy Commander. President of Germany, 1945. *10 years*.

Franz von Papen (1879–1969). Vice Chancellor. Ambassador Austria, Turkey. *Acquitted*.

Hjalmar Schacht (1877–1970). Headed Reichsbank. Economics Minister. Plenipotentiary for War Economy. *Acquitted*.

Hans Fritsche (1900–1953). Headed Radio division, Propaganda Ministry. *Acquitted*.

Robert Ley (1890–1945). Head of German Labor Front. *Committed suicide*.

Gustav Krupp (1870–1950). Military Economy Führer. *Not tried because of ill health*.[125]

All of the defendants pleaded not guilty at the beginning of the trial. Over the next ten and half months, the court heard and accepted 200 witnesses, 300,000 affidavits, and 3,000 documents, producing a trial record of 15,000 pages.[126]

The trial ended in late August 1946. The court reconvened on 30 September, and announced its sentences the following day. General Ion T. Nikitchenko, the Soviet judge, cast the only dissenting vote. He wanted to condemn all of the defendants to death and find all Nazi organizations criminal. In the end, the court only found four of the indicted organizations and groups to be criminal—the SS, the SD, the

Gestapo, and the Nazi Party leadership. This meant that it was a crime to belong to any of these groups, and that such membership could result in future prosecution. Exceptions were made for anyone below the rank of Ortsgruppenleiter (local group leader), staff members who were not office chiefs, and those who were not members of the Nazi Party leadership after the outbreak of World War II.[127]

The IMT proceedings at Nuremberg were the first and, legally speaking, the most important of a series of war crimes trials at Nuremberg and elsewhere in Europe that continued for years after the war. As Michael Bryant has noted, the trials in the American, British, and French zones in Germany operated under the jurisdiction of Allied Control Council Law No. 10, which gave them the right to investigate and try individuals "suspected of having committed a crime, including those charged with a crime by one of the United Nations."[128] These courts in turn reconfirmed the four basic IMT charges, and added that the charge of "crimes against humanity" could be used even if the crime was committed before the outbreak of World War II. Overall, the Americans, British, and French convicted more than 5,000 Germans of war crimes between 1945 and 1949. Over 800 were given the death penalty, though only about 500 were actually executed.[129]

A world away in Japan, the Allies conducted a far lengthier war crimes trial, the Tokyo IMT Trial (officially, the International Military Tribunal for the Far East). Between 3 May 1946 and 12 November 1948, 11 nations tried 28 major Japanese war criminals. The Tokyo tribunal operated under a brief Nuremberg-style "charter" that laid out the basic legal guidelines used to conduct the proceedings. The tribunal consisted of 11 judges from each of the countries that had fought the Japanese. The Tokyo charter gave General Douglas MacArthur, the Supreme Commander for Allied Powers, the right to review the court's decisions and reduce sentences. The defendants were accused of the four major war crimes cited in the Nuremberg IMT charter. Seven of the defendants were sentenced to death and 16 received life imprisonment. Others received lesser terms. Those who were condemned to death were hanged at Sugano Prison on 23 December 1948.[130]

General Kenji Doihara (1883–1948). Commander, Kwantug Army intelligence agency (1931–); mayor of Mukden; commander-in-chief Eastern Army (1943); commander-in-chief, Seventh Area Army, Singapore (1944–1945)—in charge of POWs and labor camps.

Baron Kōki Hirota (1878–1948). Foreign minister (1933–1938); prime minister (1936–1937).

General Seishirō Itagaki (1885–1948). Chief of staff, Kwantung Army; minister of war (1938–1939); chief of staff of the Army in China (1939); commander of Seventh Area Army, Singapore (1945).

General Heitarō Kimura (1888–1948). Vice minister of war (1941–1944; commander, Burma Expeditionary Force (1944). Used POWs to build Burma–Siam railway.

General Iwane Matsui (1878–1948). Commander-in-chief, all Japanese forces in China (1937–1938); advisor, Cabinet Advisory Council (1938–1940).

General Akira Mutō (1883–1948). Military Affairs Bureau (1935–1936); Army Headquarters in China (1937–); commander-in-chief, Sumatra (1943); chief of staff, Philippines Expeditionary Force Army Area (1944).

General Hideki Tōjō (1884–1948). Chief of staff, Kwantung Army (1937); minister of war (1940–1941); prime minister (1941–1944).[131]

Like the IMT trial in Germany, the Tokyo proceedings were criticized as a mere case of "victor's justice." One of the Tokyo court's judges, Indian jurist Radhabinod Pal, voted to exonerate all of the defendants because of what he considered serious jurisdictional and legal flaws in the proceedings. He joined other critics of the Tokyo trial, who pointed to earlier European colonial abuses, the firebombing of Japanese cities, and the American decision to drop atomic bombs on Hiroshima and Nagasaki as examples of the legal imbalance of such proceedings. If the Japanese were to be held accountable for their war crimes, should not the Western powers face similar judicial reviews for their "abuses"?[132]

Just as they had in Europe, the various Allied powers and the Australians, the Chinese (both nationalists and communists), the Filipinos, and other countries conducted over 2,000 war crimes trials between 1945 and 1956.[133] Over time, though, major international efforts to bring war criminals to justice fell prey to the vicissitudes of the Cold War and the political whims of the various victorious powers. In the Soviet bloc, for example, what began as legitimate Western-style trials were soon replaced by "show trials" that became more political theater than legitimate efforts to bring Nazi war criminals to justice.[134]

One legal proceeding that gained considerable international attention was the trial of Adolf Eichmann in Israel in 1961/1962. Eichmann, one of the architects of Nazi Germany's Final Solution, the program to mass murder the Jews of Europe between 1941 and 1945, was charged with 15 counts of crimes against the Jewish people, crimes against humanity, war crimes, and membership in a hostile organization. Though he pleaded innocent to all charges, he was convicted of each one and hanged in 1962. John C. Watkins Jr. and John Paul Weber consider the Eichmann trial "a milestone in international criminal justice" because it "gave rise to disputed principles of international criminal law and jurisdiction and the duty devolving upon surviving victims of the Holocaust to personally experience justice in some small but significant way."[135]

The impact of these international proceedings and the crimes committed by the accused had a considerable effect on international law. In 1948, the UN adopted its Convention on the Prevention and Punishment of the Crime of Genocide, a term coined during the war by Raphael Lemkin. It not only outlawed genocide but defined it broadly to include any act designed "to destroy, in whole or part, a national ethnical, racial, or religious group." Countries that signed the Genocide Convention agreed to enact legislation to punish such crimes.[136] And while the lessons of World War II and the Holocaust certainly seemed to have affected international law and legislation concerning genocide and various war crimes, they had little practical impact on the violation of these international statutes, at least until the end of the Cold War. What is tragically unique about many of the genocidal and war crime deaths in the second half of the twentieth century is that they took place in the midst of civil wars and other national and international upheavals.

This is certainly the case in China. R. J. Rummel calls the twentieth century "China's Bloody Century." From the time that the communists took power in 1949, Rummel claims that the "Chinese Communist Party (CCP) has probably killed 35,236,000 of its own subjects."[137] Most of these victims died as a result of failed economic and political policies. He adds that as many as 150,000 Tibetans died as a result of these policies. During the same period, Rummel charges, the Chinese authorities destroyed 80% of the country's Tibetan monasteries and burned 60% of their historical and religious literature. And by the late 1970s, he argues, "10 percent of all Tibetans ha[d] been imprisoned."[138]

The Dalai Lama, Tibet's spiritual leader and the head of the Government of Tibet in Exile, has condemned these policies, claiming what he calls "China's 'rule of terror' . . . an act of 'cultural genocide.'"[139] In 1996, a study released by his government-in-exile claimed that "over 1.2 million Tibetans have died as a direct result of the Chinese invasion and occupations of Tibet." It also asserts that between 1959 and 1976, the Chinese authorities closed 6,251 monasteries, tortured and murdered over 110,000 monks and nuns, and "forcibly disrobed another 250,000 monks and nuns." In 2008 and again in 2009, the Dalai Lama condemned these policies, claiming that while some scholars question the accuracy of such high figures, there is no question that the Tibetan people have suffered great losses under Chinese rule.[140]

The Chinese authorities, of course, will have none of this. In 1989, the Chinese government published *100 Questions about Tibet* that tried to respond to such charges. It denied charges of abuse and significant deaths, and claimed that the Tibetan population actually grew over a half million in 1953.[141] In 2000, China published a new study, *China's Tibet*, to celebrate the 40th anniversary of the liberation of Tibet from what it called degrading servitude. In 2009, the Tibetan parliament designated 28 March as Serf Emancipation Day to celebrate the end of serfdom in 1959. An article in the 22 January 2009 issue of *China Daily* noted that Tibet's population had grown from 1.29 million in 1959 to 2.84 million in 2007, while per capita income had risen from 142 yuan to 12,109 yuan during the same period.[142] And, according to *China's Tibet*,

> Tibetan Buddhism has been practiced in Tibet for some 1,000 years. Out of sincere respect for the Tibetans' religious beliefs, the Central Government [in Beijing] has invested hundreds of millions of yuan in repairing monasteries. The Central Government respects the reincarnation system of the Living Buddhas, and guarantees that the Tibetan people enjoy full freedom of religious belief.[143]

26

The troubles in Tibet mirrored similar problems in other parts of Asia after World War II. A CIA-sponsored military coup in Indonesia in 1965 toppled the dictatorship of Sukarno. He was succeeded by Suharto, who initiated an anti-communist purge that resulted in the deaths of 300,000 to 1 million Indonesians. In 1975, East Timor or (Timor-Leste) declared its independence from Portugal. Indonesia, with the backing of the US and Australia, occupied East Timor, arguing that the Timorese FRETILIN party was communist. What followed was a violent civil war that resulted in the deaths of between 60,000 and 200,000 Timorese from 1975 to 1999. A special 2006 report, *The Profile of Human Rights Violations in Timor-Leste, 1974–1999*, estimated the number of "conflict-related deaths during this period to be 102,800 $(+/-12,000)$."[144]

Similar tragedies took place in Korea, Vietnam, Cambodia, and Laos between 1950 and 1979. In many ways, Southeast Asia became the principal battleground of the Cold War. It was also the scene of some of the early post-World War II era's worst atrocities. During the Korean War, for example, the Chinese and the North Koreans adopted a number of Soviet methods of torture and used them on American POWs. The Chinese chose to avoid using "scarring tortures" since they wanted to film the "confessions" of POWs as part of their "international propaganda" campaign. Regardless, their methods were harsh and brutal. The North Koreans used methods of abuse and torture reminiscent of those used by the Germans against Soviet POWs and Jewish slave laborers during World War II. Once peace talks began in 1951, the Chinese took control of all POWs, and found new, less physically apparent ways to torture their prisoners. One of the cruelest methods of torture was "water boarding."[145] A 1954 US Senate investigation into Korean war atrocities concluded that the North Koreans and the Chinese had committed numerous war crimes and crimes against humanity, all violations of "virtually every provision of the Geneva Convention governing the treatment of war prisoners."[146] As William Peters has pointed out in his essay, a number of war crimes were committed during America's 12-year war in Vietnam. And, according to Wolfgang Form's study on the crimes against humanity tribunal in Cambodia, US involvement in Vietnam had an indirect yet tragic ripple effect on the Khmer Rouge atrocities.

Similar crimes took place in Africa and continue to haunt that continent. Many of these deaths were caused by violent tribal conflicts that erupted into civil war. Estimates are that over 2 million Ugandans have been murdered, imprisoned, injured, or forced into exile since 1962. Human Rights Watch estimated in 2005 that 1.3 million civilians in northern Uganda were living in "government-controlled displaced camps." One former UN official said in 2006 that northern Uganda was "the worst place on earth to be a child today."[147] The reason is that over the past two decades, 20,000–25,000 Ugandan children have been abducted by the terrorist-guerilla Lord's Resistance Army, described by Christopher Hitchens as "a kind of Christian Khmer Rouge."[148] Equally tragic has been the genocide in Rwanda, which took place as part of an ongoing conflict between the country's principal ethnic groups, the Hutu, the Tutsi, and the Twa. Tribal violence was an early part of post-World

War II Rwandan history and finally spun out of control after the assassination of President Habyarimana, the Hutu dictator, on 6 April 1994. His killers were possibly members of the Rwandan Patriotic Front (RPF), a Tutsi refugee group that was fearful that Habyarimana would not honor the Arusha Accords, a 1993 peace treaty that would have given the RPF territory in northern Rwanda. What followed was a carefully planned genocidal campaign waged by a new Hutu government against the Tutsi that caused the deaths of 500,000 to 1 million Rwandans over a three-month period. The RPF responded with its own massacres and quickly occupied eastern Rwanda. The UN created an international force, UNAMIR II, to deal with the crisis, though it arrived too late to stop the genocide. French forces establish a *"Zone Tourgeoise"* to halt further RPF expansion, and ultimately provided a safe haven for 2 million Rwandans. Another 2 million fled to Tanzania and Zaire. On 17 July 1994, the RPF took over the Rwandan government. By late summer, it began its own campaign against Hutu refugees, murdering thousands and imprisoning even more. In response, a guilt-ridden UN Security Council created an International Criminal Tribunal for Rwanda to try perpetrators of the 1994 genocide and RPF officials who later committed war crimes.[149]

Equally tragic is the crisis in Darfur in western Sudan where 200,000–400,000 have died. A special UN Commission report in 2005 claimed that even though "serious violations of international human rights and humanitarian law had taken place in Darfur," it was not genocide, though the crimes committed there were "no less serious and heinous than genocide."[150] In 2007, UN Secretary-General Ban Ki Moon wrote in the *Washington Post* that "amid the diverse social and political causes [of the crisis in Darfur], the Darfur conflict began as an ecological crisis, arising at least in part from climate change."[151] Gérard Prunier warns of the dangers of getting caught up in a semantic war of words over Darfur, and insists that we must see the tragedy there for what it is—a tragic, large-scale humanitarian crisis.[152]

In 2006, the UN voted to send 20,600 peacekeepers to Darfur to help a much smaller African Union force to stabilize the situation there. Prunier, who considers the international response to the Darfur tragedy impotent and "incomplete," charges that "China holds a large share of responsibility in the ongoing Darfur horror. The reason is exceedingly simple—oil."[153] China, Sudan's principal trading partner, consistently refused significantly to pressure Sudan on the Darfur crisis, which led a number of human rights groups to call for a boycott of the 2008 Beijing Olympic Games, some calling them the "Genocide Olympics."[154] Over the past year, the situation in Darfur has grown more complex, particularly after the International Criminal Court (ICC) indicted Sudanese President Omar Bashir in the spring of 2009 for war crimes and crimes against humanity in Darfur. He responded to this controversial indictment by ordering all international aid organizations out of Darfur and Sudan, creating a new humanitarian crisis there.[155]

The Middle East has suffered from similar upheavals over the past 60 years. The most serious violations of international law took place during the Iran–Iraq War between 1980 and 1988, and were initiated by Saddam Hussein, Iraq's dictator. Though estimates vary widely, it is possible that as many as a half million Iranians and Iraqis were killed or wounded in the fighting.[156] The most serious violations of international law centered on Iraqi use of chemical agents during this devastating conflict. Initially, Iraq used these weapons to counter Iranian tactics that involved sending large waves of Iranian troops into battle against Iraqi forces. But what began as a defensive tactic developed, over time, into the use of chemicals as part of an overall Iraqi strategy using jets and helicopters to drop shells filled with various forms of mustard gas and nerve agents such a tabun on Iranian forces. Iraq's use of such chemical agents violated the 1925 League of Nations *Protocol for the Prohibition of the Use in War of Asphyxiating, Poisonous, or Other Gases, and of Bacteriological Methods of Warfare* as well as the 1972 *Biological Weapons Convention*, which not only banned such weapons but also outlawed their development, acquisition, or retention, as well as weapons to deliver such chemical agents. Iraq and Iran were signatories of both agreements.[157]

A 1984 UN investigation of Iraq's use of chemical weapons verified their usage, while a later CIA study was able to document specific instances of Iraqi use of these agents between 1983 and 1988. The CIA report stated that "Iraqi forces killed or injured more than 20,000 people delivering chemical agents," while the Iranian government claimed in a 1995 report that "over 60,000 veterans of the war with Iraq were receiving medical treatment for injuries caused by Iraqi chemical agents."[158] Another source claims that during the course of the war, the Iraqis "bombarded some 2,000 villages in Iran" with a specially concocted gas compound that included "hydrogen cyanide, mustard gas, Sarin, and Tabun."[159]

While these attacks were ghastly, what received the most attention internationally were the Iraqi assaults against Kurdish villages in northern Iraq in 1987 and 1988. The Kurds, who lived in this sensitive region along the Iran–Iraq border, had mixed loyalties, and, by 1987, the pro-Iranian Kurdish Democratic Party had control of most of the northern border of Iraq. Early that year, Saddam Hussein appointed his cousin, Ali Hassan al-Majid ("Chemical Ali"), governor of northern Iraq with power to do whatever was necessary to secure the region. "Chemical Ali" initiated the *al-Anfal* ("spoils") campaign that "reached a level of brutality and killing so high and wreaked such devastation on settled life, even for a regime widely known for its brutality, that it finally resulted in international outrage and charges of genocide."[160]

Particularly heinous was the 18 March 1988 attack on the Kurdish village of Halabja, taken only a few days earlier by Iranian and Patriotic Union of Kurdistan forces. On the evening of 16 March the Iraqis began a massive bombardment of the village of 70,000 using a "hydrogen cyanide compound." Fortunately, most of the villagers had fled before the assault began. Estimates are that the Iraqis killed 3,500–8,000 Kurds in the attack, including civilians, and injured another 7,000.[161] Though it is difficult to know how many Kurds died in what Phebe Marr calls Saddam Hussein's "scorched earth campaign," estimates range from 50,000 to 100,000. It is also estimated that the Iraqis destroyed 4,000 Kurdish villages and displaced or resettled 1.5 million Kurds between 1982 and 1988. Most of this took place during the *al-Anfal* campaign.[162]

Until 1988, the international reaction to the war crimes in the Iran–Iraq War was, at best, tepid. The 1984 UN investigation of Iraq's use of chemical weapons did result in UN Security Council Resolution 582 two years later that deplored

> the escalation of the conflict, especially territorial incursions, the bombing of purely civilian centres, attacks on neutral shipping or civilian aircraft, the violation of international humanitarian law and other laws of armed conflict and, in particular, the use of chemical weapons contrary to obligations under the 1925 Geneva Protocol;
>
> Calls upon Iran and Iraq to observe an immediate cease-fire, a cessation of all hostilities on land, at sea and in the air and withdrawal of all forces to the internationally recognized boundaries without delay.[163]

To its credit, the UN had been trying since 1984 to do what it could to end the conflict. Resolution 582 was followed in 1987 by Security Council Resolution 598 which again called for an immediate ceasefire, and restated the above sections of Resolution 582. Hussein's government accepted the terms of Resolution 598, while Iran refused to do so, thinking that the international community had not done enough to condemn Iraq for its war crimes, and the general Western view that Iran was the "aggressor" in the conflict.[164]

All of this changed after the Halabjah attack. UN Secretary-General Perez de Cuellar sent Dr. Manuel Dominguez to investigate the charges of Iraqi use of chemical weapons. This ultimately convinced a hesitant Security Council to adopt Resolution 612 in the spring of 1988, which expressed dismay at the use of chemical weapons in violation of the 1925 Geneva Accords on chemical warfare. Several months later, Security Council Resolution 620 again expressed concern over the use of chemical weapons.[165] In the end, what finally convinced the Iranian government to agree to accept Resolution 598 and begin peace talks was the intense, Washington-sponsored "diplomatic, military, and economic campaign" against Iran in the aftermath of the controversial Irangate scandal. A ceasefire was declared on 20 August 1988, followed by still-unsuccessful peace talks.[166]

Sadly, Iraq remains a country haunted by death and war crimes. According to Human Rights Watch (HRW), Iraqi insurgents have killed thousands of civilians during the current conflict in Iraq. HRW also claims that US, Iraqi, and other members of the US-led coalition "have committed violations of the laws of war that raise serious doubts about their stated commitment to promoting the rule of law in Iraq." The "torture and humiliation of detainees . . . the unjustified killing of civilians . . . and the long-term detention without charge of persons apprehended" has undermined the rule of law in Iraq and earned the American-led coalition "widespread disdain . . . among ordinary Iraqis."[167]

One of the more troublesome aspects of the 9/11 tragedy and the subsequent wars in Afghanistan and Iraq, at least legally speaking, has been the question of the torture of prisoners at the Joint Task Force Guantánamo prison in Cuba and elsewhere, and the decision to try some of the prisoners under the 1996 War Crimes Act. This law, which was passed with widespread support by both houses of Congress, gives the US government the right to prosecute anyone who commits a "war crime" against a member of the US armed forces or a US national. The law defines a "war crime" as any violation of the Geneva Convention of 12 August 1949, which deals with the "Protection of Civilian Persons in Time of War" and its "Protocol Additional to ..." of 8 June 1977.[168]

Since the beginning of the war in Afghanistan, the US military has brought 775 detainees to the Guantánamo prison, releasing almost half of them after questioning. On 9 February 2008, the US government announced that it planned to try six of the detainees as members of al-Qaeda under the Military Commissions Act (MCA) of 2006, which authorizes the US military to create "military commissions" to try suspects "for violations of the law of war, and for other purposes." The law, which was aimed at members of the Taliban and al-Qaeda, states specifically that during a trial a defendant would not be required to "testify against himself" and that "statements obtained by use of torture shall not be admissible in a military commission under this chapter, except against a person accused of torture as evidence that the statement was made."[169] Such evidence, though, would be admissible if it was obtained before 30 December 2006.

Controversy has swirled around this Act since the moment it was passed. In addition to questions about the constitutionality of various measures of torture used by the military at Guantánamo, particularly "water boarding," there are basic issues about the MCA's constitutionality. Professor Marjorie Cohn, for example, feels that the MCA denies a defendant "basic due process."[170] Others have raised questions about the *ex post facto* criminalization aspects of the law, which runs counter to US constitutional and international law. Amnesty International said that the MCA "turned bad executive policy into bad law" by contravening basic "human rights principles," while the *New York Times* said in an editorial on 28 September 2006 that the MCA was "a tyrannical law that will be ranked with the low points in American democracy, our generation's version of the Alien and Sedition Acts."[171]

The various problems associated with the Allied coalition's presence in Iraq and Afghanistan are not unique to the Middle East. The 2006 war in Lebanon and in Gaza in early 2008 have raised questions about violations of international humanitarian law. The 2006 conflict began on 12 July 2006 when Israeli forces invaded southern Lebanon in response to repeated Hezbollah rocket attacks against Israeli settlements along the Israeli–Lebanese border. The "straw that broke the camel's back," at least for Israel, was Hezbollah's kidnapping of two IDF (Israeli Defense Force) soldiers from Israeli territory early on the 12th. What followed was a month-long war in which Israel tried to destroy Hezbollah's terrorist-military infrastructure in southern Lebanon. Almost immediately, war crimes charges surfaced, particularly against Israel, because of mounting Lebanese civilian deaths. Hezbollah had built its military infrastructure deep within Lebanese civilian population areas deliberately to use such populations as human shields. Of particular concern to some in the international community were questions of "proportionality" when it came to the use of missiles and other weapons by Hezbollah and Israel.[172]

Amnesty International characterized the fighting between Israel and Hezbollah as "the killing of civilians, mass forced displacement and attacks on civilian infrastructure."[173] Such attacks, HRW claimed, amounted to "war crimes," since neither side was taking "the necessary precautions to distinguish between civilian and military targets."[174] Of particular concern to international observers was the use of cluster bombs by both sides. According to the International Committee of the Red Cross, the principal concern about the use of such weapons, which is legal, is their "impact ... on civilian populations ... Since cluster munitions distribute large numbers of explosive sub-munitions over very large areas, there is a serious rise of civilian casualties when military objectives and civilians intermingle in a target area."[175]

The UN estimated that Israel "fired approximately four million U.S. and Israeli-manufactured cluster bomblets on Lebanon" during the conflict, while Hezbollah "used over a hundred Chinese-manufactured cluster munition rockets—firing them into civilian areas in Israel."[176] The Israeli government argued that its use of such weapons was in compliance with international law and that the IDF did everything possible "to minimize any incidental collateral harm to warning them [civilians] in advance of an action." It also pointed to Hezbollah's deliberate use of civilians as "human shields by storing and even firing missiles from inside their homes, something that was banned by international law."[177]

Charges of war crimes surfaced again during the Israeli invasion of Gaza in late 2008 in response to the refusal of Hamas, the Palestinian terrorist organization, to halt firing rockets into Israel from Gaza. Hamas, which is recognized internationally as a terrorist organization, took control of Gaza in elections in 2007. One of its avowed goals is the destruction of Israel. The fighting, which lasted from 27 December 2008 until 17 January 2009, resulted in the deaths of approximately 1,300 Gazans (Palestinian sources claim 1,417 killed, including 926 civilians), many of them civilians. Ten Israeli soldiers and three civilians died during the conflict. Gaza was devastated by the fighting, and the UN estimated that over 4,000 homes were destroyed and another 15,000 damaged. What followed was a serious humanitarian crisis.[178] Given the one-sided nature of the conflict, it is not surprising that Israel began to be accused of war crimes. The killing of members of the Samouni family in early January prompted the International Committee of the Red Cross to question why the Israeli military did nothing to help the wounded survivors, while Navi Pillay, the UN Commissioner for Human Rights, charged that the Samouni "killings show 'elements of what would constitute war crimes.'"[179]

Amnesty International charged that the Israeli army had used white phosphorus, a highly incendiary smokescreen, in civilian areas, but also charged Hamas with illegal rocket attacks on Israeli settlements. HRW stated that "those who wilfully conduct such attacks are responsible for war crimes."[180] HRW followed this up with a report in June 2009 that charged Israel with causing the deaths of 29 civilians during missile attacks in Gaza. The IDF spokeswoman, Lt. Col. Avital Leibovich, defended the IDF, saying that "few military forces had ever taken as many precautions to minimize civilian casualties as Israel did in Gaza, dropping 500,000 leaflets warning people that its forces were arriving and even making telephone calls to neighbors of those thought to be Hamas fighters."[181]

All of this was complicated by stories in the Israeli press based on testimony from IDF soldiers who told reporters that they had "knowingly shot civilians to death ..." and "intentionally vandalized Palestinian homes." According to Amos Harel, the *Ha'aretz* reporter who wrote a series of articles on the subject, Israel's "rules of engagement ... were exceptionally permissive."[182] An IDF investigation of these charges concluded that no war crimes had been committed by Israeli forces in Gaza and that the testimony of soldiers published in *Ha'aretz* was nothing more than "hearsay."[183] Such charges ultimately led the UN to appoint Richard Goldstone, the former chief prosecutor for the International Criminal Tribunals for Rwanda and Yugoslavia, to look into war crimes charges against both sides in the Gazan war.[184]

In many ways, Goldstone's appointment brought him full circle, given his role in the criminal proceedings against accused war criminals in the former Yugoslavia. In some ways, it could be argued that the tensions in the Middle East and in the former Yugoslavia were a byproduct of the religious, historical, and cultural differences that had brought the Ottoman Empire, which dominated the region prior to World War I, to its knees in 1918. The principal villain in all of this was Serbia, led by a former communist turned extreme nationalist, Slobodan Milosević. Serbia had always been the dominant power in the Yugoslav confederation and Milosević was willing to go to any extreme not only to maintain firm Serb control over a disintegrating Yugoslav state but also to realize the medieval dream of a Greater Serbia. This nationalistic passion, combined with additional conflicts with the region's Muslims, particularly in Bosnia and Herzegovina, led to the worst genocidal conflict in Europe since World War II.[185]

Between 1991 and 1995, fighting between Serbs, Croats, and Bosnia's large Muslim population almost destroyed Bosnia. Estimates are that 100,000–110,000 civilians were killed in the conflict, 65% of them Bosnian Muslims. The war also forced 1.3 million refugees to flee Bosnia-Herzegovina.[186] Most of the Muslims who were killed were genocidal victims of Serb forces operating in the region. Efforts to send UN peacekeepers into Bosnia to halt the violence had little impact on the conflict. In the midst of US plans to adopt a "Lift and Strike" policy against Bosnian Serb forces in 1995, Serb irregulars murdered 8,000 Muslims at Srebrenica, which led to a series of NATO air strikes against Serb forces.[187]

To the south, a growing conflict between Serbian/Yugoslav forces and the Kosovo Liberation Army exploded into civil war in Kosovo, a predominantly Albanian

Muslim enclave in southwestern Serbia. A new wave of atrocities, committed principally by Serbian forces, led to Western intervention in 1998. Efforts by the Organization for Security and Co-operation in Europe to sustain a ceasefire failed, and NATO sent troops into Kosovo to deal with what UN Security Council Resolution 1244 called "a grave humanitarian situation in Kosovo."[188] It also called for "substantial autonomy and meaningful self-administration in Kosovo" with an eye towards a "final settlement" that would determine Kosovo's fate in what was then still the Serb-dominated Federal Republic of Yugoslavia.[189]

Ethnic violence erupted again in Kosovo in 2004 and two years later special UN envoy Martii Ahtisaari began talks with Kosovar and Serbian officials on the province's ultimate status. Russia, which in the nineteenth and early twentieth centuries had claimed a special role as defender of Slavic interests in the Balkans, reassumed this role, asserting that as a member of the UN Security Council it would accept no final settlement that was not agreeable to Serbian interests. Such intransigence finally led the US, France, and the UK to support outright Kosovar independence, which was declared on 4 February 2008. Serbia immediately announced that it planned to take the case of Kosovar independence before the International Court of Justice (ICJ) in The Hague. On 8 October 2008, UN Resolution 63/3 asked the ICJ to render an advisory opinion on this question, and, as of 21 April 2009, 35 member states of the UN had submitted written statements to the ICJ about this matter.[190]

Russia's defense of Serbia's historic claims to Kosovo dovetailed with Moscow's ongoing efforts over the past 30 years to secure its sphere of influence in Muslim Central Asia and stifle any efforts by breakaway provinces within its borders to gain any significant autonomy. Russian efforts to conquer a politically unstable Afghanistan in 1979 and its ongoing war with Chechnya saw Soviet and Russian forces commit widespread war crimes between 1979 and 2008.

In fact, our first glimpse of the types of atrocities being committed in Iraq today came in the aftermath of the Soviet invasion of Afghanistan in 1979. Though the Soviets lost only 14,453 men in Afghanistan, over a million Afghans were killed during the conflict. Trapped as they were in an unwinnable conflict, Soviet forces committed widespread atrocities and war crimes in Afghanistan. Sadly, Afghanistan has continued to be plagued by civil war and accompanying violations of international law, particularly during the Taliban and post-9/11 eras. According to the Afghanistan Justice Project, each of these periods has been marked by numerous "crimes against humanity and serious war crimes."[191]

Tragically, Russian forces committed similar atrocities in Chechnya, a small Muslim province in the Caucasus Mountains that declared independence after the collapse of the Soviet Union in 1991. During the course of two Chechen Wars and the subsequent military occupation of the province, Russian troops committed a number of war crimes in Chechnya. In 2003, Peter Bouckaert, the Emergencies Researcher for Human Rights Watch, told the US Senate's Committee on Foreign Relations that "Russian forces have committed grave abuses, including war crimes, in their campaigns in Chechnya."[192] Little was done by the Russian government to stop these abuses and Western powers seemed more concerned about strengthening their ties with the country's new leader, Vladimir Putin, than raising questions about the war crimes being committed in Chechnya. As in most civil wars, atrocities were committed by both sides. Thomas Hammarberg, the Council of Europe's Commissioner for Human Rights, concluded after a trip to Chechnya in 2007 that "torture and mistreatment are widespread in Chechnya. This undermines justice."[193]

And what of justice when it comes to the various war crimes and acts of genocide committed in the decades since World War II? The collapse of the Soviet Union in 1991 and its stranglehold over much of Central and Eastern Europe helped to open the door to greater international efforts to address these issues legally.[194] In 1993, the UN Security Council created the International Criminal Tribunal for the Former Yugoslavia (ICTY) to punish "serious violations of international humanitarian laws." Over the past 16 years, the ICTY has indicted 161 individuals for one of three crimes—genocide, crimes against humanity, and violation of laws or customs of war. Though many of its investigations are still ongoing, its most prominent defendant was Slobodan Milosević, who died in the midst of his proceedings at The Hague.[195]

One of the most innovative developments, legally speaking, to come out of the creation of this tribunal was the specification of sexual violence as a crime against humanity. Though military courts in occupied Germany and Japan after World War II considered rape as a crime against humanity, such a crime was not mentioned in international statutes until 1993, when it was deemed a crime to be considered by the new ICTY. A 1993 report by the UN High Commissioner for Human Rights stated that Serb forces were using rape as "a deliberate weapon in fulfilling the policy of ethnic cleansing in the Republic of Bosnia and Herzegovina."[196] Five years later, the Rome Statute, which created the ICC, included a much broader list of sexually violent crimes that could be brought before the court.[197]

In November 1994, the United Nations Security Council created the International Criminal Tribunal for Rwanda (ICTR) to investigate and, where applicable, try Rwandan officials involved in the Rwandan genocide.[198] To date, the ICTR has tried 43 defendants for war crimes. There are another 25 trials in progress and five defendants are awaiting trial. In addition, national and local courts (*gacaca*) have tried almost 10,000 Rwandans suspected of involvement in the 1994 genocide. Though impressive, the quality of justice in these trials is quite low. Complicating all of this is Rwanda's Disarmament, Demobilization and Reintegration (DDR) program, which has tried to reintegrate tens of thousands of combatants back into Rwandan society. This, and the fact that over 800,000 Rwandans have been implicated in the *gacaca* proceedings, has further complicated this admirable exercise in transitional justice.[199]

Despite the significance of these efforts, it is the ICC in The Hague that offers the greatest promise for investigating, trying, convicting, and, through such actions, deterring war crimes and genocide internationally. As alluded to above, efforts to create an international court to try crimes of war go back almost a century. In addition to the failed efforts after World War I, there was also talk in the 1930s of creating a special tribunal to deal with war crimes, though nothing ever came of this idea until World War II. The success of the various post-1945 war crimes trials had a dramatic impact on international law.[200]

Article VI of the 1948 Genocide Convention clearly reflected this influence.

> Persons charged with genocide or any of the other acts enumerated in Article 3 [genocide; conspiracy to commit genocide; direct and public incitement to commit genocide; attempt to commit genocide; complicity in genocide] shall be tried by a competent tribunal of the State in the territory of which the act was committed, or by such international penal tribunal as may have jurisdiction with respect to those Contracting Parties which shall have accepted its jurisdiction.[201]

Simultaneously, the UN General Assembly asked its International Law Commission (ILC) to look into the prospect of creating an international tribunal to try persons accused of acts of genocide, and to determine whether this could be done through the creation of a criminal chamber for the International Court of Justice (World Court), the UN judicial branch that deals with disputes between nations. After a number of stops and starts, the ILC resumed its work on the idea of an international criminal court in 1990. Eight years later, the UN General Assembly held a conference in Rome to discuss and hopefully approve what became known as the Rome Statute (17 July 1998) of the ICC. Though 139 countries signed the Rome Statute, it required 60 nations to ratify it before the ICC could become operational. The sixtieth ratification took place on April 11, 2002, and on July 1, 2002, the ICC came into being. Unfortunately, a number of countries such as the United States, China, Iraq, and Israel have chosen not to ratify the Rome Statute, though there are now hints that the US is changing its position on this issue.[202]

The ICC, which is located in The Hague in the Netherlands, can only consider crimes committed after the Rome Statute came into force in 2002. Various limits are placed on the ICC's geographic and legal jurisdiction. Cases can be referred to the ICC by a "State Power," or the UN Security Council. In addition, the ICC's Prosecutor "may initiate charges acting *proprio motu*, that is, on his own initiative." Prosecution is limited to State Parties, or countries that either signed the Rome Statute or accept the jurisdiction of the ICC.[203] The ICC can consider four crimes— genocide, crimes against humanity, war crimes, and aggression.[204]

To date, three State Parties—Uganda, the Democratic Republic of the Congo, and the Central African Republic (CAF)—have referred potential war crimes cases to the ICC. The UN Security Council has also requested that the ICC investigate the crisis in Darfur. Three Uganda cases are currently before the ICC's Pre-Trial Chamber II, and arrest warrants have been issued for the top five leaders of the Lord's Resistance Army. Three Congolese cases are currently before the ICC as well as one CAF case. Pre-Trial Chamber I is considering three cases dealing with crimes in Darfur.[205]

Conclusion

William C. Peters reminds us in his essay on command responsibility about the hellacious, destructive nature of warfare. In many ways, it could be argued that crimes of war and genocide are a reflection of the values of the societies that engage in war and the subsequent committing of such crimes during combat. While the world in general has become a more civilized place, the horrors committed during World War I and World War II remind us that civilization, particularly in the West, has not come as far as one would hope when it comes to human values and restraints not only on the battlefield but in the broader societies engaged in such conflicts. While brutality and the mistreatment of combatants and noncombatants was certainly a characteristic of wars in antiquity and the medieval world, some changes seemed to take place, at least in the Western world, during the Renaissance and Reformation. To some extent, this was linked to changes in the nature of warfare and the greater political unity at play throughout Europe. There also began to emerge, particularly during the Enlightenment, the idea of individual human value vis-à-vis that of the state. This would lay the groundwork for the development of some important concepts in international humanitarian law.

Unfortunately, though these new values bore some fruit in the nineteenth century when it came to the development of international humanitarian law, a double standard was practiced by the Western world's various colonial powers, whether in the Americas, Asia, or Africa. Standards applicable to white Europeans or Americans at war did not apply to what many in the West viewed as the inferior peoples on these continents. Buffeted by racial and religious ideas that had long governed some aspects of the dynamics of war, Europe's major and minor colonial powers committed untold atrocities in the lands they dominated abroad.

The twentieth century held great promise for the world. The long, destructive wars of European unification and state building were now over, and, except for the distant conflicts in Asia and Africa, the Western world seemed ready to enjoy an era of peace and prosperity. Though hindsight tells us about the troublesome clouds brewing on the horizon in the decades before the outbreak of World War I, no one was prepared for the ferocity and senseless deaths of this shocking conflict. Though World War I could certainly not be cast in the same light when it came to the war crimes and acts of genocide committed during World War II, it remained a conflict that underscored the breadth and power of modern industrialized warfare. With the exception of the Armenian genocide, war crimes were minimal, particularly when compared to the large number of battlefield deaths. Regardless, the Allied victors did attempt to address these crimes, though their efforts were extremely unsuccessful.

It would take a different type of war, one more aggressive and racially driven, and, in the end, a true war to end all wars, before the Allied powers were able to bring Germany's and Japan's major war criminals to justice—World War II. The fact that it took the victorious Western powers two major, destructive world wars finally to

37

begin seriously to address questions about the specifics of war crimes and their adjudication speaks volumes about the barriers in place before such issues were addressed internationally. Laws and treaties on the books are useless without the backing of the will and mechanisms, nationally and internationally, to enforce them.

It is no accident that it was the gradual collapse of the Soviet Union and its stranglehold over Eastern Europe that finally led to the creation of various international tribunals to deal with war crimes and acts of genocide in the former Yugoslavia and Africa. In many ways, the causes of the conflicts that bred these atrocities seemed to hark back to an era when irrational religious and ethnic hatred governed the treatment of combatants and noncombatants during war. But what was different was the international political, military, and legal will of the world's major powers to enforce and create legal bodies to deal with such crimes. In this context, the lessons of history, particularly from the first half of the twentieth century, finally bore fruit.

NOTES

1. *Sun-tzu's Art of War*, 160; Sun Tzu, *The Art of War*, 46–47. This translation states that it is important to be sure that [captured] "soldiers are treated kindly when given care; this is conquest for aggrandizement."
2. Bodde, *China's First Unifier*, 5–9; Cottrell, *The First Emperor of China*, 141–45. This view of Qin Shihuangdi as a brutal emperor was perpetrated by Confucian scholars. Some contemporary Chinese scholars take a more balanced view of Qin. According to the *Basic Annals of Ch'in Shih-Huang*, at the end of his military campaigns, "all weapons were collected and brought to the capital Hsienyang, where they were melted down to make bronze bells and twelve statues of giants, and placed in the courts and palaces." Ch'ien, "Basic Annals," 269–70.
3. Lee, "Early Development of Modern International Law in East Asia," 42.
4. Cryer, *Prosecuting International Crimes*, 25–31.
5. Anand, "Universality of International Law," 23, 38.
6. *Tanakh*, 591.
7. Telushkin, *Biblical Literacy*, 165.
8. According to Charles E. Little, the origins of this phrase can be traced to a number of Roman writers who, over time, included it in the historic canon about the Punic Wars. Little, "The Authenticity and Form of Cato's Saying 'Carthago delenda Est,'" 429–35; see also Dubuisson, "'Delendo Est Carthago,'", 279–87.
9. Rawlings, "Hannibal the Cannibal?," 2–3.
10. Craven, *The Punic Wars*, 285.
11. *New Complete Works of Josephus*, 930, 933; Shayne Cohen questions some parts of Josephus' story about the mass suicide of the Jews there. Cohen, "Masada," 385–405.
12. Esposito, *Islam*, 12.
13. Ibid., 5–11, 40–48, 51–57.
14. Carey et al., *Warfare in the Medieval World*, 31–39.
15. Smith, "Islam and Christendom," 337–41; Durant, *The Age of Faith*, 585–613.
16. Nicolle, *Crusader Warfare*, 42, 49.
17. Santosuosso, *Barbarians, Marauders, and Infidels*, 224.
18. Ibid., 75.
19. Ibid., 64–65, 78.

20. Smith, "Islam and Christendom," 325.
21. Ibid., 325–26.
22. Esposito, *Islam*, 59.
23. Santosuosso, *Barbarian, Marauders, and Infidels*, 224.
24. Aboul-Enein and Zuhur, *Islamic Rulings on Warfare*, 22.
25. Kelsay, "Al-Shaybani and the Islamic Law of War," 68.
26. Rehman, "The Concept of Jihad," 329.
27. O'Donnell, *Augustine*, 259.
28. Aquinas, *Summa Theologica*, 1359–62; for more on Aquinas' work, see Torrell, *Saint Thomas Aquinas*.
29. *Die Constitutio Criminalis Carolina*, 2–3; Monter, "Witch Trials," 34; Ankarloo, "Witch Trials," 65.
30. Marius, *Martin Luther*, 267; Luther's concept of the "priesthood of the individual believer" can be found in his Luther, *Von der Freiheit eines Christenmenschen*. The paradox can be found early in Luther's essay when he states that "a Christian man is the most free lord of all, and subject to none, a Christian man is the most dutiful servant of all, and subject to every one."
31. Wedgwood, *Thirty Years War*, 491.
32. Mortimer, *Eyewitness Accounts*—see, for example, 1–2. He raises questions about the lingering idea that this was not only the most devastating war in German history prior to World War I but one filled with acts of "rapine and plunder." He traces this myth to early nineteenth-century German Romantic historians and novelists.
33. Roberts, *Gustavus Adolphus*, 240–43; American military legal scholars offer different opinions about the importance of Gustav II's Articles of War. Winthrop, *Military Law and Precedents*, the "'Blackstone' of military law," credits Gustav's Articles with forming the basis of modern military law and lists all 167 articles in the Appendix of his classic (907–17). Lieutenant Colonel William R. Hagan, who wrote the introduction to the above reprint of Winthrop's study, will have none of this. He concludes "that Gustavus Adolphus was an important, but not a revolutionary figure in the development of military law" (200); what adds to this controversy are the different versions of Gustav's laws of war. Winthrop listed 167 articles in his study, while Kenneth Ögren states that the Articles of War had 150 articles. He says that seven dealt with humanitarian issues, but then specifically cites six in his article. The difference seems to center on a revised set of the Articles issued by Gustav just before his death in 1632. The new Articles had clauses that tried to strengthen discipline in his army." Ögren, "Humanitarian Law in the Articles of War."
34. Grotius, *Rights of War and Peace*, 1021.
35. Meron, *War Crimes Law*, 124.
36. Roberts, *Gustavus Adolphus*, 423, 639.
37. Locke, *Essay Concerning Human Understanding*, 11–12, 30–32, 39.
38. Locke, *Two Treatises*, 101, 166, 172.
39. Ibid., 224, 249.
40. "Declaration of the Rights of Man," 1–2.
41. Bass, *Stay the Hand of Vengeance*, 49–50.
42. Bell, *First Total War*, 7.
43. Bass, *Stay the Hand of Vengeance*, 37, 56–57.
44. Thornton, *American Indian Holocaust*, 22.
45. Churchill, *Indians Are Us?*, 38; Stannard, *American Holocaust*, 146.
46. De las Casas, *Short Account of the Destruction of the Indies*, xx.

47. Ibid., 29.
48. Ignatieff, "Legacy of Raphael Lemkin," 9.
49. Oswalt and Neely, *This Land was Theirs*, 4.
50. Thornton, *American Indian Holocaust*, 43–44.
51. Ibid., 47, 49.
52. Beeching, *Chinese Opium Wars*, 199–200, 286–87, 305–06; Fairbank, *Great Chinese Revolution*, 81. For Taiping regulations on the conduct of its armies, see Spence, *God's Chinese Son*, 147–48, 165–68.
53. Hsü, *Rise of Modern China*, 373–80, 387–406; Spence, *Search for Modern China*, 230–35.
54. Esherick, *Origins of the Boxer Rebellion*, 123–24; Schrecker, *Imperialism and Chinese Nationalism*, 91, 130–39; *Yi Ho Tuan Movement*, 1–14 *passim*; MacDonough, *Last Kaiser*, 234–35.
55. Brandt, *Massacre in Shansi*, 223–33; Purcell, *Boxer Uprising*, 240–62.
56. Edgerton, *Warriors of the Rising Sun*, 323.
57. Ibid., 324.
58. Ward, *Our Bones are Scattered*, 428–29.
59. Ibid., 437.
60. Ibid., 442.
61. Laband, *Kingdom in Crisis*, 87.
62. Ibid., 88.
63. Ibid., 107–08.
64. Cope, *Ploughshares of War*, 250.
65. Hochschild, *King Leopold's Ghost*, 225, 233.
66. Conrad, *Heart of Darkness*, 89.
67. Ó Slocháin and O'Sullivan, *The Eyes of Another Race*, 1, 28–32. This volume contains not only Casement's full official report but also his 1903 diary detailing his research travels in the Congo; Hochschild, *King Leopold's Ghost*, 250–59.
68. Stern, *Gold and Iron*, 411.
69. Pakenham, *Scramble for Africa*, 608–09.
70. Ibid., 609–10.
71. Ibid., 615.
72. Ibid., 611.
73. Ibid., 615.
74. Hull, *Absolute Destruction*, 332–33.
75. Pakenham, *Scramble for Africa*, 284–85.
76. Gay, *Cultivation of Hatred*, 85–86.
77. Ibid., 87.
78. Hull, *Absolute Destruction*, 332.
79. Laws of War: General Orders No. 100, 12–13.
80. Friedel, *Francis Lieber*, 331–35; Meron, *War Crimes Law Comes of Age*, 132; Krammer, *Prisoners of War*, 88.
81. Meron, *Humanization of International Law*, 5.
82. Laws of War: General Orders No. 100, 9; Meron, *War Crimes Law Comes of Age*, 133.
83. Burlingame, *Abraham Lincoln*, 540–41.
84. *Report of Charles S.P. Bowles*, 6–8.
85. Benvenisti, "The Origins of the Concept of Belligerent Occupation," 641.
86. Hertigan, *Lieber's Code*, 23; Friedel, *Francis Lieber*, 340; Meron, *War Crimes Law Comes of Age*, 138–39.

87. Laws of War: Laws and Customs of War on Land (Hague II), 2–3. The wording of the Martens Clause was slightly changed in the 1907 Hague Convention on the Laws and Customs of War on Land. The final phrase now read "and the dictates of the public conscience." Laws of War: Laws and Customs of War on Land (Hague IV), 2.

88. Kramer, *Dynamic of Destruction*, 5.

89. Hankel, *Die Leipziger Prozesse*, 15; Kramer, "The First Wave of International War Crimes Trials," 447.

90. *Treaty of Versailles*, Part VIII, Articles 227–30, Part VIII, Article 231.

91. Horne and Kramer, *German Atrocities*, 74–76.

92. Kramer, "The First Wave of International War Crimes Trials," 448–49.

93. Hankel, *Die Leipziger Prozesse*, 507–17; Horne and Kramer, *German Atrocities*, 351; Matthäus, "The Lessons of Leipzig," 19–20.

94. Akçam, *A Shameful Act*, 125–29.

95. Lewy, *The Armenian Massacres*, 20–26; "Another Armenian Holocaust," 1.

96. Bloxham, *The Great Game of Genocide*, 51, 60.

97. Akçam, *A Shameful Act*, 159; Dadrian, *History of the Armenian Genocide*, 221.

98. Balakian, *The Burning Tigris*, 182–83.

99. Theriault, "Rethinking Dehumanization in Genocide," 28–31.

100. Akçam, *A Shameful Act*, 214; Balakian, *The Burning Tigris*, 278; Payaslian, *United States Policy toward the Armenian Question*, 89–95.

101. *The Treaty of Peace between the Allied and Associated Powers and Turkey Signed at Sèvres*, Part III, Articles 88–93.

102. Suny, *Looking toward Ararat*, 122–32, 239–46; Kurkjian, *History of Armenia*, 474–88; Herzig, "Armenians," 147–49; Dudwick, "Armenia," 265–66, 275–80; Shaw, *History of the Ottoman Empire*, II, 356–57; *Treaty of Kars*, 1–14.

103. Dadrian, *History of the Armenian Genocide*, 304–05.

104. *The Treaty of Peace at Sèvres*, Part IV, Article 144, and Part VII, Articles 226–30.

105. Dadrian, *History of the Armenian Genocide*, 310–11.

106. Ibid., 311.

107. Taylor, *Anatomy of the Nuremberg Trials*, 18.

108. *Covenant of the League of Nations*.

109. Shaw, *International Law*, 848.

110. Conquest, *Harvest of Sorrow*, 4.

111. Khrushchev, *Khrushchev Remembers*, 74.

112. Wolowyna, "Famine-Genocide," 5.

113. Krawchenko, *Social Change and National Consciousness*, 116; Conquest, *Harvest of Sorrow*, 306.

114. Subtelny, *Ukraine*, 413.

115. Liber, "Ukraine," 12.

116. *Documents on the Tokyo International Military Tribunal*, 537.

117. Chang, *Rape of Nanjing*, 4; Li, "Nanjing Holocaust," 231. The Japanese claim that there were only 38,000–42,000 "illegal murders" by their forces in Nanjing.

118. Rummel, *China's Bloody Century*, 149.

119. Tanaka, *Hidden Horrors*, 79–109; Rummel, *China's Bloody Century*, 166, n. 71.

120. Osmanczyk and Mango, *Encyclopedia of the United Nations*, 4, 2663.

121. Kochavi, *Prelude to Nuremberg*, 45–54; Harris, *Tyranny on Trial*, 4.

122. Office of United States Chief Counsel, *Nazi Conspiracy and Aggression*, 5.

123. Taylor, *Anatomy of the Nuremberg Trials*, 45.

124. *Nazi Conspiracy and Aggression*, 114.

125. Crowe, *The Holocaust*, 399.
126. Ibid., 399.
127. Ibid., 401–02.
128. *Nuremberg Trials Final Report Appendix D*, 3.
129. Crowe, *The Holocaust*, 402.
130. Boister and Cryer, *Tokyo International Military Tribunal*, 22–32.
131. Ibid., 54–59, 252.
132. Justice Pal's full dissenting opinion can be found in Boister and Cryer, *Documents on the Tokyo International Military Tribunal*, 809–1420; Boister and Cryer, *Tokyo International Military Tribunal*, 32–40; Chang and Barker, "Victor's Justice," 40, 47–49, 53; Dower, *Embracing Defeat*, 461–69.
133. Ball, *Prosecuting War Crimes and Genocide*, 70–85; Welch, *The Tokyo Trial*, 113–14.
134. For a more detailed look at the trials in the occupied parts of Germany and the Soviet bloc, see Crowe, *The Holocaust*, 397–435.
135. Watkins and Weber, *War Crimes and War Crimes Trials*, 369, 371.
136. Office of the High Commissioner for Human Rights, "Convention," 1.
137. Rummel, *China's Bloody Century*, 205.
138. Ibid., 272–73.
139. Government of Tibet in Exile, *Tibet*, Human Rights Section, 1–3, Religion and National Identity Section, 2, 7; Eimer, "Dalai Lama Condemns China's 'Cultural Genocide,'" 1; Wang, "Report Says Valid Grievances at Root of Tibet Unrest, A4; in 1960, the International Commission of Jurists reported that China had committed "acts of genocide" in Tibet in "an attempt to destroy the Tibetans as a religious group." But since there was not "sufficient proof of the destruction of Tibetans as a race, nation, or ethnic group," the report went on, such policies could not "be regarded as genocide in international law"; International Commission of Jurists, *Tibet and the Chinese People's Republic*, 1.
140. French, *Tibet, Tibet*, 279–83. French, who is very sympathetic to Tibetan suffering, estimates that as many as a half million Tibetans may have died as a "direct result" of Chinese policies.
141. Wei, *100 Questions*, 38–45.
142. Yinan, "Release from a Cycle of Servitude," 7.
143. Zhonglu et al., *China's Tibet*, iv.
144. *The Profile of Human Rights Violations in Timor-Leste*, 1–2.
145. Rejali, *Torture and Democracy*, 83–86.
146. *Korean War Atrocities*, 15.
147. Human Rights Watch, *Uganda*, 1; Boston, "Genocide in Uganda," 1.
148. Hitchens, "Childhood's End," 1.
149. Des Forges, *"Leave None to Tell the Story,"* 38–40, 123–30, 181–85, 199–302, 595–690; Prunier, *The Rwanda Crisis*, 74–92, 159–91; Dallaire, *Shake Hands with the Devil*, 421–60; Peskin, *International Justice in Rwanda*, 151–69.
150. International Commission of Inquiry on Darfur, *Report of the International Commission*, 3, 160–61.
151. Ban, "Climate Culprit in Darfur," A15.
152. Prunier, *Darfur*, 148–58.
153. Ibid., 178–80.
154. "China and Darfur," A30.
155. "A Warrant for Bashir," 20; "Compounding the Crime," 3–4.
156. Hiro (*The Longest War*, 250) estimates that the total war dead is, conservatively, 262,000 Iranians and 105,000 Iraqis. Official Iranian estimates claim that 194,931 Iranians died

during the war, while the Iraqi government claimed afterwards that 800,000 were killed during the conflict; Charles Tripp says over 250,000 Iraqis died during the war. Tripp, *History of Iraq*, 239; Marr, *Modern History of Iraq*, 207. Marr says that Iraq suffered 380,000 casualties: 125,000 dead and 255,000 wounded.

157. Ali, "Chemical Weapons," 43–49; *Protocol for the Prohibition of the Use in War*, 1; *Convention on the Prohibition of the Development*, 1–4.

158. Central Intelligence Agency, *Iran's Weapons of Mass Destruction*, 8–9; "News Chronology," 20.

159. Timmermann, *Death Lobby*, 146.

160. Marr, *Modern History of Iraq*, 200; this was not the first instance of such brutality. In 1982, Shiite Muslim rebels tried to assassinate Saddam Hussein while he was riding through the village of Dujail. In retaliation, Hussein ordered the execution of 148 Dujaili residents, including many children.

161. Timmerman, *Death Lobby*, 293–94; Ali, "Chemical Weapons," 52.

162. Marr, *Modern History of Iraq*, 202; in 2005, the district court in The Hague declared the *al-Anfal* campaign an act of genocide as defined by the 1948 Genocide Convention during the trial of Franz van Anraat, who was accused of selling to Iraq chemicals that were used against the Kurds. The charge against Anraat was later changed to war crimes.

163. United Nations, *Resolution 582*, 1.

164. Ali, "Chemical Weapons," 52–53.

165. United Nations, *Resolution 598*, 1–2; idem, *Resolution 612*, 1; idem, *Resolution 620*, 1–2.

166. Hiro, *The Longest War*, 240, 248, 270.

167. Human Rights Watch, *A Face and a Name*, 12.

168. *War Crimes Act of 1996*, 18 U.S.C.2441; War Crimes, *Convention (IV)*, 1–39; "Protocol Additional," 1–55.

169. *Military Commissions Act*, 1, 11.

170. Cohn, "Injustice at Guantanamo," 1–2.

171. "Rushing off a Cliff," 2.

172. "UN Warning on Mid-East Crimes," 1.

173. Amnesty International, *Israel/Lebanon*, 1.

174. Council on Foreign Relations, "Bouckaert," 1.

175. International Committee of the Red Cross, *Observations*, 1.

176. Maslen and Wiebe, *Cluster Munitions*, 18.

177. Israel Ministry of Foreign Affairs, "Behind the Headlines," 1–2.

178. "Counting the Cost," 53; "Not Nearly Back to Normal," 49; "UN Appoints Jewish Judge," 2.

179. "A Thousand Tragedies," 49.

180. Amnesty International, *Israel/Opt*, 3–14; McCarthy, "Hamas Accused of War Crimes," 1–2.

181. Human Rights Watch, *Precisely Wrong*, 1–32; Drew, "Human Rights Groups Says," A14; Katz, "IDF Doubts Credibility," 1–2.

182. Jewish Peace News, "IDF," 1–4.

183. Pidd, "Gaza Offensive," 1–2.

184. Human Rights Watch, "UN," 1–3.

185. Janjić, "Serbia," 63–65; Malcolm, *Bosnia*, 213–15; Cohen, *Broken Bones*, 51–54; Ramet, "A Theory," 769–71.

186. Sarajevo's Research and Documentation Center (*Human Losses*, Slides 1–32) writes that 39,684 civilians and 57,523 soldiers were killed during the conflict. Of this number, 66% were Bosnian Muslims; Tabean and Bijak, "War Related Deaths," 206, 210.

187. Burg and Shoup, *War in Bosnia-Herzegovina*, 324–28.
188. United Nations Security Council, *Resolution 1244*, 1.
189. Ibid., 2–3.
190. United Nations, General Assembly, *Resolution, 63/3*, 1; International Court of Justice, Press Release No. 2009/17, 1–2.
191. Afghan Justice Project, *War Crimes*, 4.
192. "War Crimes in Chechnya," 1.
193. Council of Europe, *Initial Conclusions*, 2.
194. Satkauskas, "Soviet Genocide Trials," 388–409.
195. Lopez-Terres, "Arrest and Transfer of Indictees," 1, 8; Wilson, "Judging History," 923–24; by the summer of 2009, there were still eight ongoing trials and three upcoming trials, including one of the court's most sought-after criminal, Radovan Karadžić. *Calendar of Court Proceedings*, 1–2.
196. *Statute of the International Tribunal for the Former Yugoslavia*, 1–2; United Nations High Commissioner for Human Rights, "Rape and Abuse of Women," 1–3; in 2003, the Office of the High Representative in Bosnia and Herzegovina and the ICTY recommended the creation of a War Crimes Chamber Project and the Registry for War Crimes and Organized Crimes. In early 2006, the War Crimes Chamber opened its first trial of 11 members of the Republika Srpska's Ministry of International Affairs, who were accused of genocide and conspiracy to commit genocide during the Srebrenica massacre.
197. *Rome Statute of the International Criminal Court*, Part 2, Article 7, section (g), defines as a crime against humanity "rape, sexual slavery, enforced prostitution, forced pregnancy, enforced sterilization, or any other form of sexual violence of comparable gravity."
198. Des Forges, *"Leave None to Tell the Story"*, 737–40.
199. UN Office of the Special Adviser on Africa, "DDR and Transitional Justice," 13–14, 30–31; for more on the controversies surrounding the ICTR, see Del Ponte, *Madame Prosecutor*; courts in Belgium and Switzerland have also convicted a handful of individuals for crimes committed in Rwanda.
200. Schabas, *Introduction to the International Criminal Court*, 3–5.
201. *Convention on the Prevention and Punishment of the Crimes of Genocide*, 1–2.
202. Schabas, *Introduction to the International Criminal Court*, 22–23, 465–69. A complete copy of the Rome Statute can be found on pages 381–464.
203. *Rome Statute*, Articles 1–16; Schabas, *Introduction to the International Criminal Court*, 141–43.
204. *Rome Statute*, Article 5, sections (a)–(c). Articles 6–8 define more specifically each of these crimes.
205. International Criminal Court, "Situations and Cases," 1–2.

REFERENCES

Aboul-Enein, Youssef H., and Sherifa Zuhur. *Islamic Rulings on Warfare*. Carlisle: Strategic Studies Institute, US Army War College, 2004.

Afghan Justice Project. *War Crimes and Crimes against Humanity, 1978–2001: Documents and Analysis of Major Patterns of Abuse in the War in Afghanistan*. Kabul: Afghan Justice Project, 2005.

Akçam, Taner. *A Shameful Act: The Armenian Genocide and the Question of Turkish Responsibility*. New York: Metropolitan Books, 2006.

Ali, Javed. "Chemical Weapons and the Iran–Iraq War: A Case Study of Noncompliance." *The Nonproliferation Review* 8, no. 1 (2001): 43–58.

Amnesty International. *Israel/Lebanon: Israel and Hezbollah Must Spare Civilians: Obligations under International Humanitarian Law of the Parties to the Conflict in Israel and Lebanon/N/N.* New York: Amnesty International, 2006.

———. *Israel/Opt: Fuelling [sic] Conflict: Foreign Arms Supplies to Israel/Gaza.* New York: Amnesty International, 2009.

Anand, R. P. "Universality of International Law: An Asian Perspective." *Essays in International Law,* no. 23 (2007): 21–40.

Ankarloo, Bengt. "Witch Trials in Northern Europe, 1450–1700." In *Witchcraft and Magic in Europe,* edited by Bengt Ankarloo and Stuart Clark. Philadelphia: University of Pennsylvania Press, 2001.

"Another Armenian Holocaust." *New York Times,* 10 September 1895.

Aquinas, St. Thomas. *Summa Theologica.* Translated by Fathers of the English Dominican Province. 2. New York: Benziger Brothers, 1947.

Balakian, Peter. *The Burning Tigris: The Armenian Genocide and America's Response.* New York: HarperCollins, 2003.

Ball, Howard. *Prosecuting War Crimes and Genocide: The Twentieth Century Experience.* Lawrence: University of Kansas Press, 1999.

Ban, Ki Moon. "A Climate Culprit in Darfur." *Washington Post,* 16 June 2007, A15.

Bass, Gary Jonathan. *Stay the Hand of Vengeance: The Politics of War Crimes Tribunals.* Princeton: Princeton University Press, 2000.

Beeching, Jack. *The Chinese Opium Wars.* San Diego: Harcourt Brace Jovanovich, 1975.

Bell, David. *The First Total War: Napoleon's Europe and the Birth of Warfare as We Know It.* Boston: Houghton Mifflin, 2007.

Benvenisti, Egal. "The Origins of the Concept of Belligerent Occupation." *Law and History Review* 26, no. 3 (2008): 621–48.

Bloxham, Donald. *The Great Game of Genocide: Imperialism, Nationalism, and the Destruction of the Ottoman Armenians.* Oxford: Oxford University Press, 2005.

Bodde, Derk. *China's First Unifier: A Study of the Chi'in Dynasty as Seen in the Life of Li Ssū, 280?–208 B.C.* Hong Kong: Hong Kong University Press, 1967.

Boister, Neil, and Robert Cryer, eds. *Documents on the Tokyo International Military Tribunal: Charter, Indictment, and Judgements.* Oxford: Oxford University Press, 2008.

———. *The Tokyo International Military Tribunal: A Reappraisal.* Oxford: Oxford University Press, 2008.

Boston, Daniella. "Genocide in Uganda: The African Nightmare Christopher Hitchens Missed." *Huffington Post,* 17 May 2006, 1, <http://www.huffingtonpost.com/daniella.boston/genocide-in-uganda-the-af_b_21150.html>.

Brandt, Nat. *Massacre in Shansi.* Syracuse: Syracuse University Press, 1994.

Burg, Steven L., and Paul S. Shoup. *The War in Bosnia-Herzegovina: Ethnic Conflict and International Intervention.* Armonk: M. E. Sharpe, 2000.

Burlingame, Michael. *Abraham Lincoln: A Life.* 2. Baltimore: Johns Hopkins University Press, 2008.

Calendar of Court Proceedings before the ICTY (November 2008). "International Criminal Tribunal for the Former Yugoslavia," 1–2, <http://www.haguejusticeportal.net/eCache/DEF/10/019.html>.

Carey, Brian Todd, Joshua B. Allfree, and John Cairns. *Warfare in the Medieval World.* Barnsley: Pen & Sword, 2006.

De las Casas, Bartolomé. *A Short Account of the Destruction of the Indies*. Edited and translated by Nigel Griffin. London: Penguin Books, 1992.

Central Intelligence Agency. *Iraq's Weapons of Mass Destruction Programs*. Washington, DC: Central Intelligence Agency, 2002.

Chang, Iris. *The Rape of Nanking: The Forgotten Holocaust of World War II*. New York: Basic Books, 1997.

Chang, Maria Hsia, and Robert P. Barker "Victor's Justice and Japan's Amnesia: The Tokyo War Crimes Trial Reconsidered." In *Japanese War Crimes: The Search for Justice*, edited by Peter Li. New Brunswick: Transaction, 2006.

Ch'ien, Ssu-ma. "Basic Annals of Ch'in Shih-huang." In *The First Emperor of China*, edited by Li Yu-ning. White Plains: International Arts and Sciences Press, 1975.

"China and Darfur: The Genocide Olympics?" *Washington Post*, 14 December 2006, A30.

Churchill, Ward. *Indians Are Us? Culture and Genocide in Native North America*. Monroe, ME: Common Courage Press, 1994.

Cohen, Leonard J. *Broken Bones: The Disintegration of Yugoslavia*. Boulder: Westview Press, 1993.

Cohen, Shayne. "Masada: Literary Tradition, Archaeological Remains, and the Credibility of Josephus." *Journal of Jewish Studies* 33 (Spring–Autumn, 1982): 385–405.

Cohn, Marjorie. "Injustice at Guantanamo: Torture Evidence and the Military Commissions Act." GlobalResearch.ca, 5 April 2008, 1–2, <http://www.globalresearch.ca/index.phpcontext=va&aid=8090>.

"Compounding the Crime." *The Economist*, 14–20 March 2009, 3–4.

Conquest, Robert. *The Harvest of Sorrow: Soviet Collectivization and the Terror-Famine*. New York: Oxford University Press, 1986.

Conrad, Joseph. *Heart of Darkness*. New York: Dell, 1960.

Die Constitutio Criminalis Carolina. <http://www.latein-pagina.de/iexplorer/hexen1/carolina.htm>.

Convention on the Prevention and Punishment of the Crimes of Genocide. 9 December 1948, United Nations General Assembly, <http://www.hrweb.org/legal/genocide.html>.

Convention on the Prohibition of the Development, Production and Stockpiling of Bacteriological (Biological) and Toxin Weapons and in their Destruction, Harvard Sussex Program on CBW Armament and Arms Limitation, <http://www.fas.harvard.edu/~hsp/1972.html>.

Convention (IV) Relative to the Protection of Civilian Persons in Time of War. Geneva, 12 August 1949, <http://www.icrc.org/ihl.nsf/385ec082b509e76c41256739003e636d/6756482d86146898c125641e004aa3c5>.

Cope, Richard. *The Ploughshares of War: The Origins of the Anglo-Zulu War of 1879*. Pietermaritzburg: University of Natal Press, 1999.

Cottrell, Arthur. *The First Emperor of China*. New York: Holt, Rinehart, & Winston, 1981.

Council of Europe. "Initial Conclusions of the Visit of the Commissioner for Human Rights in the Chechen Republic of the Russian Federation." Strasbourg, 6 March 2007, <https://wcd.coe.int/ViewDoc.jsp?id=1103233>.

Council on Foreign Relations. "Bouckaert: Both Israel and Hezbollah Committing War Crimes," <http://www.cfr.org/publication/11252>.

"Counting the Cost." *The Economist*, 24–30 January 2009, 53.

The Covenant of the League of Nations. <http://avalonlaw.yale.edu/20th_century/leagcov.asp>.

Craven, Brian. *The Punic Wars*. New York: St. Martin's Press, 1980.

Crowe, David M. *The Holocaust: Roots, History, and Aftermath*. Boulder: Westview Press, 2008.

Cryer, Robert. *Prosecuting International Crimes: Selectivity and the International Criminal Law Regime*. Cambridge: Cambridge University Press, 2005.

Dadrian, Vahakn N. *The History of the Armenian Genocide: Ethnic Conflict from the Balkans to Anatolia to the Caucasus*. 6th ed. New York: Berghahn Books, 1995.

Dallaire, Lt. Gen. Romeó. *Shake Hands with the Devil: The Failure of Humanity in Rwanda*. New York: Da Capo Press, 2003.

Declaration of the Rights of Man—1789. The Avalon Project, Yale Law School, <http://avalon.law.yale.edu/18th_century/rightsof.asp>.

Des Forges, Alison. *"Leave None to Tell the Story": Genocide in Rwanda*. New York: Human Rights Watch, 1999.

Documents on the Tokyo International Military Tribunal: Charter, Indictment and Judgements. Edited by Neil Boister and Robert Cryer. Oxford: Oxford University Press, 2008.

Dower, John W. *Embracing Defeat: Japan in the Wake of World War II*. New York: W. W. Norton, 1999.

Drew, Christopher Drew. "Human Rights Group Says 29 Civilians Were Killed by Israeli Air Attacks in Gaza." *New York Times*, 1 July 2009, A14.

Dubuisson, M. "'*Delendo Est Carthago*': remise en question d'un stéréotype." In *Studia Phoenicia. X, Punic Wars*, edited by H. Devijver and E. Lipiński. Leuven: Vitgeverij Peeters, 1989.

Dudwick, Nora. "Armenia: The Nation Awakens." In *Nations & Politics in the Soviet Successor States*, edited by Ian Bremmer and Ray Taras. Cambridge: Cambridge University Press, 1993.

Durant, Will. *The Age of Faith: A History of Medieval Civilization—Christian, Islamic, and Judaic—from Constantine to Dante: A.D. 325–1300*. New York: Simon & Schuster, 1950.

Edgerton, Robert B. *Warriors of the Rising Sun*. New York: W. W. Norton, 1997.

Eimer, David. "Dalai Lama Condemns China's 'Cultural Genocide.'" *The Telegraph*, 16 March 2008, <http://www.telegraph.co.uk/news/worldnews/1581875/Dalai-Lama-condemns-Chinas-cultural-genocide-of-Tibet.html>.

Esherick, Joseph W. *The Origins of the Boxer Rebellion*. Berkeley: University of California Press, 1987.

Esposito, John I. *Islam: The Straight Path*. Rev. 3rd ed. New York: Oxford University Press, 2005.

Fairbank, John King. *The Great Chinese Revolution, 1800–1985*. New York: Harper & Row, 1986.

French, Patrick. *Tibet, Tibet: A Personal History of a Lost Land*. New York: Vintage, 2003.

Friedel, Frank. *Francis Lieber: Nineteenth Century Liberal*. Gloucester: Peter Smith, 1968.

Gay, Peter. *The Cultivation of Hatred. III, The Bourgeois Experience—Victoria to Freud*. New York: W. W. Norton, 1993.

Government of Tibet in Exile. *Tibet: Proving Truth from Facts*. Dharamsala: Government of Tibet in Exile, 1996, <http://www.tibet.com/WhitePaper/white7.html>.

Grotius, Hugo. *The Rights of War and Peace*. Book II. Edited by Richard Tuck, from the edition of Jean Barbeyrac. Indianapolis: Liberty Fund, 2005.

Hagan, Lieutenant Colonel William R. "Overlooked Textbooks Jettison some Durable Military Law Legends." *Military Law Review*, no. 163 (1986): 163–202.

Hankel, Gerd. *Die Leipziger Prozesse: Deutsche Kriegsverbrechen und ihre strafrechtliche Verfolgung nach dem Ersten Weltkrieg*. Hamburg: Hamburger Edition, 2003.

Harris, Whitney R. *Tyranny on Trial: Trial of the Major German War Criminals at the End of World War II at Nuremberg, Germany, 1945–1946*. Rev ed. Dallas: Southern Methodist University Press, 1999.

Hertigan, Richard Shelly. *Lieber's Code and the Law of War*. Chicago: Precedent, 1983.

Herzig, Edmund M. "Armenians." In *The Nationalities Question in the Soviet Union*, edited by Graham Smith. London: Longman, 1990.

Hiro, Dilip. *The Longest War: The Iran–Iraq Military Conflict*. New York: Routledge, 1992.

Hitchens, Christopher. "Childhood's End." *Vanity Fair*, January 2006, http://www.vanityfair.com/politics/features/2006/01/hitchens200601.

Hochschild, Adam. *King Leopold's Ghost: A Story of Greed, Terror, and Heroism in Colonial Africa*. Boston: Houghton Mifflin, 1999.

Horne, John, and Alan Kramer. *German Atrocities, 1914: A History of Denial*. New Haven: Yale University Press, 2001.

Hsü, Immanuel C. Y. *The Rise of Modern China*. 6th ed. New York: Oxford University Press, 2000.

Hull, Isabel V. *Absolute Destruction: Military Culture and the Practices of War in Imperial Germany*. Ithaca, NY: Cornell University Press, 2005.

Human Rights Watch. *A Face and a Name: Civilian Victims of Insurgent Groups in Iraq*. New York: Human Rights Watch, 2005.

———. *Uganda: Country Summary (January 2005)*. New York: Human Rights Watch, 2005.

———. *Precisely Wrong: Gaza Civilians Killed by Israeli Drone-Launched Missiles*. New York: Human Rights Watch, 2009.

———. "UN: Support Goldstone Investigation into Gaza War Violations." 6 May 2009, 1–3, <http://www.hrw.org/en/news/2009/05/06/un-support-goldstone-investigation-gaza-war-violations>.

Ignatieff, Michael. "The Legacy of Raphael Lemkin." Lecture, the United States Holocaust Memorial Museum, Washington, DC, 13 December 2000, <http//www.ushmm.org/conscience/analysis/details.php?content=2000-12-13>.

International Commission of Inquiry on Darfur. *Report of the International Commission of Inquiry on Darfur to the United Nations Secretary-General*. Geneva: United Nations, 2005.

International Commission of Jurists. *Tibet and the Chinese People's Republic*. Geneva: Government of Tibet in Exile, 1960, <http://www.com/Resolution/icj60.html>.

International Committee of the Red Cross. *Observations on the Legal Issues Related to the Use of Cluster Munitions*. Geneva: International Committee of the Red Cross, 2007.

International Court of Justice. The Hague, Press Release No. 2009/17, 21 April 2009.

International Criminal Court. "Situations and Cases," 1–2, <http://www.icc-cpi.int/menus/ICC/Situations+and-cases/>.

Israel Ministry of Foreign Affairs. "Behind the Headlines: Legal and Operational Aspects of the Use of Cluster Bombs," 5 September 2006, 1–2, <http://www.mfa.gov.il/MFA/About+the+Ministry/Behind+the+headlines/legal+and+oper>.

Janjić, Dušan. "Serbia between the Past and Future." In *The Yugoslav War, Europe and the Balkans: How to Achieve Security?*, edited by Stefano Bianchini and Paul Shoup. Ravenna: Longo Editore, 1995.

Jewish Peace News. "IDF Ends Investigation into Gaza War Crimes Investigations." 3 April 2009, 1–4, <http://jewishpeacenews.blogspot.com/2009/04/idf-ends-investigation-into-gaza-war.html>. This article lists Harel's articles in *Ha'aretz*. These are all available online in English.

Katz, Yaakov. "IDF Doubts Credibility of Gaza Report." *Jerusalem Post* (online ed.), 30 June 2009, 1–2, <http://www.jpost.com/servlet/Satellitecid=1246296537077&pagename=JPost%2FJPArticle%2FPrinter>.

Kelsay, John. "Al-Shaybani and the Islamic Law of War." *Journal of Military Ethics* 2, no. 1 (2003): 63–75.

Khrushchev, Nikita. *Khrushchev Remembers*. Translated by Strobe Talbot. Boston: Little, Brown, 1970.

Kochavi, Arieh J. *Prelude to Nuremberg: Allied Wear Crimes Policy and the Question of Punishment*. Chapel Hill: University of North Carolina Press, 1998.

Korean War Atrocities: Report of the Committee on Government Operations made through its Permanent Subcommittee on Investigations by its Subcommittee on Korean War Atrocities pursuant to S. Res. 40, January 11, 1954. Washington, DC: United States Government Printing Office, 1954.

Kramer, Alan. "The First Wave of International War Crimes Trials: Istanbul and Leipzig." *European Review* 14, no. 4 (2006): 441–55.

———. *Dynamic of Destruction: Culture and Mass Killing in the First World War*. Oxford: Oxford University Press, 2007.

Krammer, Arnold. *Prisoners of War: A Reference Handbook*. New York: Praeger, 2007.

Krawchenko, Bohdan. *Social Change and National Consciousness in Twentieth-Century Ukraine*. New York: St. Martin's Press, 1985.

Kurkjian, Vahan M. *A History of Armenia*. New York: Armenian General Benevolent Union, 1958.

Laband, John. *Kingdom in Crisis: The Zulu Response to the British Invasion of 1879*. Manchester: Manchester University Press, 1992.

Laws of War: General Orders No. 100. *Instructions for the Government of Armies of the United States in the Field*, 24 April 1863. The Avalon Project at Yale Law School, <http://www.yale.edu/lawweb/avalon/lieber.htm>.

Laws of War: Laws and Customs of War on Land (Hague II). 29 July 1899. The Avalon Project at Yale Law School, <http://www.yale/edu/lawweb/avalon/lawofwar/hague02.htm>.

Laws of War: Laws and Customs of War on Land (Hague IV). 18 October 1907, <http://www.yale.edu/lawweb/avalon/lawofwar/hague04.htm>.

Lee, Eric Yong-Joong. "Early Development of Modern International Law in East Asia—With Special Reference to China, Japan, and Korea." *Journal of the History of International Law* 4, no. 1 (2002): 42–76.

Lewy, Guenter. *The Armenian Massacres in Ottoman Turkey: A Disputed Genocide*. Salt Lake City: University of Utah Press, 2005.

Li, Peter. "The Nanking Holocaust: Memory, Trauma, and Reconciliation." In *Japanese War Crimes: The Search for Justice*, edited by Peter Li. New Brunswick: Transaction, 2003.

Liber, George. "Ukraine and Three Twentieth-Century Cataclysms." Paper presented at "The Ukrainian Famine-Genocide: Reflections after 75 Years" conference, University of North Carolina at Chapel Hill, 12 September 2008.

Little, Charles E. "The Authenticity and Form of Cato's Saying 'Carthago delenda Est.'" *The Classical Journal* 29, no. 6 (1934): 429–35.

Locke, John. *An Essay Concerning Human Understanding*. Abridged and edited with an Introduction and Notes, by Kenneth P. Winkler. Indianapolis: Hackett, 1996.

———. *Two Treatises of Government and a Letter Concerning Toleration*. Edited by Ian Shapiro. New Haven: Yale University Press, 2003.

Lopez-Terres, Patrick. "Arrest and Transfer of Indictees: The Experiences of the ICTY." Paper presented at the 2006 ICLN "International Cooperation on Transnational Crime" conference, 15 December, 2006.

Luther, Martin. *Von der Freiheit eines Christenmenschen* [The Freedom of a Christian], <http://wsu.edu/~dee/REFORM/FREEDOM.HTN>.

MacDonough, Giles. *The Last Kaiser: The Life of Wilhelm II*. New York: St. Martin's Press, 2000.

Malcolm, Noel. *Bosnia: A Short History*. New York: New York University Press, 1994.

Marius, Richard. *Martin Luther: The Christian between God and Death*. Cambridge, MA: The Belknap Press of Harvard University Press, 1999.

Marr, Phebe. *The Modern History of Iraq*. Boulder: Westview Press, 2004.

Maslen, Stuart, and Virgil Wiebe. *Cluster Munitions: A Survey of Legal Responses*. London: Landmine Action, 2007.

Matthäus, Jürgen. "The Lessons of Leipzig: Punishing German War Criminals after the First World War." In *Atrocities on Trial: Historical Perspectives on the Politics of Prosecuting War Crimes*, edited by Patricia Heberer and Jürgen Matthäus. Lincoln: University of Nebraska Press, 2008.

McCarthy, Rory. "Hamas Accused of War Crimes in Gaza." guardian.uk.co, 23 March 2009, 1–2, <http://www.guardian.co.uk/world/2009/mar/23/gaza-war-crimes-hamas/print>.

Meron, Theodore. *War Crimes Law Comes of Age: Essays*. Oxford: Clarendon Press, 1998.

———. *The Humanization of International Law*. Leiden: Martinus Nijhoff, 2006.

Military Commissions Act of 2006. 3 January 2006, <http://thomas.loc.gov/cgi-bin/query/C?c109:./temp/~c1099Zil9a>.

Monter, William. "Witch Trials in Continental Europe." In *Witchcraft and Magic in Europe*, edited by Bengt Ankarloo and Stuart Clark. Philadelphia: University of Pennsylvania Press, 2002.

Mortimer, Geoff. *Eyewitness Accounts of the Thirty Years War, 1618–48*. New York: Palgrave, 2002.

The New Complete Works of Josephus. Translated by William Whiston. Grand Rapids: Kregel, 1999.

"News Chronology." *Chemical Weapons Convention Bulletin*, no. 28 (June 1995): 20.

Nicolle, David. *Crusader Warfare*. I, *Byzantium, Europe and the Struggle for the Holy Land, 1050–1300*. London: Continuum, 2007.

"Not Nearly Back to Normal." *The Economist*, 30 April 2009, 49.

Nuremberg Trials Final Report Appendix D: Control Council Law No. 10: Punishment of Persons Guilty of War Crimes Against Peace and Against Humanity. The Avalon Project at Yale Law School, <http://www.yalelaw.edu/lawweb/avalon/int/imt10.htm>.

O'Donnell, James J. *Augustine: A New Biography*. New York: HarperCollins, 2005.

Ó Siocháin, Séamas, and Michael O'Sullivan, eds. *The Eyes of Another Race: Roger Casement's Congo Report and 1903 Diary*. Dublin: University College Dublin Press, 2003.

Office of the High Commissioner for Human Rights. *Convention on the Prevention and Punishment of the Crime of Genocide*. 9 December 1948, <http://www.unhchr.ch/html/menu3/b/p_genocid.htm>.

Office of United States Chief Counsel for Prosecution of Axis Criminality. *Nazi Conspiracy and Aggression*. I. Washington, DC: United States Government Printing Office, 1946.

Ögren, Kenneth. "Humanitarian Law in the Articles of War Decreed in 1621 by King Gustavus II Adolphus of Sweden." *International Review of the Red Cross*, no. 313 (1996): 1–3, <http://www.icrc.org/Web/Eng/siteeng0.nsf/html/57JN8D>.

Osmanczyk, Edmund Jan, and Anthonhy Mango. *Encyclopedia of the United Nations and International Agreements*. Volume 4. London: Routledge, 2004.

Oswalt, Wendell H., and Sharlotte Neely. *This Land was Theirs: A Study of North American Indians*. 5th ed. Mountain View, CA: Mayfield, 1996.

Pakenham, Thomas. *The Scramble for Africa: White Man's Conquest of the Dark Continent from 1876 to 1912*. New York: Perennial/HarperCollins, 2003.

Payaslian, Simon. *United States Policy toward the Armenian Question and the Armenian Genocide*. New York: Palgrave Macmillan, 2005.

Peskin, Victor. *International Justice in Rwanda and the Balkans: Virtual Trials and the Struggle for Cooperation*. Cambridge: Cambridge University Press, 2008.

Pidd, Helen. "Gaza Offensive: Israeli Military Says No War Crimes Committed." guardian. co.uk. 1–2, <http://www.guardian.co.uk/world/2009/mar/31/israeli-military-denies-war-crimes-gaza/print>.

Ponte, Carla Del. *Madame Prosecutor: Confrontations with Humanity's Worst Criminals and the Culture of Impunity: A Memoir*. New York: Other Press, 2008.

The Profile of Human Rights Violations in Timor-Leste 1974–1999. A Report by the Benetech Human Rights Analysis Group to the Commission on Reception, Truth, and Reconciliation of Timor-Leste, <http://www.hrdag.org/resources/timor_chapter_graphs/timor_chapter_page_01.shtml>.

Protocol Additional to the Geneva Convention of 12 August 1949, and Relating to the Protection of Victims of International Armed Conflicts (Protocol 1), <http://www.unhchr.ch/html/menu3?b/93.htm>.

Protocol for the Prohibition of the Use in War of Asphyxiating, Poisonous, or Other Gases, and of Bacteriological Methods of Warfare (Geneva Protocol), 17 June 1925.

Prunier, Gérard. *The Rwanda Crisis: History of a Genocide*. New York: Columbia University Press, 1995.

———. *Darfur: A 21st Century Genocide*. 3rd ed. Ithaca, NY: Cornell University Press, 2008.

Purcell, Victor. "*The Boxer Uprising: A Background Study*. Cambridge: Cambridge University Press, 1963.

Ramet, Sabrina P. "A Theory about the Yugoslav Meltdown: The Serbian National Awakening as a 'Revitalization Movement.'" *Nationalities Papers* 32, no. 4 (2004): 765–79.

Rawlings, Louis. "Hannibal the Cannibal? Polybius on Barcid Atrocities." *Cardiff Historical Papers*, 1–11, <http://174.125.47.132/search?q.cache.neOxygYip9wJ:www.ct.ac.uk/hisar/resources/CHP9>.

Rehman, Javaid. "The Concept of Jihad in Islamic International Law." *Journal of Conflict and Security Law* 10, no. 3 (2005): 321–43.

Rejali, Darius. *Torture and Democracy*. Princeton: Princeton University Press, 2007.

Report of Charles S.P. Bowles Foreign Agent of the United States Sanitary Commission. New York: Thomson Gale Reprint, 1969.

Roberts, Michael. *Gustavus Adolphus: A History of Sweden, 1611–1632*. II, *1626–1632*. London: Longman, Green, 1958.

Rome Statue of the International Criminal Court (U.N. Doc. A/CONF.183/9).

Rummel, R. J. *China's Bloody Century: Genocide and Mass Murder since 1900*. New Brunswick: Transaction, 2007.

"Rushing off a Cliff.". *New York Times*, 28 September 2006, 2, <http://www.truthout.org/cgi-bin/artman/exec/view/cgi/64/22818>.

Santosuosso, Antonio. *Barbarians, Marauders, and Infidels*. Boulder: Westview Press, 2004.

Sarajevo Research and Documentation Center (Istraživačko dokumentacioni centar). *Human Losses in Bosnia and Herzegovina 91–95*. Sarajevo: Sarajevo Research and Documentation Center, 2007.

Satkauskas, Rytis. "Soviet Genocide Trials in the Baltic States: The Relevance of International Law." *Yearbook of International Humanitarian Law* 7 (2004): 388–409.

Schabas, William S. *An Introduction to the International Criminal Court*. 3rd ed. Cambridge: Cambridge University Press, 2007.

Schrecker, Joseph E. *Imperialism and Chinese Nationalism: Germany in Shantung*. Cambridge, MA: Harvard University Press, 1971.

Shaw, Malcolm N. *International Law*. 5th ed. Cambridge: Cambridge University Press, 2003.

Shaw, Stanford. *History of the Ottoman Empire and Modern Turkey.* II, *Reform, Revolution, and Republic. The Rise of Modern Turkey, 1808–1975.* Cambridge: Cambridge University Press, 1977.

Smith, Jane I. "Islam and Christendom: Historical, Cultural, and Religious Interaction from the Seventh to the Fifteenth Centuries." In *The Oxford History of Islam,* edited by John L. Esposito. Oxford: Oxford University Press, 1999.

Spence, Jonathan D. *The Search for Modern China.* New York: W. W. Norton, 1990.

———. *God's Chinese Son: The Taiping Heavenly Kingdom of Hong Xiuquan.* New York: W. W. Norton, 1996.

Stannard, David E. *American Holocaust: The Conquest of the New World.* New York: Oxford University Press, 1992.

Statute of the International Tribunal for the Former Yugoslavia (25 May 1993).

Stern, Fritz. *Gold and Iron: Bismarck, Bleichröder, and the Building of the German Empire.* New York: Vintage Books, 1979.

Subtelny, Orest. *Ukraine: A History.* 2nd ed. Toronto: University of Toronto Press, 1994.

Sun-tzu's Art of War. In *The Seven Military Classics of Ancient China.* Translated by Ralph D. Sawyer. Boulder: Westview Press, 1993.

Sun, Tzu. *The Art of War: The New Translation.* Translated by J. H. Huang. New York: Quill, 1993.

Suny, Ronald Gregor. *Looking toward Ararat: Armenia in Modern History.* Bloomington: Indiana University Press, 1993.

Tabean, Ewa, and Jakub Bijak. "War Related Deaths in the 1992 Armed Conflicts in Bosnia and Herzegovina: A Critique of Previous Estimates and Recent Deaths." *European Journal of Population* 21 (2005): 187–215.

Tanaka, Yuki. *Hidden Horrors: Japanese War Crimes in World War II.* Boulder: Westview Press, 1998.

Tanakh: The Holy Scriptures. Philadelphia: Jewish Publication Society, 1985.

Taylor, Telford. *The Anatomy of the Nuremberg Trials.* Boston: Little Brown, 1992.

Telushkin, Rabbi Joseph. *Biblical Literacy: The Most Important People, Events, and Ideas of the Hebrew Bible.* New York: HarperCollins, 1997.

Theriault, Henry C. "Rethinking Dehumanization in Genocide." In *The Armenian Genocide: Cultural and Ethical Legacies,* edited by Richard Hovannisian. New Brunswick: Transaction, 2007.

Thornton, Russell. *American Indian Holocaust and Survival: A Population History since 1492.* Norman: University of Oklahoma Press, 1987.

"A Thousand Tragedies. But is it a Crime?" *The Economist,* 17–23, January 2009, 49.

Timmerman, Kenneth R. *The Death Lobby: How the West Armed Iraq.* Boston: Houghton Mifflin, 1991.

Torrell, Jean-Pierre. *Saint Thomas Aquinas.* I, *The Person and his Work.* Translated by Robert Royal. Washington, DC: Catholic University of America Press, 2005.

Treaty of Kars (23 October 1921). Text in Russian and English, <http://en.wikisource.org/Treaty_of_Kars>.

The Treaty of Peace between the Allied and Associated Powers and Turkey Signed at Sèvres August 10, 1920, <http://history.acusd.edu/gen/versaillestreaty.html>.

Treaty of Versailles (28 June 1919). <http://firstworldwar.com/source/versailles.hte>.

Tripp, Charles. *A History of Iraq.* 3rd ed. Cambridge: Cambridge University Press, 2007.

"UN Appoints Jewish Judge to Head Gaza Inquiry into Alleged War Crimes." *Mail Online,* 3 April 2009, 1–4, <http://www.dailymail.co.uk/news/worldnews/article-1167138/UN-appoints-Jewish-judge-head-Gaza-inquiry-alleged-war-crimes.html>.

UN Office of the Special Adviser on Africa (OSAA). "DDR and Transitional Justice." Issue Paper presented at the Second International Conference on DDR and Stability in Africa, Kinshasa, Democratic Republic of Congo, 2007, 12–14 June.

"UN Warning on Mid-East Crimes." *BBC News*, 20 July 2006, 1, <http://news.bbc.co.uk/2/hi/middle_east/5197544.stm>.

United Nations. *Resolution 582 (1986)*. Adopted by the Security Council at its 2666th meeting, 24 February, 1986.

———. *Resolution 598 (1987)*. Adopted by the Security Council at its 2750th meeting, 20 July 1987.

———. *Resolution 612 (1988)*. Adopted by the Security Council at its 2812th meeting, 9 May 1988.

———. *Resolution 620 (1988)*. Adopted by the Security Council at its 2825th meeting, 26 August 1988.

United Nations, General Assembly. Resolution 63/3.*Request for an advisory opinion on the International Court of Justice on whether the unilateral declaration of independence of Kosovo is in accordance with international law*, 8 October 2008.

United Nations High Commissioner for Human Rights. "Rape and Abuse of Women in the Territory of the Former Yugoslavia." Commissioner on Human Rights Resolution 1993. United National Human Rights Commission, Geneva, 2003.

United Nations Security Council. *Resolution 1244*, S/RES/1244(1999), 10 June 1999.

Wang, Edward. "Report Says Valid Grievances at Root of Tibet Unrest." *New York Times*, 6 June 2009, A4.

War Crimes: Convention (IV) Relative to the Protection of Civilian Persons in Times of War. Geneva, 12 August 1949, <http://www.icrc.org/ihl.nsf/385ec082b509e76c41256739003e636d/6756482d86146898c125641e004aa3c5>.

"War Crimes in Chechnya and the Response of the West. Testimony before the Senate Committee on Foreign Relations." Human Rights Watch, 2004, <http://hrw.org/english/docs/2000/03/01/russia11094_txt.htm>.

Watkins, John C., Jr., and John Paul Weber, eds. *War Crimes and War Crime Trials: From Leipzig to the ICC and Beyond: Cases, Materials and Comments*. Durham, NC: Carolina Academic Press, 2006.

Ward, Andrew. *Our Bones are Scattered: The Cawnpore Massacre and the Indian Mutiny of 1857*. New York: Henry Holt, 1996.

"A Warrant for Bashir." *The Economist*, 7–13 March 2009, 20.

Wedgwood, C. V. *The Thirty Years War*. New York: Anchor Books, 1961.

Wei, Jing. *100 Questions about Tibet*. Beijing: Beijing Review Press, 1989.

Welch, Jeanie M. *The Tokyo Trial: A Bibliographic Guide to English-Language Sources*. Westport: Greenwood Press, 2002.

Wilson, Richard Ashby. "Judging History: The Historical Record of the International Criminal Tribunal for the Former Yugoslavia." *Human Rights Quarterly* 27 (2005): 908–42.

Winthrop, William. *Military Law and Precedents*. 2nd ed. Washington, DC: Government Printing Office, 1920.

Wolowyna, Oleh. "The Famine-Genocide of 1932–1933: Estimation of Losses and Demographic Impact." Paper presented to "The Ukrainian Famine-Genocide: Reflection after 75 Years" conference University of North Carolina at Chapel Hill, 12 September 2008.

The Yi Ho Tuan Movement of 1900. Peking: Foreign Languages Press, 1976.

Yinan, Hu. "Release from a Cycle of Servitude." *China Daily*, 22 January 2009, 7.

Zhonglu, Liu, Chu Lizhong, and the Information Office of the State Council, People's Republic of China. *China's Tibet*. Beijing: China Intercontinental Press, 2000.

"The Last Bullet for the Last Serb":[1] The Ustaša Genocide against Serbs: 1941–1945[2]

Michele Frucht Levy

While participating in Hitler's Holocaust against Jews and Roma, wartime Croatia's collaborationist government, the Ustaša (Insurgent),[3] conducted its own genocide against the Serbs within its territories. As the title of Marco Rivelli's 1978 text, *Le Génocide occulté*, makes clear, this phenomenon remained largely unknown in the West until the 1990s. Of the principal external actors, post-war German attention focused on the Holocaust. Italy still resists fully confronting its less than pristine role in the Balkans, so that Rivelli's work, completed in 1978, was not published in Italy until 1999.[4] The Vatican, meanwhile, has yet to release its documents on the subject.

Within Yugoslavia itself, Ustaša perpetrators strove to conceal their crimes once it became clear that Tito's Partisans would win the Yugoslav Civil War. After the Partisans executed the *Četnici* (Cetniks or Chetniks, Serbian paramilitary forces) and Ustaša troops they had captured, Tito encouraged all ethnicities to bury their war memories so that Yugoslavia could build a new nation based on brotherhood and unity.[5] While politically expedient, this policy initially limited public discussion and scholarly discourse on the subject. The West, meanwhile, bankrolled prominent Ustaše reborn as anti-communist agents, while America's popular consciousness all but forgot about the Balkans until Yugoslavia imploded.

Despite Tito's attempts to forge a single national identity, ethnic tensions surfaced in Yugoslavia as early as the 1960s. After his death in 1980, nationalist intellectuals and writers produced a spate of books, articles, and novels on the genocide, much of it propagandistic. Power-hungry politicians used these works to stir latent memories and manipulated wildly inflated or deflated numbers to garner power. Thus Vladimir Žerjavić, a Croat scholar whose calculations significantly revised the earlier numbers, observed: "Our polemics about our [World War II] losses escalated so much that they threaten a new war, to avenge those killed 50 years ago."[6] Then in 1991–1995, sites of Serb mass deaths again became places of violence. In 1992, when Croats blew up a monument in Šurmanci to Serbs murdered by the Ustaša, one explained: "We killed the dead because they kept them alive."[7] Thus, as Kerstin Nyström suggests, "... it is reasonable to argue that the Second World War was resumed in 1991."[8]

This violent eruption rekindled Western interest in the area.[9] A number of histories appeared, many by journalists who had covered the war. But most alluded to the Ustaša genocide only briefly or suggested that rival ethnic and political groups massacred each other's civilian populations, which, while true, managed to obscure the history of that phenomenon. As Marko Attila Hoare suggests:

> The Ustaša genocide of Serbs, Jews and Gypsies in the territory of the so-called "Independent State of Croatia" in the period 1941–1945 is a subject about which historians in the West have to date had little to say. English-language accounts by journalists and others have often been as empty of serious analysis as they are full of gory descriptions of atrocities.[10]

Indeed, a recent genocide textbook designed for university students contains a case study on Serbian ethnic cleansing in Bosnia that mentions only World War II "massacres" as historical background.[11] Even though Western scholars have at last begun to examine seriously the Ustaša and its genocidal program, their works are mostly studies that address a single facet of this complex event.[12] I therefore intend my essay as a broad overview of the genocide in its various aspects, that we may glimpse its full extent and better understand both the event itself and its role in the history of post-war Yugoslavia and its successor states.

Yugoslavia's signing of the Tripartite Treaty with Italy and Germany on 25 March 1941 initiated that sequence of events which led to the creation of the Nezavisna Država Hrvatska (NDH—Independent State of Croatia). On 27 March, angry pro-British officers of the Yugoslav army and navy overthrew the government of Prince Paul, and installed his 17-year old cousin, Peter II, as ruler. On 6 April, German planes bombed Belgrade as part of Operation Marita. Originally intended to remove the British from Greece, and then expanded to punish the errant Yugoslavs, the Axis invasion successfully dismembered the Kingdom of Yugoslavia. Over the next few days, the Ustaša, led by Ante Pavelić, infiltrated the paramilitary arm of the Hrvatska seljačka stranka (HSS—Croatian Peasant Party), while on 9 April, in a radio broadcast to Croatia from Berlin's Kaiserhof Hotel, Andrija Artuković ("the Butcher of the Balkans") exhorted Croats to kill Serbs. The ultra-nationalist Ustaša sought support from Croats angered by their perceived inferior status in Yugoslavia. For Serbia had a long tradition of political independence and supplied pre-World War II Yugoslavia with its core political system and ruling dynasty.

The next day, Slavko Kvaternik, who would become commander-in-chief of the Croatian armed forces (the military arm of the Ustaša state), announced the creation of the NDH. Many members of this small group of nationalist Croatian terrorists had recently returned from exile, most of them from Italy, where the Organizzazione per la Vigilanza e la Repressione dell'Antifascismo (OVRA—Organization for Vigilance and the Repression of Anti-Fascism), Mussolini's secret police, had supported them. Others returned from Yanka Puszta, a small Hungarian town and fascist stronghold on the Yugoslav border, and Germany. Kvaternik then administered the new government until Pavelić, the architect of Yugoslav King Aleksandar's assassination in 1934, returned to Zagreb from Italy on 15 April and declared himself *poglavnik*, or *Führer*. To the chagrin of many Croats, Germany let Italy keep Dalmatian territory it claimed during the invasion (Korčula, Mljet, Krk and some smaller islands, as well as the hinterland of Zadar and Split and some territories that Italy had controlled since 1918, including Zara/Zadar and Lastovo). But since the NDH received most of Bosnia-Herzegovina, an area larger than Tomislav I's tenth-century kingdom, Croats could still idealize its romantic origins.[13]

With relatively few members in April 1941, the Ustaša enhanced its narrow base by drawing support from nationalists, students, intellectuals, the petit bourgeoisie, peasants, and Catholic clergy.[14] Pavelić's agents also successfully recruited from among the diasporic populations in Italy, Germany, Belgium, and South America, appealing to those who embraced the Ustaša goal of a pure Catholic Croatia.[15] Interestingly, Croat scholar Branimir Anzulović asserts that Croats from the Dinaric Alps, which straddle the Adriatic coast of the Balkan Peninsula from Croatia to Albania, joined the movement in numbers much higher than their ratio to the general population. The high percentage of Dinaric Serbs who fought in the recent Bosnian War mirrors this, as nationalist Serb media encouraged post-Tito Serbs to "remember" the earlier atrocities against Serbs in the Dinaric regions of Croatia and Bosnia-Herzegovina—a historical quid pro quo.[16]

Ustaša headquarters served as the center of the hastily erected NDH government infrastructure designed to secure its idealized utopia. It included three branches: one dealing with political and organizational matters; the Ustaška vojnica (Ustaša Corps), a Nazi-like paramilitary group separate from the *Domobranstvo*, or regular army; and the Ustaška nadzorna služba (UNS—Ustaša Supervisory Service). The latter coordinated the implementation of government policies with a branch of the Interior Ministry, the Ravnateljstvo za javni red i sigurnost (RAVSIGUR—Office for Public Order and Security), that housed *Ustaška* obrana (Ustaša Defense) and Ustaška redarstvo (Ustaša Supervision), its security arm. Slavko Kvaternik's son, Eugen, known as Dido, headed both the UNS and RAVSIGUR, thereby controlling all internal security and intelligence agencies, even those under Andrija Artuković, the Interior Minister. Vjekoslav "Maks" Luburić led the Ustaša Defense, which would manage Pavelić's extensive concentration camp system.[17]

Eager to distance itself from the Serbs, cement ties with Germany, and claim a Western identity,[18] the Ustaša tried to claim that Croats had Gothic roots. There were approximately 1.8 million Serbs, 700,000 Bosnian Muslims (Bosniaks), 40,000 Jews, 28,500 Roma, 300,000 from other minority groups, and 4.8 million Croats in the NDH. The Bosnian Muslims were declared "the blood of our blood ... the flower of our Croatian Nation"[19] and granted rights and privileges. But according to Education Minister Mile Budak, "1/3 of Serbs we shall kill, another we shall deport, and the last we shall force to embrace the Roman Catholic religion and thus meld them into Croats."[20] Indeed, Croat historian Branka Prpa-Jovanović suggests that "the Ustaša, although a small minority of the Croatian people, also recruited among the Slavic Muslims of Bosnia-Hercegovina for a program of brutal repression of communists as well as outright genocide against the Serbian population within the 'independent state.'"[21] Once the Jews and the Roma were effectively eliminated, such a policy would finally enable the Ustaša to claim that it had created a nation of ethnically pure Catholic and Muslim Croats.[22]

Before addressing the genocide itself, let us first explain the use of that loaded term, which Serb nationalists appropriated and aggressively deployed for ideological purposes in the 1980s and 1990s. Indeed, throughout World War II, Yugoslavia fought a bloody civil war in which Serb *Četnici*, Croat and Muslim Ustaše, and communist partisans of all ethnicities brutally massacred one another and destroyed their respective villages. All sides inflicted brutal violence against civilians. One might then question the virtue of applying "genocide" to one particular group and not the rest. Here I find Tomislav Dulić's classifications helpful:

> *Genocide* is the total or substantial destruction of a religious or ethnic group by a state or similar political actor by a method that includes but is not limited to intentional, continuous and systematically organized annihilation.
>
> *Attempted Genocide* is the attack against a religious or ethnic group by a state or similar political actor, where the perpetrator has attempted but not succeeded in total or substantial destruction, by a method that includes but is not limited to intentional, continuous and systematically organized annihilation.
>
> *Ethnocide ("ethnic cleansing")* is the intentional and systematic forced removal of a religious or ethnic group by a method that includes the commission of organized massacres.
>
> *Massacre* is the incidental mass killing of members of a religious or ethnic group in a local community that may or may not be organized by a central political actor.[23]

According to these definitions, the *Četnici*, who possessed a rudimentary ideology, no state apparatus, a decentralized, territorially dispersed leadership, and the lack of an effective media network for propaganda, engaged in ethnocide and massacre in an effort to create their own imagined community of Orthodox Serbs. On the other hand, the Ustaša controlled the NDH with strong Italian and Germany backing.[24] Its ideology was based on Pavelić's Seventeen Principles (institutionalized through legal codes enacted at the local and national level, and expanded in 1942), while its central leadership, with its clearly defined bureaucratic and military hierarchy, dominated the Catholic Church and the media. The NDH was thus positioned to commit either genocide or attempted genocide, depending on how one weighs the number of those annihilated, a fiercely contested figure that reputable scholars generally agree will remain elusive because of the absence of credible records.[25] Indeed, according to Generalmajor Edmund von Glaise-Horstenau, the German Plenipotentiary General in Zagreb, Kvaternik had privately promised that the Ustaša would ultimately exterminate "the remaining one and a half million Serbs, including women and children."[26] His son Dido suggested that Anti-Serbdom was "the quintessence of the Ustaša doctrine, its *raison d'être*."[27] More recently, Croat scholar Jozo Tomasevich has suggested that "only the resistance of the Partisans and, to a much lesser extent, Serb *Četnici*, saved the Serbs in the territory of the NDH from total disaster."[28]

A brief examination of Pavelić's Seventeen Principles, written during his Italian exile and revised after the NDH was formed, should clarify the ideological foundation of the Ustaša movement and the laws of the NDH:

1. The Croatian nation is an independent ethnic and national unit, a nation by itself, and in that sense it is not identical with any other nation nor is it a part or a tribe of any other nation.

2. The Croatian nation has its original and historical name, Croat, under which it came 1300 years ago to its present territory, and under which it lives today. That name cannot and must not be replaced by any other name.

3. The Croatian nation made its present country its homeland already in ancient times, inhabiting it permanently, becoming one with it and giving it the original and natural name Croatia. That name cannot and must not be replaced by any other name.

4. The land which was occupied in ancient times by the Croatian people, and which became their Croatian homeland, extends over several provinces, many of which had their names even before the arrival of the Croats and some of which were given their names later, but all of them constitute one single Croatian homeland, and therefore nobody has the right to claim for himself any of those provinces.

5. The Croatian people came to their homeland of Croatia as a completely free nation in the time of the Great Migrations, by their own will, thus conquering that land and making it their own forever.

6. The Croatian nation was completely organized when it came to its Croatian homeland, not only in a military sense but also in a familial sense, so that it immediately founded its own state with all of the attributes of statehood.

7. The state of Croatia was already formed when many other nations lived in complete chaos. The Croatian nation preserved its state through the centuries until the end of the World War, and never abandoned it, not by any act or by any legal resolution, nor did it give away its rights to anyone else, but at the end of the World War foreign forces prevented the Croatian people from exercising their sovereign right to form their own Croatian State.

The first seven principles stated that Croatia was an ancient state with claims to land within its historic boundaries and with a people bound by a single ethnicity. They also had a right to exist freely as a nation without the threat of outside intervention. Thus Pavelić simultaneously repudiated post-World War I Croatia's existence as part of the Kingdom of Serbs, Croats, and Slovenes and the Kingdom of Yugoslavia, and affirmed that the NDH was the historic nation-state of the Croatian people.

8. The Croatian nation has the right to revive its sovereign authority in its own Croatian State in its entire national and historical area, that is to say to reconstitute a complete, sovereign and independent Croatian state. This reconstitution may be accomplished by any means, including force of arms.

Pavelić rewrote this eighth principle after April 1941 to reflect the new national reality and reject any obligations, whether internal or external, which did not strictly adhere to the Seventeen Principles.

9. The Croatian nation has the right of happiness and prosperity, and every single Croat has that right as a part of the Croatian nation. Happiness and prosperity can be revived and fulfilled for the nation in general and for individuals as members of the nation only in a complete, sovereign and independent Croatian state which must not and cannot be a component of any other state or any creation of a foreign power.

10. The Croatian nation is sovereign, therefore only it has the right to rule an independent state of Croatia and to manage all state and national affairs.

11. In the Croatian state and in the national affairs of a sovereign and independent state of Croatia no one can make decisions who is not by origin and by blood a member of the Croatian nation, and in the same way no other nation or state can decide the destiny of the Croatian people and the Croatian state.

12. The Croatian nation belongs to western culture and to western civilization.

The tenth and eleventh principles implicitly excluded Serbs, Jews, and Roma, who were not Croat "by blood," from political activity in the NDH, while the twelfth officially asserted the Croatian identity as Western, an important step in distancing itself from negative Western constructs of Eastern Europe and the Balkans.[29] This further isolated Croats from other Yugoslav groups, who were now seen as non-Western and, hence, Eastern.

13. The peasantry is not only the foundation and source of life, but it alone constitutes the Croatian nation, and as such it is the bearer and agent of all state authority in the Croatian state.

14. All classes of the Croatian people constitute one unified whole, defined by their Croatian blood, who can trace back their origins and who maintain a permanent familial connection with the village and the land. In ninety-nine out of a hundred cases someone in Croatia who does not originate from a peasant family is not a Croat at all, but a foreign immigrant.

15. The material and moral wealth of the Croatian state is the property of the people, therefore the people are the only ones authorized to possess and to use it.

16. The essence of the moral strength of the Croatian people is found in an orderly and religious family; its economic strength is in agriculture, communal life and the natural wealth of the Croatian land; its defensive strength is in its valor, and its educational and cultural progress is based on a natural genius and proven ability in the fields of science and learning. Craftsmanship is the helping hand of the entire peasant economy.

17. Balanced breeding, the promotion and perfect of these virtues and branches of national life, is the goal of all public welfare and of state authority as such, because they have guaranteed survival for centuries of existence and will guarantee the prosperity of future generations of the Croatian nation and the existence of that security in the independent Croatian State.[30]

Principle Thirteen articulated one of the Ustaša's "creation myths," the centrality of the peasant,[31] which, among other things, labeled the *krajina* Serbs who had migrated to the frontier between Bosnia and Croatia several hundred years earlier as immigrants and non-Croats.[32] The fourteenth principle better defined the idea of "racial purity," while the sixteenth linked the Ustaša to the Catholic Church by stating that "the essence of the moral strength of the Croatian people is found in an orderly and religious family life." Finally, the seventeenth principle's reference to "balanced breeding" echoed Nazi racial ideas about blood purity.

The 17 April 1941 Law for the Defense of the People and the 30 April Law Decree on Citizenship provided the legal basis for the NDH's policies towards Serbs, Jews, Roma, and unpatriotic Croats. Though the Ustaša would murder over 80% of the NDH's Jews and Roma, their principal target was the Serbs. According to Milovan Žanić, the Minister of Justice:

> This has to be a country of Croats and nobody else, and the method does not exist which we as *Ustaša* would not use in order to make this country truly Croatian and cleanse it from the Serbs, who have threatened us for centuries and would threaten us at the first opportunity.[33]

Such statements laid the groundwork, ideologically, for the genocide against the Serbs.

Given the traditionally strong presence of Serbs in the Yugoslav army, the Ustaša attacked that institution first. Shortly before Kvaternik announced the creation of the NDH, Pavelić broadcast a radio speech from Florence calling for Croat soldiers to "remove Serbian officers, pledge allegiance to the Ustaša flag, and turn your rifles against those who had captured the Croatian people, desecrated all things sacred to Croats, and taken over Croatian homes and Croatian land."[34] On 6 April, Foreign Minister Mladen Lorković reported that a group of Croat soldiers, "following the call of the *Poglavnik* and the voice of our Croatian blood, rose against the Serb officers and the Serbian army units," an action that prevented Yugoslavia's Fourth Army from proceeding to the military front. Finally, on 11 April, one day after declaring the birth of the NDH, Kvaternik announced the exclusion of "undesirables" from the military.[35]

On 13 April, after disarming Serb officers and soldiers, the Ustaša created Croat gendarmeries, units that were later augmented with Croat *Volksdeutsche*, ethnic Germans descended from colonists originally sent by Vienna in the eighteenth century to repopulate demographically weakened regions of their Balkan territories. Of the approximately 500,000 *Volksdeutsche* throughout Yugoslavia, most of whom were deeply loyal to the Third Reich, about 170,000 resided in Croatia, where they lived in a virtual state-within-a-state during the war.[36] The exclusion of Serbs in the NDH army meant that 30% of military-aged youth, a group known for its military prowess, could not be called upon to serve when manpower shortages later occurred.[37]

Between 13 and 30 April, the Ustaša used these new laws to strip Serbs of their citizenship, livelihoods, and possessions. Those who tainted Croatia's purity could now be legally killed—which clearly applied to impure Serbs, now labeled "Greek

Easterners," because of their purported link to the East. Serbs were purged throughout the judicial system, in all levels of government, the diplomatic corps, the medical profession, and so on. This caused havoc throughout the NDH, since incompetent zealots often replaced experts. A revamped legal system allowed for "courts of three," essentially kangaroo courts, to adjudicate legal matters. In time, even this façade faded away; once tried, the accused could be summarily executed or sent to a concentration camp. The Ustaša then ordered its legal structures meshed with those of the now entirely "pure" Croat government, disrupting local jurisdictions and further alienating many Croats. The Cyrillic alphabet was likewise banned and, on 30 April, the Ustaša defined a citizen of the NDH as an Aryan who was actively loyal to the NDH, threatening those Croats who questioned Ustaša practices.

By May 1941 the Ustaša had Aryanized the bureaucracy, the professions, and the currency (the Croatian kuna replaced the banned Yugoslav dinar). Unofficially banned from civic and public social activities, Serbs had to wear blue armbands bearing a large P, for *pravoslavac* (Orthodox). This was later replaced by yellow tin neckplates. In June 1941, efforts were made to purify the Croatian language of all "Eastern" (i.e. Serbian) words, and to close all Serbian schools. Serb businesses were likewise seized, and in August the Ustaša nationalized all Serbian real estate and property, which was to be turned over to the Croats and *Volksdeutsche*.[38]

Expulsions, the first pillar of the tripartite Ustaša plan to create a pure Croat state, began on 18 April, when the government seized land in Slavonia and Srem from Serb veterans who had fought in the Yugoslav army during World War I. Between May and June 1941, more than 5,000 Serbs fled or were driven into German-occupied Serbia.[39] The government established the Office of Colonization to resettle Croats on reclaimed land, but the steady stream of battered refugees strained the resources of the German authorities in occupied Serbia, who wanted to exchange Serbia's Slovenes for Croatia's Serbs. The Ustaša complied and began nocturnal raids to round up Serbs, which often left families just half an hour to gather papers and no more than 50 kilos of property. The elites, which included Serbian community leaders, intellectuals, and particularly Orthodox clergy, the backbone of the Orthodox communities, went first. By the end of 1941, half of 577 Serbian Orthodox clergymen in the NDH were dead, imprisoned, or deported.[40]

The Ustaša opened holding camps, which allowed them to round up large numbers of Serbs and deport them to Serbia. Many, though, were robbed and killed by the Ustaše before reaching the camps. While poor record keeping makes it impossible to determine the exact number of deportees, Jozo Tomasevich suggests that by the summer of 1942 almost 200,000 Serbs had crossed into Nazi-occupied Serbia as transferees or refugees.[41]

Forced conversion to Catholicism was another way to rid the NDH of Serbs.[42] It also highlights the problematic role of the Vatican and the Croatian Catholic Church in the Ustaša's genocide. The Vatican had long supported the idea that Croatian Catholics guarded the religious boundary between East and West. Croats shared this view of themselves as a heroic bulwark against both Islam and Orthodoxy. Education Minister Budak stated in August 1941:

> The Drina is the border between the East and West. God's Providence placed us to defend our border, which our allies are well aware and value, because for centuries we have proven that we are good frontiersmen. Therefore, we were dubbed "Antemurale Christianitatis."[43]

But the rise of the Soviet Union underscored the importance of the Croats as a defense against communism, which Pius XII identified as an immediate and dangerous threat to global Catholicism. This strengthened his interest in Croatia.[44]

To legitimize his government, Pavelić sought full diplomatic relations with the Vatican. His request for a papal audience was turned down several times. The Vatican explained that it had to remain neutral towards states created during the war. But on the evening of 18 May 1941, four days after the infamous Ustaša murder of hundreds of Serbs in the Orthodox Church in Glina, the Pope gave Pavelić, who had come to Rome on political business, a brief private audience.[45] Though the meeting stopped short of fulfilling Pavelić's wish, many among the Allied and Axis powers felt it meant that the Vatican had granted the NDH de facto recognition. A memorandum from the Yugoslav government-in-exile's Legation in London, for example, strongly protested the Pope's audience on 12 June.[46] On 3 October 1942, London's Minister to the Vatican, Sir Godolphin Francis d'Arcy Osborne, worried that Pavelić would seek another audience with the Pope while on a scheduled visit to Rome, since "his reception in 1941 by His Holiness caused a very bad impression in official and unofficial circles in England . . ."[47]

In August 1941, the Vatican appointed Giuseppe Ramiro Marcone as an "apostolic visitor" to the NDH. Pavelić had earlier requested a papal nuncio.[48] But this allowed the Vatican to maintain close contact with the NDH while stopping just short of diplomatic recognition. Thus, while the Pope may not have known the extent of the Ustaša's violence against its minorities during his May meeting with Pavelić, Marcone was now able to keep him well informed. In addition, the Vatican began receiving reports from Italian and German sources that claimed that as many as 300,000 Serbs had already been killed. In March 1942, for instance, Cardinal Eugène Tisserant told Nicola Rusinović, one of two "unofficial" Croatian representatives to the Vatican:

> I know for a fact that it is the Franciscans themselves, as for example Father Simic of Knin, who have taken part in attacks against the Orthodox populations so as to destroy the Orthodox Church. In the same way you destroyed the Orthodox Church in Banja Luka. I know for sure that the Franciscans in Bosnia and Herzegovina have acted abominably, and this pains me. Such acts should not be committed by educated, cultured, civilized people, let alone by priests.[49]

Indeed, according to German, Italian, and eyewitness reports, many Catholic clergymen in the NDH, particularly in Bosnia-Herzegovina, encouraged, took part in, or led massacres and acts of brutal violence against Serbs.[50] Pius XII refused to see Pavelić again, even privately.[51] But in response to pleas on behalf of endangered Jews and Serbs, the Vatican issued only discrete recommendations that the Ustaša moderate its behavior.[52]

Finally, while some clergy in the NDH committed war crimes in the name of the Catholic Church and others protested the genocidal actions of their government, the nationalistic young Archbishop of Zagreb, Alojzije Stepinac, practiced a wary ambivalence. He was an early supporter of Pavelić and the Ustaša's goal of an independent Catholic Croatia. He proclaimed in a letter to his clergy:

> Honourable brothers! There is not one among you who recently has not been a witness to the greatest events in the life of the Croatian people, among whom we work as the harbingers of Christ's Gospel. These are events which have brought our people to embrace a long dreamed and yearned for ideal. These are moments in which the tongue does not speak, but the blood through its mysterious connection with the soil, in which we have become aware of God's light, and with the people from which we have emerged.[53]

As the highest Catholic official in the NDH, Stepinac advised Croatian clergy not to tolerate Orthodox Christianity, which Pavelić considered a political force rather than a religion.[54] This was linked to the fact that the Serbs had enjoyed political dominance in Yugoslavia, with the Orthodox Church wielding considerable political power. Yet neither Pavelić nor Stepinac acknowledged similar aspirations for their own Church and its powerful mother Church in Rome.

Scholars debate the degree of Stepinac's contact with the Ustaša. Vladimir Dedjier, Tito's colleague, alleges that Stepinac entertained the Poglavnik and his inner circle, blessed the military and police, and publicly performed services as the highest Catholic official in the NDH.[55] But while some Western sources cite Dedjier's claim, his strident anti-Catholicism renders it suspect, and little objective evidence exists in its support. In any case, despite his initial enthusiasm for the NDH, Stepinac soon began to question the regime's mandate of forced conversion. Many clergymen embraced these conversions as a way to increase the number of Church members; some even sought to convert already doomed Serbs and Jews at the very last moment, to be certain that they died as members of the "true faith." But the Vatican recognized only "good faith" conversions, rather than conversions forced upon desperate individuals. To complicate the matter further, on 14 July 1941, the Ustaša's Ministry of Justice decreed that no educated Orthodox Christian artists, intellectuals, or merchants could be converted, despite its campaign of forced conversion. This made it even more difficult for clergy to determine the appropriate action to take. Nevertheless, whole villages of Serbs were forcibly converted. Of those, most were later murdered despite their conversions.[56] In the end, the forced conversions that had begun sporadically in the spring of 1941, intensifying in late autumn of that year, faded by 1942 as Serb resistance grew and Serbs saw that conversion did not guarantee security.[57] Both Yugoslav and Western historiographers cite the figure of 240,000 Orthodox Serb converts.[58]

Loyal to Rome and Pavelić, Stepinac at first sought to uphold the positions of both, but reports of large-scale massacres caused him to shift his stance on conversion.

Rather than enforcing the Vatican's insistence that conversion was only appropriate "for the salvation of the soul," he began to advocate those that might save lives.[59] In November 1941, he convened a Bishops' Synod to discuss this question. It concluded that government authorities should not harm Jewish converts to Catholicism—though the Ustaše frequently disregarded the bishops' stand.[60]

Stepinac now worked privately to limit the impact of Pavelić's policies. Pavelić complained to the Germans about his less-than-supportive archbishop and asked that the Vatican remove him from his post.[61] On 24 May 1942, Stepinac spoke out against genocide from his pulpit, mentioning Jews and Roma, though not Serbs.[62] He also questioned the government's authority to make policy regarding Catholic rites such as baptism and conversion. But his private protests did not deter Pavelić. At his trial in 1946, Stepinac stated that his conscience was clear: "I say, before God, the people, the diplomatic corps so far as they are present here ... that I am completely innocent, and history will fairly judge my whole work."[63]

The end of Stepinac's story resembles that of Pope Pius XII, who was later praised and denounced for his actions during the war. In 1946, Stepinac was tried and found guilty as a Nazi collaborator with strong ties to the Ustaša. He was sentenced to 16 years' hard labor, but released after five years. He was placed under house arrest in Krašić, where he was born, and died of a blood clot in 1960. Pope John Paul II beatified him as a Martyr to the Faith in 1998. The campaign for his beatification collected and publicized a number of testimonies about his work on behalf of the Jews, though not on behalf of Serbs.[64] But his supporters have so far failed to get Yad Vashem to declare him a "Righteous Gentile (Righteous among the Nations)." Stepinac remains an ambiguous, controversial figure who is still esteemed by nationalist Croats and reviled by nationalist Serbs.

Extermination, the third and most chilling Ustaša method for cleansing the NDH of Serbs, included massacres throughout Serb-populated areas of Croatia's *krajina* and Bosnia-Herzegovina as well as a network of concentration camps. Hundreds of Catholic clergy played central roles in these efforts to murder Serbs. For example, eyewitness and survivor testimony as well as Italian and *Wehrmacht* reports note the enthusiastic participation of some Franciscan priests (the order that brought Catholicism to Bosnia) in massacres, while the management of Jasenovac, Croatia's most brutal concentration camp, fell twice to priests. One, Miroslav "Majsterović" Filipović (his nickname meaning master or craftsman) commanded the Jasenovac concentration camp and later its Stara Gradiška subcamp for women. Filipović, a Franciscan monk, was warned by his religious superiors about his role as an Ustaša chaplain. In 1942, Marcone suspended him for his chaplaincy. Filipović had a reputation in Jasenovac and Stara Gradiška as a master sadist. After the war, Filipović was tried and convicted as a war criminal. He was hanged wearing his Franciscan robe and cross. In spring 1943, the former priest Ivica Brkljačić replaced Filipović.[65]

One Ustaša emblem, a dagger superimposed on a Catholic crucifix, symbolized the power of force with faith, while new recruits swore oaths of loyalty on daggers, knifes, and crosses.[66] Given Pavelić's sixteenth principle, which stated that the "essence of the moral strength of the Croatian people is found in an orderly and religious family," and Stepinac's early enthusiasm for the Ustaša, strongly nationalist priests and monks could consider themselves latter-day Crusaders, holy warriors fighting to preserve the sanctity of their Catholic state against Orthodoxy and communism. For example, Mate Mugos, a pastor from Udbina, remarked: "Until now we have worked for the Catholic faith with the prayer book and with the cross. Now the time has come to work with knife and revolver."[67]

Massacres, often accompanied by looting, began just a few weeks after the NDH came into existence in April 1941, and continued for its duration. However, by 1943, the Ustaša military had to face increasing attacks from the Partisans, whose ranks were swollen with recruits from all ethnicities. Ideologically motivated militias, working with local Croats and Muslim recruits, generally carried out the massacres against Serbs. This frequently created tension with the less ideologically motivated *Domobranstvo*, which sometimes participated in killings but more often than not attempted to restore order after violence had devastated an area. By the fall of 1944, the Ustaša sought to unite the two branches, and on 1 December the *Domobranstvo* had come under the *Obrana*, an arm of the secret police that maintained security for the concentration camp system, staged raids on villages, and engaged in heavy fighting near the end of the war. This meant fewer checks on violence.[68]

The first significant attack, on 27 April 1941, near Bjelovar in Croatia proper, was justified by the local Ustaša authorities as retaliation for a falsely alleged Serb massacre of Croats, a policy that the Ustaša employed throughout that spring and early summer.[69] At first only Serb men were singled out for murder, usually beginning with the most influential members of the community. On 12 May, six days prior to the Pope's private audience with Pavelić, Ustaša forces killed 260 men at Glina, south of Zagreb. At Otocac, another 331 men had their heads bashed in with axes, while on 31 May, near Trebinje, between 120 and 270 Serbs were rounded up and killed, again ostensibly because they were *Četnici* who had killed Ustaše. An outraged von Glaise-Horstenau reported that 2,300 men were murdered after a round-up of villagers near Banja Luka.[70] Moreover, the Muslim commander of the regional gendarmerie, Muharem Aganović, reported that, in fact, these were unprovoked assaults on Serb civilians in their homes,[71] which eyewitnesses confirmed. But the massacres continued, including one led by Leo Tongl on 24 May against villages near Ljubinje. The Ustaše murdered all of the Serb men they arrested, including many new Catholic converts. On 2 and 3 June, between 120 and 170 men from the Trebinje area were similarly murdered.[72]

The same month, the Ustaša executed large numbers of Serb civilians in the Karst region, shooting them and tossing their bodies into nearby limestone pits. Some were still alive when they were thrown into the pits. On 3 June, local recruits led by Herman Tongl, Leo's brother, rounded up 167 Serb men from two villages near Korita, imprisoned them on the pretext that they would stand trial, and transported them to the Golubnjača pit, where they were killed.[73] Informed of the Korita incident by the bishop of Mostar, Alojzije Mišić, Stepinac protested to Pavelić privately. But Tongl told wary local Muslims in eastern Herzegovina:[74] "We cannot be satisfied and will not stop until the total extermination of the last Serb from our Independent State of Croatia. The last bullet for the last Serb."[75]

On 22 June, the Ustaša initiated the so-called Vidovdan massacres, spreading rumors that the Serbs planned a major offensive against Croats and Muslims on Vidovdan (St. Vitus Day), 28 June. Particularly important to Serbs, Vidovdan commemorates the date in 1389 on which, according to Serbian myth, Serbia lost the Battle of Kosovo to the Ottoman Turks. Using this ruse, Tongl enlisted local Croats and Muslims to massacre Serb farmers in four districts. Once the attacks began, the Croats targeted women, whom they raped and brutalized, and children. Some were killed and thrown into pits; others were transported to spots along the Neretva River near the Adriatic Coast and executed there. When local Muslims in Bileča, a predominantly Serbian area, interceded to win the release of Serbs who had been arrested,[76] the Ustaša realized its success in carrying out the massacres depended upon its "ability to pacify the Muslims and Croats," i.e. to secure their support and trust. As Dulić suggests, "Where such pacification succeeded, they [the Ustaše] were more or less free to initiate the destruction process."[77] Attacks in southeastern Bosnia killed fewer Serbs than those in eastern Herzegovina, except near Višegrad, where Serbs and Jews were executed along the Drina River for a month.[78]

Once Pavelić abruptly ordered an end to the massacres on 27 June, the Ustaša began massive deportations of Serbs. The Ustaše blamed the Vidovdan "rumors" on Jews, asked Serbs to return to their farms, and decreed that 100 Serbs would be killed for every dead Ustaše. But despite Pavelić's order, the mass killings continued throughout the summer, as did the deportations to newly constructed concentration camps. In the villages around Prebilovći, Ustaše operatives arrested all Serbs and sent them to a collection camp at Čapljina, where they were killed and thrown into a pit near Šurmanci.[79]

In addition to Tongl's group, so-called "wild Ustaše" units, answerable to no one, terrorized the area. Some were led by Franciscan monks carrying crosses, while others, made up of Croat zealots from the diaspora, murdered 260 Serbian community leaders between 1941 and 1942.[80] Outraged at the barbarity, and fearful that such violence would spur Serb resistance and destabilize the region, *Wehrmacht* commanders protested bitterly to Pavelić.[81] On 9 August, he ordered the killings stopped, though they continued throughout the rest of the war. Herbert von Troll-Oberfell, Chargé d'Affaires in the German legation in Zagreb, wrote the Foreign Ministry in Berlin that

> The Serbian question has become considerably more acute in the last few days. The ruthless carrying out of the resettlement with many unfortunate bi-products, and numerous other acts of terror in the provinces ... are giving even the sober-minded Croatian circles reason for serious concern.[82]

And he was right. Over the previous few months, a Yugoslav army Serbian colonel, Dragoljub Draža Mihailović, had formed the nucleus of a Serb guerilla army, the

Četnićki odredi jugoslovenske vojske (Chetnik Detachments of the Yugoslav Army). What followed were *Četnik* massacres of Croat and Muslim villages. By July, the Muslims and Croats generally held the towns, while the Serbs held sway in the forests and countryside. The resulting chaos prevented Germany from gaining full control of the region.[83]

The *Obrana* (Ustaša Defense Brigade) units caused more problems by committing acts so horrific that the Germans urged Pavelić to disband them.[84] In a desperate effort to see order reestablished in NDH-controlled territory, the Germans even suggested that the Ustaša allow Serbs to become "Croats of the Orthodox faith." By September 1942, Pavelić had removed Jure Francetić, the head of the Crna legija (Black Legion), and "officially" dissolved it, though it remained active under Major Rafael Boban.[85] Another division of the *Obrana*, led by Vjekoslav "Maks" Luburić, who was in charge of all NDH camps, ordered all Orthodox villages razed near Jasenovac. The Germans distrusted Luburić, whom one *Wehrmacht* report described as a "neurotic, pathological personality."[86]

Continued German criticism of *Obrana* initiatives forced Dido Kvaternik, Chief of Ustaša Internal Security, to resign in September 1942.[87] Regardless, between 10 June and 30 July, *Wehrmacht* units, supported by Ustaša troops, conducted their own extensive "pacification" campaign against Partisans in the Kozara Mountains of western Bosnia. One of the officers involved in this operation was Kurt Waldheim, who was serving as a communications officer with a *Kampfgruppe* in Bosnia. He later became Secretary-General of the United Nations and President of Austria. In July, Pavelić awarded Waldheim the Order of King Zvonimir (an eleventh-century king linked to the Ustaša myth of the glorious Croatian medieval kingdom), following the first successful wave of massacres. During the operation, the Germans and the Croats displaced some 60,000 predominantly Serb civilians, many of whom were ultimately killed or sent to the camp that came to embody the horrors of the Ustaša regime, Jasenovac. Of those sent to Jasenovac, most died.[88] The extent of the campaign caused Glaise to write, "Kozara was cleared to the last man, and likewise, the last woman and last child."[89] Waldheim's involvement in Operation Kozara did not come to light until 1986, when he was running for the presidency of Austria. The Austrian government appointed a special commission to look into the charges, which were later found to be true. These revelations did not stop his election as Austria's president, nor Pope John Paul II from making him a Knight of the Order of Pius IX.[90]

The deteriorating situation in Bosnia and Herzegovina adversely affected Bosnian Muslims. Vulnerable to radicalized Serbs, they could no longer afford to remain neutral and began to join Ustaša, German, or Partisan units as well as the Muslim Volunteer Legion, and, in a few cases, the *Četnici*. Like those *Četnici*, Ustaše and *Domobrani* who later joined the Partisans, some Muslims shifted allegiances as the need arose. On paper, the Ustaša guaranteed Muslims equal rights as pure Croats. Indeed, to highlight Muslim inclusion within the NDH, Pavelić built a mosque in Zagreb and named Osman Kulenović, a Muslim leader from a powerful Bosnian family, as his vice president. In 1941, Osman's brother, Džafer, replaced him, remaining in that position until 1945. But Kulenović was viewed by many Muslims as a figurehead, and Pavelić ignored Muslim pleas on behalf of their community.[91]

Muslims saw themselves as increasingly endangered by the brutal behavior of the Ustaša troops in Bosnia-Herzegovina and the complicity of the Catholic Church.[92] Throughout 1941, Muslim leaders sent letters and petitions to various higher Muslim, Croat, Italian and German authorities that criticized the unnecessary bloodshed and the discrimination they experienced, despite the government's guarantee of equality.[93] The petitions also pointed out Bosnia's unique history of tolerance as a Muslim kingdom under the Ottoman Turks. A letter of protest signed by 200 Sarajevan Muslims, dated 12 October 1941, accused the Ustaše of using "fezzes and Muslim names" to provoke Serbs against Muslims.[94] A memorandum from Banja Luka Muslims, dated 22 November 1941, criticized the regime's violent treatment of Serbs and accused some Catholic Croats of encouraging Muslim "*ološ*" (scum) to murder Serbs and to force Serbs who had earlier adopted Islam to convert to Catholicism.[95]

Ustaša indifference to the plight of Muslims led many to place their hopes in the Germans. A group of Bosnian Muslims sent Hitler a memorandum dated 1 November 1942, that stressed their Gothic roots, decried Ustaša killings in Bosnia, asked to expand the Muslim Volunteer Legion, and sought "an autonomous Bosnian region under the direct supervision of the *Wehrmacht*."[96] While Germany could not afford to do anything that would further affect its uneasy relationship with Pavelić's government, Jozo Tomasevich links Himmler's desire to create a Bosnian Muslim SS division to the November memorandum. Three months later, on 10 February 1943, Hitler gave the order to begin recruiting.[97]

Many Muslims, however, did participate enthusiastically in attacks on Serbs. Some joined the Ustaša directly, while others fought in the Prinz Eugen Waffen SS division, which was made up principally of *Volksdeutsche* from Yugoslavia. In 1943, Himmler signed an agreement in Sarajevo with the Grand Mufti of Jerusalem, Hadj Amin el Husseini, to form the first non-Germanic SS unit, the 13th Waffen Mountain division, the SS Handžar (1st Croatian), named for the celebrated Turkish battle knife, the scimitar. The Grand Mufti hoped to create a pan-Islamic force that would join the Muslims of Europe with those elsewhere. Himmler, who believed the Arabs were fierce fighters, thought that the Bosnian Muslims would make good soldiers.[98] When Pavelić objected to the plan, the Germans allowed more than 1,000 Croat officers to join the Handžar division. Nearly 21,000 Muslims enlisted to fight for their homeland under German and Croat leadership. They mutinied when they were sent to France for training.[99] Some later served in Silesia, others on the Russian Front. In 1944, the division returned to Bosnia, where it became involved in large-scale actions against Serbs in the eastern and northeastern areas. After heavy desertions, the Handžar division was transferred from northeastern Bosnia to northern Croatia in September of the same year. Other Muslim recruits were attracted to the 23rd or "Kama" (a Turkish short knife) Waffen SS division, though these were later placed in the Handžar division, which continued to wreak havoc in Bosnia until both units were disbanded at the end of 1944.

The Ustaša also opened more than 20 transit, containment and concentration camps throughout its territories in the summer of 1941. That following July, the Ustaše rounded up civilians of all ages and began to intern entire families in these camps.[100] On 25 November 1941, Pavelić, Andrija Artuković, and other Ustaša leaders signed an order decreeing the building of camps for "undesirables", legitimizing this tactic.

Women and children faired poorly in the Ustaša camps. Those who could work were frequently sent to Germany as "slaves." Others were killed or died of disease. But children had an especially difficult time because they were often separated from their mothers and were sent to special camps such as Jastrebarsko and Sisak. Professor Ruža Rupčić, a Croat prisoner at Stara Gradiška, reported that "In July 1942, the Ustaša selected 2000 children whom they said were incapable of living, put them in one room, and killed them with cyanide."[101] Mara Vejnović-Smiljanić, a Serb professor from Croatia, recalled having seen nuns "apply liquid to children's mouths with brushes," which caused the children to scream, writhe in pain, and at last die.[102] Božo Švarc

> saw the *Ustaše* grab small children [from Kozara] and whirl them in the air above their head so fast until they ripped their arms off, leaving the Ustaše holding only the arm. The other *Ustaše* would try to catch the flying bodies of the children on their bayonets.[103]

A few child prisoners were adopted by Croats, who hoped to reeducate them. After the Kozara murders, "Maks" Luburić tried to organize an Ottoman Turkish *devirsme*, an annual tax on Orthodox villagers that involved rounding up and sending 12-year-old boys to Istanbul for conversion to Islam and training them as Janissaries, an elite Turkish military unit. He arranged to have 450 Serbian boy prisoners "adopted," labeled as Janissaries, and trained as Ustaše in the camp. Not surprisingly, the experiment failed.[104] A former child prisoner at Jasenovac, Dragoje Lukić, has documented that 19,554 children, the majority of them Serbs, died at Jasenovac.[105]

Though there were between 22 and 26 camps in the NDH network, Jasenovac has come to represent the horrors of genocide in wartime Yugoslavia.[106] Questions and controversies about the number who died there have led to the creation of separate Serb and Croat historiographies marked by vitriolic exchanges between scholars, as well as opposing "victim" myths.[107] Official records are limited, either missing or destroyed. German and Italian reports from that period as well as eyewitness testimony offer figures too high for credibility. A *Wehrmacht* document dated 6 December 1943, for example, informed Berlin that 120,000 had been "liquidated" (*liquidiert*) at Jasenovac.[108] But whereas Nazi efficiency and a distant bureaucracy was able methodically to record the deaths of millions, Ustaša incompetence, inefficiency, conflicts over camp oversight, and random acts of violence resulted in poor records. In addition, Ustaša officials burned camp records in 1943 and 1945.[109]

The number of dead has become a weapon in a political game played to serve ethno-national ends. For as noted above, Croat and Serb nationalists generally deflate or inflate figures according to their respective political needs. Estimates range from Croat leader Franjo Tuđman's 30,000 to the more than a million cited by Serb nationalist and anti-Milošević novelist Vuk Drašković. For this reason, many contemporary scholars now cite Žeravić's more balanced estimate of 85,000 deaths in Jasenovac, which he admits excludes the 28,000 who died in transit or were murdered directly outside of the camp walls.[110] But it is generally conceded that historians will likely never be able to determine the exact number of murders there.

Jasenovac was located about 100 kilometers southeast of Zagreb in a marshy area down river from the Dubički lime pits. The Zagreb–Belgrade railroad ran nearby, which facilitated prisoner transports, while the Sava, Una, and Velika Struga Rivers, which bounded the camp, created a triangular piece of land with watery borders. The Sava's western side, meanwhile, was a sparsely populated plain susceptible to flooding, which made it easy to dispose of bodies but difficult to escape and survive. These constraints, as well as the two barbed wire fences that surrounded Jasenovac III and the Sava on the unfenced side, meant that breakouts were unlikely until the final days of Jasenovac in April 1945.[111]

Jasenovac was divided into five camps: I, Bročice, and II, Krapje (August 1941–December 1941); III, Ciglana—the brickyards, the central killing ground (November 1941–late April 1945); IV, Kozara, the work camp, which, with Ciglana, operated until the Partisans liberated it at the end of the war (February 1941–late April 1945); and V, Stara Gradiška, originally intended for political prisoners (summer 1941 until late April 1945, just before III and IV). More than 5,000 children were sent to Stara Gradiška after the mass deportations from Kozara and other areas in the summer of 1942. By the winter of 1942/1943, women and children from the Đakovo camp were sent to Stara Gradiška.[112]

Dido Kvaternik's Office III of the Ustaša Intelligence Service administered Jasenovac until June 1943, when it was placed under the main public security office. Maks Luburić's defense forces were in charge of its security, and in September and October 1941, Luburić and his forces rounded up the Serbs in neighboring villages, sent them to Jasenovac, and built a military garrison in the area. Following the German model, the Ustaša appointed foremen and deputies from among the prisoners to manage camp life. Ex-police and imprisoned Ustaše formed a willing circle of informers that kept a tight rein on prisoners.[113]

Though lacking German technology, Jasenovac III became a death camp for most of those sent there. Its 88% mortality rate was higher than that of Auschwitz, where 84.6% of the inmates died.[114] Moreover, while most Ustaša camps were closed by 1942 or 1943, Camps III, IV, and V continued operations until late April 1945, and received prisoners from other camps. Luburić, who toured Nazi camps in July 1941, modeled Jasenovac after Sachsenhausen.[115] Since the camp had once been a brickyard, its commandant, Ivica Matković, Luburić's first deputy, directed engineer

Hinko Pičili (later a camp commandant) to design a furnace there in 1942. It functioned as a crematorium for dead prisoners, although survivor testimony suggests that some, including children, were thrown in alive. Eduard Šajer described the "stench of burning human bodies" that spread across the camps, adding that, "Many Jews I recognized from Sarajevo were all burned alive in this way ..."[116] Sadik Danon remembered a sudden "smell of grilled meat" that reminded him of the kebabs of Belgrade restaurants. Nearby, the Ustaše were "throwing people into the blazing brickyard furnace alive; that was the smell of human flesh."[117]

Luburić also had a gas-chamber built at Jasenovac's Camp V after unsuccessful experiments with gas vans. A considerable number of inmates were gassed during the three-month experiment with sulfur dioxide and Zyklon B. This method was abandoned because of poor construction of the gassing chamber. In the end, such technologies proved unnecessary. For by far the largest number of men, women, and children who were murdered in this so-called "political" or "labor" camp died from starvation, disease (especially typhus), and beatings or assaults with mallets, maces, axes, poison, and knives. One, the *srbosjek*, or Serb-cutter, was a long, curved knife attached to a partial glove and designed for cutting throats. In addition, guards regularly executed large groups en masse outside the camp itself when they arrived and threw the bodies into the Sava River.[118]

Unlike the German-run camps, which emphasized anonymity and efficiency, Jasenovac specialized in one-on-one violence of a particularly brutal kind. From 25 to 27 December 1941, for example, guards attacked the Serbian barracks with mallets, assaulted the prisoners, tied their hands together, and killed them with knives and mallets. They then threw their bodies into nearby trenches.[119] Guards were allowed to beat inmates indiscriminately, while camp commandants like Filipović (dubbed "Fra Sontona," or Brother Satan) and Dinko Šakić and his wife, Nada Luburić-Šakić (sister of Maks Luburić),[120] sated their appetites with acts of ingenious torture.[121] Jewish survivor Eta Najfeld called Filipović "the very personification of evil," because of his notorious one-on-one crimes against men and murder of women and children. On one occasion, Majfeld reported that Filipović "summoned all Serbian women and children to the cellar of a prison and then had some kind of dam opened so that water from the Sava River flooded the cellar," trapping and drowning them all.[122]

From December 1943 through August 1944, conditions at Jasenovac eased somewhat under the command of Ivica Brkljačić, though executions continued. But after several inmates escaped, the camp authorities clamped down again. Prisoners continued to be sent to Jasenovac and were usually killed upon arrival.[123] By fall 1944, Camps III and IV held between 3,000 and 3,500 prisoners. After the Ustaše discovered a resistance plot in III and hanged its leaders, the authorities began to dismantle Stara Gradiška (where another cell went undetected) and sent the remaining prisoners to Camps III and IV. The liberation of Belgrade on 20 October 1944 forced the camp authorities to begin eradicating evidence of the murders. Prisoner crews exhumed mass graves and burned old corpses before being killed and burned by the next crew.[124]

In late 1944, the numbers of inmates in Jasenovac dwindled. But prisoners still arrived, and 200–300 prisoners were sent to Germany to provide additional labor to the Third Reich. In the winter of 1944/1945, prisoners noticed allied bombers in the area. Then on 30 March 1945, Good Friday, Partisan aircraft bombed the camp, accurately hitting buildings rather than prisoners, and bombed again on 5 and 7 April. Blaming prisoner deaths on the allies and the Partisans, who were even then advancing on the camp, the Ustaše began mass liquidations. On 21 April, they marched perhaps 700 women and children to their deaths and locked the remaining 1,000 to 1,400 men into the *šusteraj* (shoemakers' building). When the doors opened the next morning, unarmed prisoners rushed the guards and tried to escape. Most were shot before reaching the Sava. Only 80 survived the escape attempt. Afterwards, the Ustaše torched records and buildings before fleeing. After the Partisans arrived on 25 April, they forced captured *Domobrani* to level what remained of Jasenovac.[125]

The story of how the principal Ustaša leaders fled the NDH—replete with trunks of loot, secret hiding places, Vatican accomplices, murderous betrayals, and ratlines— belongs in a spy novel. The records of the US State Department and Counter-Intelligence Corps (CIC) ironically remain reliable sources because of the direct involvement of these agencies in the escape of these war criminals.[126] Although Yugoslavia captured and executed Filipović in 1946, many in the Ustaša high command escaped immediate captivity, some for years. Luburić fled to Spain, where an agent of Uprava državne bezbednosti (UDBA—the Yugoslav secret police) assassinated him in 1969.[127] Artuković escaped to Ireland and later settled in southern California, where he lived until his extradition to Yugoslavia in 1986. Tried and sentenced to death, he died in prison of natural causes in 1988. He said during his trial that he did not have any knowledge of killings beyond those necessary to protect the NDH. Dinko Šakić and his wife Nada lived comfortably in Argentina until 1998, when they were extradited to Croatia. He was tried and found guilty in 1999 and sentenced to 20 years' confinement. He died in a prison hospital on 20 July 2008.[128] Nada was found innocent and released.

Many of the Ustaša leaders who fled the NDH found shelter in the College of San Girolamo degli Illirici, a monastery for Croatian monks near the Vatican.[129] Fr. Krunoslav Draganović, an Ustaša lieutenant-colonel, directed the fugitive enterprise at San Girolamo. As vice chief of the Ustaša's Bureau of Colonization, Draganović had overseen the confiscation of Serb property in Bosnia-Herzegovina. He also served as the army chaplain at Jasenovac until Stepinac sent him to Rome in mid-1943 as the Ustaša's second unofficial representative.[130] At San Girolamo, Draganović worked with the US CIC to send Ustaše abroad. He also arranged Klaus Barbie's (the Gestapo's infamous "Butcher of Lyon") successful flight to South America.[131] Through his efforts, many of those responsible for the NDH's mass murders found refuge in Argentina, Chile, Paraguay, Portugal, Spain and the US, where they became the heroes of the Croatian diaspora.[132] Interestingly, just a few days after the death of Pius XII in 1958, the Vatican Secretary of State asked Draganović to leave San Girolamo. He then began to work for US Army Intelligence until they dismissed him in 1962, when they found his information no longer worth their investment. He then retired to Vienna, only to resurface inexplicably in Tito's Yugoslavia, where he lived and worked quietly in Zagreb until his death in 1979.[133]

Ante Pavelić, the architect of the Ustaša genocide, fled to Austria disguised as a priest. From there he was smuggled into Italy, where he, too, established contact with San Girolamo. When the US explored the possibility of extraditing him, the CIC warned that such a move could hurt the Vatican and expose US anti-communist agents. The US military agreed and backed off.[134] In 1948, Pavelić fled to Argentina, where he remained until 1957. On 9 April of that year, one day before the anniversary of the founding of the NDH, he was shot twice either by an agent of the Yugoslav secret police, or perhaps by a former Četnik, Blagoje Jovović, a Montenegrin by birth, who claimed responsibility in his memoir. Pavelić, who survived the assassination attempt, sought refuge in fascist Spain to avoid potential extradition. Franco granted him asylum to reciprocate the support that Croats had shown him during the Spanish Civil War.[135] Before his death in 1959, Pope John XXIII blessed the former NDH dictator.[136] A leading Croatian newspaper in Buenos Aires printed the following eulogy:

> May the Spanish soil weigh lightly on our brave head of state until the day the Croatian patriots will have taken him to the liberated Independent State of Croatia, which he had resurrected through his unflinching struggle and which he through his great sacrifice had held out as an everlasting goal of the whole Croatian people for all times![137]

This passage clearly reveals the powerful ethno-nationalist sentiments harbored by some in the diasporic Croatian community, which 30 years later would play a vital role in the birth of the new Croatian state, the death of Yugoslavia, and the Bosnian debacle. They supplied money, publicity, and arms to fulfill, at last, their dream of a free, independent nation of Croatian Catholics.

Forgotten in all of this was the Ustaša genocide of the Serbs and other ethnic minorities during World War II. The actual number murdered by the Ustaša regime remains a source of controversy: some nationalist Croats suggest a figure of 60,000, while some nationalist Serbs cite 1,500,000. The United States Holocaust Memorial Museum in Washington, DC, suggests a figure of between 300,000 and 400,000. The numbers most widely accepted today are those of the Croat Žerjavić and the Montenegrin Serb Kočović. The former cites 307,000 Serb victims (1989) and 322,000 (1997), while the latter in 1985 projected 333,000.[138] Whatever the actual count, the relatively large number of men, women, and particularly children massacred or sent to Jasenovac and other camps neutralizes the official Ustaša claim that the dead were combatants fighting to destroy the NDH, except in the sense that, as non-Croats, they threatened "the national interests and the preservation of the biological survival of the Croatian people."[139]

Finally, then, if Tito's goal of a multi-ethnic communist state demanded that Yugoslavs forget the past, Freud taught us the power and cost of memories repressed.

As noted above, even before Tito died, cracks had appeared in the golden façade of his state. After 1980, nationalist Serbs began to exhume bodies and memories in the lands of the former NDH—Croatia and Bosnia-Herzegovina—to stir up renewed fear of their Muslim and Croat neighbors among *krajina* and Bosnian Serbs. As Monroe Price suggests, "Spurious reports of new atrocities were bolstered by reference to past genuine ones."[140] Meanwhile, the former Partisan, Franjo Tuđman, the so-called "Father of Croatia" who became its first president in 1990, pronounced the NDH "not simply a quisling creation and a fascist crime" but rather "the expression of the historical aspirations of the Croat people."[141]

Ilana Bet-El stresses the authoritative power of the words "I remember" for "allocating blame and defining justice in terms of personal and national memory."[142] Yet if Croat and Serb mythographers alike embellished truth and distorted history for the sake of nationalist ideals, the buried truths—ever fragmentary, like the bones that once were bodies in the limestone pits—demand our scrutiny. In the 1990s and even today, potent Ustaša-era symbols still stir emotion in the former Yugoslavia: Jasenovac, graphic images of Serbian war dead, the checkerboard-*šahovnica*,[143] the *kuna*, and black T-shirts commemorating the infamous Black Legion. Croat rock-star Thompson (Marko Perković) performs concerts attracting as many as 40,000 at a time and highlighting his nationalist, often explicitly pro-Ustaša lyrics, Black Legion shirts, the Nazi salute, and the Ustaša rallying cry, "*Za dom—Spremni* [For the homeland—Ready]." Arguing that the "grand narratives" of Croatian histories since independence pay little attention to the NDH and Jasenovac and portray Croats as "the victims of other national groups and history," Maja Brkljačić states:

> The history of the twentieth century in Croatia is depicted as a continuous line of events, people, and historic institutions that all serve as prototypes and are not recognized for their uniqueness. They are, as Funkenstein has pointed out about collective memory, links in an ongoing past that has never ended.[144]

Thus, whether in Serbia, Croatia or the West, an important but neglected or manipulated chapter in the history of Croatia, Bosnia, and Serbia remains the Ustaša genocide, whose major components and issues I have sought to introduce here.

NOTES

1. This constitutes the last phrase of a frequently cited speech by which Hermann Tongl, Ustaša operative in Eastern Bosnia, sought to enlist Croat and Muslim villagers in actions against their Serb neighbors. See n. 5.
2. The research for this paper was supported by a grant from the Department of Research and Development, North Carolina Agricultural and Technical State University, and a fellowship from the United States Holocaust Memorial Museum.
3. The noun Ustaša refers to the government itself, while its plural, Ustaše, designates members of the various branches of that government.
4. Italian soldiers in Mostar helped Jews reach Italian camps on the Adriatic, where, despite Mussolini's orders, they generally treated Serbs and Jews comparatively well, enabling

many of the latter to reach Italy. But Italy had sheltered and supported the Ustaše in their exile, invaded Ethiopia in 1936, invaded Albania in 1939, with Albania entered Greece in 1940, and in 1941 allied with Germany in Operation Maritsa, annexing much of the Dalmatian Coast (thereby angering Croats and precipitating mutual hostility), as well as parts of Montenegro, Kosovo, Bosnia and Herzegovina. Moreover, Italians failed to intervene in the Ustaša massacres of Serbs and Jews, stood by as the Ustaša on Pag carried out genocidal operations there, and helped round up the Jews near Rjeka. Between 1941 and 1943, moreover, Italy struggled fiercely with Germany over territory and authority in the NDH, often using Serb *Cetnici* to help defeat the Partisans, an alliance that included supplying food and arms to Serbs, which angered Croats.

5. The *Cetnici* had existed since the nineteenth century, when bands of 10, *četi*, hid in the forests of Ottoman-occupied Serbian lands to raid Ottoman targets and thus achieve Serbia's independence. On 5 June 1941, after the Korita incident, Serbs began forming units to resist the *Ustaši*. Initially royalists, most later became Serb nationalists, collaborating with the Germans or Italians when it served their cause.

6. Job, *Yugoslavia's Ruin*, 8. Žerjavić and Bogoljub Kočović, a Montenegrin Serb scholar, have produced the most credible work on the numbers of dead in Yugoslavia during World War II.

7. Bax, "Mass Graves, Stagnating Identification, and Violence," 11.

8. Nyström, "The Holocaust and Croatian National Identity," 272.

9. Indeed, the West actively intervened in Bosnia despite having only a fragmentary knowledge of its peoples' history.

10. Hoare, "The Ustaša Genocide," 29.

11. See Hewitt, "Ethnic Cleansing," 296–318.

12. Ramet explicitly suggests of her edited volume: "The collection of articles in this volume is an attempt to remedy this deficit." See "The NDH," 403.

13. Redžić, *Bosnia and Herzegovina*, 84.

14. Dulić cites a number between 2,000 and 4,000 in *Utopias of Nation*, 81. Biondich suggests a core group "not exceeding 10,000 members" in "Religion and Nation," 79.

15. Paris, *Genocide in Satellite Croatia*, 22.

16. Anzulović, *Heavenly Serbia*, 142–43.

17. Dulić, *Utopias of Nation*, 82.

18. During and after the eighteenth century, the West essentialized and racialized Balkan ethnicities, advancing the notion of two Europes, the civilized West and the barbaric, atavistic East. Enlightenment travel narratives commonly figured Eastern Europe as oriental, irrational, and barbaric, its people dark and degenerate. Indeed, while historically and geographically peripheral to the West, Eastern Europe proved vital to its psyche. For this trope of the West's internal opposite, like the *topos* of Europe's external other, Africa, enhanced Western claims to civilization and reason. To escape the sting of Western stereotypes, the west of Eastern Europe named itself Mitteleuropa, Central Europe, thereby gaining distance from the Balkans, the "true threshold to the Orient," replete with barbarism, tribalism and "ancient hatreds." Maria Todorova calls this discourse "Balkanism," akin to Said's Orientalism. See such works as Jezernik, *Wild Europe*; Todorova, *Imagining the Balkans*; Wolff, *Inventing Eastern Europe*.

19. This position emerged partially from the mythic view articulated by nineteenth-century Croat nationalists that Bosnian Muslims were descendants of medieval Croat settlers in Bosnia who had embraced the Bogomil sect before converting to Islam. Here, Dulić quotes Pavelić (Dulić, *Utopias of Nation*, 85).

20. Many scholars cite this quote, variously attributing it to Budak or Kvaternik, often crediting as its source Dedijer's *The Yugoslavian Auschwitz and the Vatican*. But Dulić, Utopias, suggests that he has found no primary source that can confirm its reality (101).
21. Prpa-Jovanović, "The Making of Yugoslavia," 58.
22. Later in the war, the Ustaše would target Muslims, as also happened during the Bosnian War—as, for example, when Croats and Muslims ethnically cleansed Mostar of Serbs, then took separate sides of the city (divided by the Neretva River) and attacked one another. This suggests that while paying lip service to the ideal of Muslims as "blood brothers," Croats in fact saw them as potential rivals.
23. Dulić, *Utopias*, 22.
24. The fascist governments and armies of Germany and Italy played a considerable role in the NDH as they variously fought and allied with *Četnici*, battled Partisans, and vied with one another for power in the region.
25. The Serbian Milan Bulajić cites a figure of 1,850,000 dead Serbs, a quote even higher than the inflated total Tito's representative presented to the International Reparations Commission in 1946, which purported to include all the war dead. Croatian revisionists cite figures as low as 35,000 for the total number of Serb war dead. But most contemporary scholars find the figures of the Montenegrin Serb Bogoljub Kočović and the Croat Vladimir Žerjavić more digestible. David Bruce MacDonald cites the figures of 487,000 and 530,000, respectively. See *Balkan Holocausts?*, 162. However, Žerjavić himself sets 322,000 as a likely figure for Serb dead, with 85,000 of those in camps and the remainder in villages. See "The Most Likely Numbers of Victims Killed in Jasenovac," 21.
26. Dulić, *Utopias*, 100.
27. See Biondich, "Religion and Nation in Wartime Croatia," 72.
28. Tomasevich, *The Chetniks*, 106.
29. Indeed, the Balkans themselves internalized negative Western stereotypes from Balkanist discourse. Thus, Todorova declares that *Imagining the Balkans*, her pioneering work on the subject, "emphasizes the extent to which the outside perception of the Balkans has been internalized in the region itself" (39). Within Yugoslavia, Eastern Orthodox Serbs came to believe themselves the last proud Christian warriors in the land of the infidel Turk, while Westernized Catholic Croats projected onto Serbs the worst aspects of Eastern civilization. That the Ustaša labeled Serbs "Greek Easterners" aptly demonstrates this point.
30. "Principles of the Ustaša Movement."
31. For while Croat nationalism, like its Serb counterpart, depended upon the "*volk*" for support, it was historically framed and promulgated by the intellectual elite.
32. The government, however, viewed the *Volksdeutsche* as kinsmen. See discussion on page 813.
33. Dulić, *Utopias*, 88.
34. Tomasevich, *The Chetniks*, 58.
35. Ibid., 78.
36. Tomasevich, *Occupation and Collaboration*, 282.
37. As *domobrani* increasingly deserted to join the Partisans after 1943, it appears that the government may have conscripted Serbs, some of whom were ultimately liquidated in Jasenovac. See the testimony of Miloš Despot, "Death and Survival in Jasenovac," 138. Hoare, moreover, notes that the Ustaša conscripted Serbs in Bosanska Gradiška region; see "The Ustaša Genocide," 34.
38. Tomasevich, *Occupation and Collaboration*, 381–87.

39. Ibid., 393.
40. Three were in prison, five died of natural causes, 217 were killed by the Ustaše, 334 were deported to Serbia, and 18 fled to Serbia on their own. Ramet, *Balkan Babel*, 104.
41. Tomasevich suggests that at least 300,000 Serbian refugees or deportees had come to Serbia by the end of the war. See *Occupation and Collaboration*, 219.
42. While most scholars see this practice as emerging from the Catholic foundation of Ustaša ideology, Mark Biondich suggests that the Ustaša acted from a secular desire to achieve the "neutralization of Orthodoxy in the western Balkans." Thus, he argues that these conversions were essentially a political tactic. He nonetheless maintains that "the 'marriage' between the Church and Ustaša state was consummated during the Second World War." See "Religion and Nation," 114, 81.
43. Dulić, *Utopias*, 85.
44. Phayer, *The Catholic Church*, 32.
45. *Actes et documents du Saint Siège relatifs à la seconde guerre mondiale*, Book 4, 500.
46. Ibid., 545.
47. Ibid., Book 5, 736.
48. Mgr. Tardini, aide to Pius XII in the Secretariat, in a note dated 13 June 1941, suggests that Pavelić was "furioso" about this, since the Pope had granted Slovakia a nuncio. See *Actes et documents du Saint Siège*, Book 4, 547.
49. Cornwell, *Hitler's Pope*, 259.
50. Early sources include Dedijer, *The Yugoslavian Auschwitz*; Paris, *Genocide in Satellite Croatia*. Innumerable eyewitness accounts can be found today, including several cited within this paper.
51. A note from Montini dated 5 July 1943 suggests that while Pavelić seeks a papal audience, even if private, the Pope will attempt to avoid an encounter "si verifichi a Roma." See *Actes et documents du Saint Siège*, Book 7, 404. As to the alleged meetings, I have not been able to verify them, though they may be noted in papal memoranda from Tardini or Montini.
52. When, for example, Sarajevo's Chief Rabbi Freiberger wrote regarding the plight of Sarajevo's Jews under Bishop Šarić's anti-Semitic and anti-Serb reign, the Vatican instructed Marcone to respond "prudently, tactfully, in accordance with the circumstances." See Shelah, "The Catholic Church in Croatia," 332.
53. Dulić, *Utopias*, 80.
54. This would seem to validate Biondich's position.
55. Dedijer, *The Yugoslavian Auschwitz*, 103.
56. Dulić, *Utopias*, 95.
57. Mark Biondich offers compelling evidence that while many scholars date the mass conversions from the spring, the main thrust did not take place until late autumn. See "Religion and Nation in Wartime Croatia," 88–90.
58. Ibid., 111.
59. Ibid., 94.
60. Breitman notes that Stepinac served as the Ustaša military chaplain; see Breitman et al., *US Intelligence*, 205. See also Shelah, "The Catholic Church in Croatia," 330.
61. One German report by Herr Dörnberg, dated 20 April 1942, states: "Er [Pavelic] ä-üsserte sich dabei in ablehnender Form über den Agramer Erzbischof. Auf den Papst war er sichtlich sehr schlecht zu sprechen und bemerkte, die Kroaten seien zwar zum grossen Teil Katholiken, aber gar keine Anhänger des Papstes und der päpstlichen Kirche." [Büro des Staatssekretärs, Bind 3:32]
62. Jansen, *Pius XII*, 151.

63. Tomasevich, *Occupation and Collaboration*, 563.
64. So, for example, Esther Gitman, a Croatian-born Israeli, wrote a dissertation on Stepinac and is currently publishing articles that document his work on behalf of Jews.
65. According to Miloš Despot, that spring Brkljačić briefly eased camp conditions, before resuming oppressive policies that summer. See "Death and Survival in Jasenovac," 136.
66. Gumz, "*Wehrmacht* Perceptions of Mass Violence," 1025.
67. *Novi List* (Croatia), 24 July 1941.
68. See Allen Milcic, "Croatian Axis Forces in WWII," <http://www.feldgrau.com/a-croatia.html> (accessed 16 September 2009).
69. According to Tomasevich, Siegfried Kasche, the German envoy to the NDH, learned this from Croatian Minister of Foreign Affairs Lorković. See Tomasevich, *Occupation and Collaboration*, 397–98.
70. Popovich, "Primary Sources," 93.
71. Dulić, *Utopias*, 125.
72. Again, the Ustaša used Chetnik attacks as a pretext for the executions. Ibid., 126.
73. Ibid., 129.
74. The Muslims rightly worried that such massacres would mobilize Serb resistance and that they themselves would likely serve as the targets.
75. Dulić, *Utopias*, 127.
76. Ibid., 144.
77. Ibid., 145.
78. Ibid., 179.
79. Šurmanci is the location highlighted in the article by Bax, cited at the beginning of the present paper.
80. Again, Dedijer and Paris address this. As both a high-ranking communist under Tito and a Serb, Dedijer had strong political reasons to disparage the Church. But Edmund von Glaise-Horstenau, the German commanding officer in the NDH in 1941, likewise condemned both Ustaša atrocities in Bosnia and the highest official of the Church in Bosnia, Ivan Šarić, whom he identified as a Croat extremist who supported genocide as a solution to the Serbian problem. See Adeli, "From Jasenovac to Yugoslavism," 121.
81. In "*Wehrmacht* Perceptions of Mass Violence," Gumz explores the *Wehrmacht*'s perceptions of Ustaša violence compared to its sense of its own strategies against Serbs. He pays particular attention to the Germans' language, suggesting that "words like 'cleansed' or 'elimination' bestowed on German efforts a clinical and restrained appearance; an appearance undermined in fact by the wholesale brutality associated with these operations." See 1029.
82. Adeli, "From Jasenovac to Yugoslavism," 137.
83. Gumz discusses this at length in "*Wehrmacht* Perceptions of Mass Violence" and "German Counterinsurgency Policy." See also Tomasevich, *The Chetniks*, 122–25.
84. Its first and fifth divisions, the Crna legija, or Black Legion, were led by Jure Francetić and composed of some 1,000–1,500 Muslim and Croat refugees from villages in Bosnia-Herzegovina that *Četnici* or Partisans had raided.
85. Tomasevich, *Occupation and Collaboration*, 422.
86. Rosenbaum, "Jasenovac as Encountered in OSI's Investigations," 72.
87. Pavelić had both Kvaterniks removed. Tomasevich suggests that he perceived Slavko as his rival, Dido as a cause of tension with the Germans, and realized that he might blame army failures on both of them. See Tomasevich, *Occupation and Collaboration*, 439–42.
88. Rosenbaum, "Jasenovac as Encountered in OSI's Investigations," 83.

89. Gumz, "*Wehrmacht* Perceptions," 1023.
90. Herzstein, *Waldheim*, 71–78, 233–47.
91. See Dulić, *Utopias*, 237–40; Jelinek, "Bosnia-Herzegovina at War," 279.
92. See Jelinek, "Bosnia-Herzegovina at War," for a general discussion of the Muslim response to the genocide and Biondich, who examines the negative Muslim response to forced conversions, in "Religion and Nation," 107–09.
93. For specific names, see Dulić's section on "Muslim Resolutions," in *Utopias*, 228–36. Jelinek mentions that Dr. Lemr, local representative of the Company for South-Eastern Europe Ltd (a front agency for the German secret service), petitioned his superiors, Deputy Prime Minister Kulenović wrote the local governments in the Sana and Luka districts, and prominent Muslims in Sarajevo wrote Kulenović (284).
94. Dulić, *Utopias*, 231.
95. Jelinek, "Bosnia-Herzegovina at War," 279.
96. Tomasevich, *Occupation and Collaboration*, 495–96.
97. Ibid., 496.
98. Ibid., 500.
99. This incident is referred to as the Mutiny at Villefranche.
100. Rosenbaum, "Jasenovac as Encountered in OSI's Investigations," 68.
101. Goldstein, *Anti-Semitism; Holocaust; Anti-Fascism*, 97.
102. Vejnović-Smiljanić, "The Suffering of Children," 226.
103. Švarc, "The Testimony of a Survivor," 140.
104. Dulić, *Utopias*, 249–50.
105. Lukić, *Rat i djeca Kozare*. Lukić has written a number of volumes detailing the fates of children across the NDH whose lives were caught in the Ustaša net.
106. The figure is cited by Goldstein and Goldstein, *Jews in Jasenovac*, 9. Ramet states that "there were some 26." See "The NDH—An Introduction," 402. Among the camps were: Loborgrad, in northern Croatia, administered by *Volksdeutsche*, Krušcica, near Travnik (mainly for women and children, sent to Loborgrad and finally to Auschwitz when the camp was closed in 1942), Đakovo, near Sarajevo (also for women and children), and Jadovno, near Gospić (which may have held as many as 35,000 prisoners).
107. To counter Serbian propagandists' egregious inflation of the dead at Jasenovac, Croat strategists exaggerated the numbers of dead Croats in the Bleiberg incident in fall 1945.
108. Rosenbaum quotes from a "heavily footnoted" OSI report housed in the US National Archives and originally classified as "Secret": T-120/5793/H306076-87. See "Jasenovac as Encountered in OSI's Investigations," 72.
109. Miletić, "Establishing the Number of Persons Killed," 6. See also the United States Holocaust Memorial Museum Jasenovac website, <http://www.ushmm.org/museum/exhibit/online/jasenovac/frameset.html> (accessed 16 September 2009).
110. Žerjavić, "The Most Likely Numbers," 18.
111. Sabolevski, "Jews in the Jasenovac Group," 102.
112. Erlih, "Kula," 158.
113. Indeed, since 6 of 22 foremen were Jews, Franjo Tudjman blamed them, not Ustaše, for Jasenovac brutalities. Since the publication of his "history," *Bespuća*, many Serb and Croat eyewitness testimonies have directly refuted this.
114. Dulić, *Utopias*, 280.
115. Goldstein and Goldstein, *Jews in Jasenovac*, 15. But Lituchy cites Dachau as the influence; see Lituchy, *Jasenovac*, xxxix.
116. Šajer, "The Stench of the Crematorium," 80.
117. Danon, "Recollections of Jasenovac," 181.

118. Kennedy et al., *The Library of Congress World War II Companion*, 683.

119. Goldstein and Goldstein, *Jews in Jasenovac*, 20. See also Novaković, *Crimes in the Jasenovac Camp*, 63.

120. Several survivors note the particular brutality of the Ustaše women. See, for example, the testimonies of Erlih and Štefica Serdar Sabolić in *Jasenovac and the Holocaust in Yugoslavia*, 155, 173, and Šajer in "The Stench of the Crematorium," 85.

121. Among other sites, the United States Holocaust Memorial Museum library houses both oral and written eyewitness testimony and photographs that document the particularly ghastly nature of the killings at Jasenovac.

122. See Despot, "Death and Survival in Jasenovac," 132. Indeed, innumerable accounts now exist. Thus, for instance, Gaon's two-volume collection, *We Survived*, compiles survivor testimony from Jasenovac and other camps, including Dachau and Auschwitz, while Lituchy's *Jasenovac* also includes a number of eyewitness testimonies by Serbs, Jews, and Croats detailing the horrors of the camp. See also the online sites of the United States Holocaust Memorial Museum: <http://www.ushmm.org/museum/exhibit/online/jasenovac/frameset.html> (accessed 16 September 2009) and <http://www.ushmm.org/wlc/article.php?ModuleId=10005449> (accessed 16 September 2009).

123. Delibašić, "Varieties of Psychopathological Behavior among the Ustashe at Jasenovac," 233.

124. Despot, "Death and Survival in Jasenovac," 139; Erlih, "Kula," 160.

125. "The Jasenovac Extermination Camps," Holocaust Education and Archive Research Team, <http://www.holocaustresearchproject.org/othercamps/jasenovac.html> (accessed 16 September 2009).

126. See such works as: Neitzke, Ustaša *Gold*; Milan and Brogan, *Soldiers, Spies and The Ratline*; Aarons and Loftus, *Unholy Trinity*; Eizenstat, *U.S. and Allied Wartime and Postwar Relations and Negotiations*.

127. In Spain he operated a printing press, "Drina," a symbolic name for diaspora Croats since Budak famously stated in 1941: "The Drina is the border between East and West" (Dedijer, *The Yugoslavian Auschwitz*, 130). Interestingly, his publications also included the diaries of Marcone's Zagreb secretary. See Dulić, "Tito's Slaughterhouse," 92.

128. In his weblog a month after the funeral of Sakić, Marko Atilla Hoare noted that he was buried in full Ustaša uniform and that the presiding clergyman, Vjekoslav Lasić, had said that "the court that convicted Dinko Sakić convicted Croatia and the Croatian nation," that "the NDH is the foundation of the modern Croatian homeland," and that "every honorable Croat should be proud of Sakić's name." See Hoare, <http://greatersurbiton.wordpress.com/2008/08/05/croatias-ustashas-from-treason-and-genocide-to-simple-national-embarrassment> (accessed 16 September 2009).

129. Cornwell, *Hitler's Pope*, 266.

130. Breitman et al., *US Intelligence*, 211.

131. Records of the Counter-Intelligence Corps (CIC) show that government funds helped provide maintenance and travel for these exiles, seen as potentially useful weapons in the Cold War against the growing communist threat. See Neitzke, Ustaša *Gold*, 3, 8; US Department of Justice, Criminal Division, *Klaus Barbie and the U.S. Government: A Report to the Attorney General of the United States*.

132. Thus, for example, Yossi Melman suggests in "Tied up in the Rat Lines" that Juan Peron granted entry visas to 34,000 Croats.

133. Breitman et al., *US Intelligence*, 217. The circumstances under which Draganović came to Yugoslavia remain a mystery.

134. Neitzke, Ustaša *Gold*, 149–50.

135. That event split an increasingly divided Croatia, with nationalist Catholics supporting Franco and those who leaned communist favoring his rivals.
136. This, at least, according to the Argentine newspaper *Hrvatska*, February 1960. See Paris, *Genocide*, 279.
137. Dedijer, *The Yugoslav Auschwitz*, 313.
138. For Žerjavić, see *Gubici stanovništva Jugoslavije u drugom svjetskom ratu*, 61–66 and "The Most Likely Numbers of Victims Killed in Jasenovac," 21. For Kočović, see "Žrtve Drugog svetskog rata u Jugoslaviji." Interestingly, each gave a lower number for his own ethnicity. For a good overview on the numbers issue, see Srđan Bogosavlje-vić, "The Unresolved Genocide," 146–59.
139. Dinko Šakić made this assertion at his trial. See Croatian News Agency (HINA), "The Trial of Dinko Šakić."
140. Price, "Memory, the Media, and Nato," 143.
141. Nyström, "The Holocaust and Croatian National Identity," 269.
142. Bet-El, "Unimagined Communities," 206.
143. The *šahovnica* pre-dates and differs slightly from the flag of the NDH, but its red and white checkerboard clearly evokes the latter.
144. Brkljačić, "What Past is Present?," 50.

REFERENCES

Aarons, Mark, and John Loftus. *Unholy Trinity; The Vatican, The Nazis, and The Swiss Banks*. New York: St. Martin's Press, 1998.

Actes et documents du Saint Siège relatifs à la seconde guerre mondiale. Edited by Pierre Let, Angelo Martini, Robert A. Graham, and Burkhart Schneider. Rome: Libreria Editrice Vaticana, 1967.

Adeli, Lisa M. "From Jasenovac to Yugoslavism: Ethnic Persecution in Croatia during World War II." Diss. in history, University of Arizona, 2004.

Anzulović, Branimir. *Heavenly Serbia: From Myth to Genocide*. New York: New York University Press, 1999.

Bax, Mart. "Mass Graves, Stagnating Identification, and Violence: A Case Study in the Local Sources of 'The War' in Bosnia/Hercegovina." *Anthropology Quarterly* 70, no. 1 (1997): 11–19.

Bet-El, Ilana R. "Unimagined Communities: The Power of Memory and the Conflict in the Former Yugoslavia." In *Memory and Power in Post-War Europe*, edited by Jan-Werner Müller. Cambridge: Cambridge University Press, 2002.

Biondich, Mark. "Religion and Nation in Wartime Croatia." *Slavic and East European Review* 83, no. 1 (2005): 71–116.

Bogosavljević, Srđan. "The Unresolved Genocide." In *The Serbian Road to War*, edited by Nebojsa Popov and Drinka Gojković. Budapest: Central European University Press, 1999.

Breitman, Richard, et al, eds. *US Intelligence and the Nazis*. Cambridge: Cambridge University Press, 2005.

Brkljačić, Maja. "What Past is Present?" *International Journal of Politics, Culture and Society* 17, no. 1 (2003): 41–52.

Cornwell, John. *Hitler's Pope: The Secret History of Pius XII*. New York: Viking Press, 1999.

Croatian News Agency (HINA). "The Trial of Dinko Šakić." Croatian Institute for Culture and Information, 1999, <http://public.carnet.hr/sakic/hinanews/arhiva/9909/hina-29-d.html> (accessed 16 September 2009).

Danon, Sadik. "Recollections of Jasenovac." In *Jasenovac and the Holocaust in Yugoslavia: Analyses and Survivor Testimonies*, edited by Barry Lituchy. New York: Jasenovac Research Institute, 2006.

Dedijer, Vladimir. *The Yugoslavian Auschwitz and the Vatican*. Buffalo: Prometheus Books, 1992.

Delibašić, Savo. "Varieties of Psychopathological Behavior among the Ustashe at Jasenovac." In *Jasenovac and the Holocaust in Yugoslavia: Analyses and Survivor Testimonies*, edited by Barry Lituchy. New York: Jasenovac Research Institute, 2006.

Despot, Miloš. "Death and Survival in Jasenovac." In *Jasenovac and the Holocaust in Yugoslavia: Analyses and Survivor Testimonies*, edited by Barry Lituchy. New York: Jasenovac Research Institute, 2006.

Dulić, Tomislav. "Tito's Slaughterhouse: A Critical Analysis of Rummel's Work on Democide." *Journal of Peace Research* 41, no. 4 (2004): 85–102.

———. *Utopias of Nation*. Uppsala: Studia Historica Upsaliensia 218, Acta Universitatis Upsaliensis, 2005.

Eizenstat, Stuart E. *U.S. and Allied Wartime and Postwar Relations and Negotiations with Argentina, Portugal, Spain, Sweden and Turkey on Looted Gold and German External Assets and U.S. Concerns about the Fate of the Wartime Treasury*. Washington, DC: Department of State, June 1998.

Erlih, Josip. "Kula: The Prison in the Concentration Camp Stara Gradiška." In *Jasenovac and the Holocaust in Yugoslavia: Analyses and Survivor Testimonies*, edited by Barry Lituchy. New York: Jasenovac Research Institute, 2006.

Gaon, Aleksandar, ed. *We Survived: Yugoslav Jews on the Holocaust*. Translated by Stephen Agnew and Jelena Babšek. Belgrade: Jewish Historical Museum, Federation of Jewish Communities in Yugoslavia, 2005.

Goldstein, Ivo, ed. *Anti-Semitism; Holocaust; Anti-Fascism*. Translated by Nikolina Jovanović. Zagreb: Zagreb Jewish Community, 1997.

Goldstein, Slavko, and Ivo Goldstein. *Jews in Jasenovac*. Translated by Nikolina Jovaniović. Jasenovac Memorial Area, 2001.

Gumz, Jonathan. "German Counterinsurgency Policy in Independent Croatia, 1941–1944." *Historian* 61, no. 1 (1998): 33–51.

———. "*Wehrmacht* Perceptions of Mass Violence in Croatia, 1941–1942." *Historical Journal* 44, no. 4 (2001): 1015–38.

Herzstein, Robert Edwin. *Waldheim: The Missing Years*. New York: Paragon House, 1989.

Hewitt, William L. "Ethnic Cleansing: Bosnia." In *Defining the Horrific: Readings on Genocide and Holocaust in the Twentieth Century*. New York: Prentice Hall, 2003.

Hoare, Marko Attila. <http://greatersurbiton.wordpress.com/2008/08/05/croatias-ustashas-from-treason-and-genocide-to-simple-national-embarrassment> (accessed 16 September 2009).

———. "The *Ustaša* Genocide." *South Slav Journal* 25, no. 1–2 (2004): 29–38.

———. *Genocide and Resistance in Hitler's Bosnia: The Partisans and the Chetniks, 1941–1943*. London: Oxford University Press, 2006.

Jansen, Hans. *Pius XII. Chronologie van een onophoudelijk protest*. Kampen: Uitgeverij Kok, 2003.

Jelinek, Yeshayahu A. "Bosnia-Herzegovina at War: Relations between Moslems and Non-Moslems." *Holocaust and Genocide Studies* 5, no. 3 (1990): 275–93.

Jezernik, Bozidar. *Wild Europe: The Balkans in the Gaze of Western Travelers*. London: Saqi Press, 2003.

Job, Cvijeto. *Yugoslavia's Ruin: The Bloody Lessons of Nationalism, a Patriot's Warning*. Lanham, MD: Rowman & Littlefield, 2002.

Kennedy, David M., Margaret E. Wagner, Linda Barrett Osborne, and Susan Reyburn *The Library of Congress World War II Companion*, edited by David M. Kennedy, Margaret E. Wagner, Linda Barrett Osborne and Susan Reyburn. New York: Simon & Schuster, 2007.

Klaus Barbie and the U.S. Government: A Report to the Attorney General of the United States. Washington, DC: Criminal Division, US Department of Justice, 1983.

Kocovic, Bogolub. *Zrtve Drugog svetskog rata u Jugoslaviji*. London: Nase delo, 1985.

Lituchy, Barry, ed. *Jasenovac and the Holocaust in Yugoslavia: Analyses and Survivor Testimonies*. New York: Jasenovac Research Institute, 2006.

Lukić, Dragoje. *Rat i djeca Kozare*. Belgrade: Književne novine, 1990.

MacDonald, David. *Balkan Holocausts? Serbian and Croatian Victim-Centred Propaganda and the War in Yugoslavia*. Manchester: Manchester University Press, 2002.

Melman, Yossi. "Tied up in the Rat Lines." *Ha'aretz*, <www.haaretz.com/hasen/spages/670245.html> (accessed 16 September 2009).

Milan, James V., and Patrick Brogan. *Soldiers, Spies and The Ratline: America's Undeclared War against the Soviets*. New York: St. Martin's Press, 1998.

Miletić, Antun. "Establishing the Number of Persons Killed in the Jasenovac Concentration Camp 1941–1945." In *Jasenovac and the Holocaust in Yugoslavia: Analyses and Survivor Testimonies*, edited by Barry Lituchy. New York: Jasenovac Research Institute, 2006.

Neitzke, Ron. *Ustaša Gold*. Washington, DC: Office of the Historian, Department of State, April 1999.

Novaković, Nenad., ed. *Crimes in the Jasenovac Camp*. Translated by Dragica Banja. Banja Luka: Croatian Commission for Establishing Crimes of Occupying Forces and their Assistants, 2000.

Nyström, Kerstin. "The Holocaust and Croatian National Identity: An Uneasy Relationship." In *The Holocaust on Post-War Battlefields: Genocide as Historical Culture*, edited by Klas-Göran Karlsson and Ulf Zander. Malmo: Sekel Baförlag, 2006.

Paris, Edmond. *Genocide in Satellite Croatia, 1941–1945*. Chicago: American Institute for Balkan Affairs, 1961.

Phayer, Michael. *The Catholic Church and the Holocaust, 1930–1965*. Bloomington: Indiana University Press, 2005.

Popovic, Thomas. "Primary Sources on the Persecution of Minorities in the Independent State of Croatia, 1941–1945." In *Jasenovac and the Holocaust in Yugoslavia: Analyses and Survivor Testimonies*, edited by Barry Lituchy. New York: Jasenovac Research Institute, 2006.

Price, Monroe. "Memory, the Media, and Nato: Information Intervention in Bosnia/Hercegovina." In *Memory and Power in Post-War Europe: Studies in the Presence of the Past*, edited by Jan-Werner Müller. Cambridge: Cambridge University Press, 2002.

"Principles of the *Ustaša* Movement." Translated by Sinisa Djuric. In *The Pavelić Papers*, <http://pavelic-papers.com/documents/pavelic/ap0040.html> (accessed 16 September 2009).

Prpa-Jovanović, Branka. "The Making of Yugoslavia: 1830–1945." In *Burn this House: The Making and Unmaking of Yugoslavia*, edited by Jasmina Udovički and James Ridgeway. Durham, NC: Duke University Press, 2000.

Ramet, Sabrina. *Balkan Babel: The Disintegration of Yugoslavia from the Death of Tito to the War for Kosovo*. Boulder: Westview Press, 1999.

———. "The NDH—An Introduction." *Totalitarian Movements and Political Religions* 7, no. 4 (2006): 399–408.

Redžić, Enver. *Bosnia and Herzegovina in the Second World War*. Abingdon: Routledge, 2005.

Rivelli, Marco Aurelio. *Le Génocide occulté: État indépendent de Croatie 1941–1945*. Translated from the Italian by Gaby Rousseau. Lausanne: L'Age d'Homme, 1998.

Rosenbaum, Eli M. "Jasenovac as Encountered in OSI's Investigations." In *Jasenovac and the Holocaust in Yugoslavia: Analyses and Survivor Testimonies*, edited by Barry Lituchy. New York: Jasenovac Research Institute, 2006.

Sabolevski, Mihael. "Jews in the Jasenovac Group of Concentration Camps." In *Anti-Semitism, Holocaust, Anti-Fascism*. Zagreb: Jewish Community, 1997.

Sabolić, Štefica Serdar. "Stara Gradiška: Camp V of the Jasenovac System of Concentration Camps—The Croatian Women's Camp." In *Jasenovac and the Holocaust in Yugoslavia: Analyses and Survivor Testimonies*, edited by Barry Lituchy. New York: Jasenovac Research Institute, 2006.

Šajer, Eduard. "The Stench of the Crematorium." In *We Survived: Yugoslav Jews on the Holocaust*, edited by Aleksandar Gaon. Belgrade: Jewish Historical Museum, Federation of Jewish Communities in Yugoslavia, 2005.

Shelah, Menachem. "The Catholic Church in Croatia, the Vatican and the Murder of the Croatian Jews." *Holocaust and Genocide Studies* 4, no. 3 (1989): 323–39.

Švarc, Božo. "The Testimony of a Survivor of Jadovno and Jasenovac." In *Jasenovac and the Holocaust in Yugoslavia: Analyses and Survivor Testimonies*, edited by Barry Lituchy. New York: Jasenovac Research Institute, 2006.

Todorova, Maria. *Imagining the Balkans*. New York: Oxford University Press, 1997.

Tomasevich, Jozo. *War and Revolution in Yugoslavia, 1941–45: The Chetniks*. Stanford: Stanford University Press, 1975.

———. *War and Revolution in Yugoslavia, 1941–1945: Occupation and Collaboration*. Stanford: Stanford University Press, 1981.

Vejnović-Smiljanić, Mara. "The Suffering of Children and their Mothers in the Stara Gradiška Ustaše Concentration Camp." In *Jasenovac and the Holocaust in Yugoslavia: Analyses and Survivor Testimonies*, edited by Barry Lituchy. New York: Jasenovac Research Institute, 2006.

Wolff, Larry. *Inventing Eastern Europe: The Map of Civilization on the Mind of the Enlightenment*. Stanford: Stanford University Press, 1994.

Žerjavić, Vladimir. *Gubici stanovništva Jugoslavije u drugom svjetskom ratu*. Zagreb: Naprijed, 1989.

———. "The Most Likely Numbers of Victims Killed in Jasenovac." In *Jasenovac and the Holocaust in Yugoslavia: Analyses and Survivor Testimonies*, edited by Barry Lituchy. New York: Jasenovac Research Institute, 2006.

Hitler's *Rassenkampf* in the East: The Forgotten Genocide of Soviet POWs

Thomas Earl Porter

The sheer enormity of Soviet losses at the hands of German forces during the Second World War staggers the mind. During the immediate post-war period, Stalin did not want the West to know just how badly the Soviet Union had been mauled or the fact that far more Soviet soldiers had died than German ones (up to three times as many); consequently, the Soviets clamed that the *total* number of dead was 7 million, while Western estimates were between 10 and 15 million Soviet dead. It was only during the Khrushchev era that the true scale of the disaster was revealed and the more accurate figure of 20 million dead was generally accepted.[1] Of these, only half were soldiers. The rest were at least 10 million civilians, including 2 million who died as slave laborers in Nazi Germany.[2] The death toll has more recently been put at 25, 27 and even 30 million, though I suspect the latter figures also take into consideration the decline in birth rates. In April 2009 Russian President Dmitrii Medvedev appointed yet another commission to give a final accounting of Soviet losses.

Soviet military records are not particularly accurate but it is estimated that the total number of its dead in combat, hospital, or captivity was at least 8 million and possibly as high as 10 million. An exhaustive investigation by M. Ellman and S. Maksudov puts the figure at 8,668,000.[3] The Germans captured between 5 and 6 million Soviet troops, and executed many after their surrender. Between 3.3 and 3.5 million Soviet prisoners of war (POWs), or well over one third of the military dead, would perish in captivity. Stalin supposedly said the death of one person is a tragedy, whereas the death of millions is but a statistic.[4] The true horrors of Hitler's policies are almost incomprehensible to us, but our duty as scholars is to understand the motives behind the Nazi phenomenon and the reason why so many participated in its implementation. Numbers matter, and, more important, the identities and faces behind each and every one of these numbers matter.

Most accounts of the Holocaust, of course, focus upon its principal victims, the Jews. Approximately 5.8 million of them were murdered. In the popular mind, the figure of 6 million is given as the sum total of Nazi atrocities. This is literally only half the story, since almost that many more non-Jews perished, including Soviet POWs, Roma, homosexuals and others. It is imperative that we honor the memory of *all* the victims of Nazi persecution by exploring these "forgotten" genocides of the Holocaust. This article will address the fate of Soviet POWs, and cover not only the horrors and atrocities they suffered in German captivity but also the lesser known experiences of the repatriated soldiers who were shipped directly to the GULAG (Glavnoe upravleniie ispravitel'no-trudovykh lagerei, or Main Administration of Corrective Labor Camps) up to another decade of incarceration after the war ended.

I should pause here to mention that not all the Soviets captured and executed by the Germans or sent to the camps were soldiers. While most scholars are familiar with the "commissar" order which called for all communists and Jews to be summarily shot after interrogation, even males not in uniform between the ages of 15 and 65 could also be executed or sent to the camps as partisans. But many of the Red Army soldiers who surrendered were turned over to the SS and summarily executed.[5] Jurgen Forster agrees that the documentary evidence proves that at least half a million POWs were handed over to the SS between June 1941 and May 1943; Christian Streit has asserted that all of these men were simply shot, but Forster is not as certain. It must be kept in mind, however, that since the exhibition "The German Army and Genocide" in Germany in 1995, the role that the *Wehrmacht* played in the Holocaust has been extensively researched and documented by many scholars, including Forster, who found that in one month the 707th Infantry division, deployed in Belarus, shot 10,431 captives (including soldiers, partisans, and civilians) out of a total of 10,940, while suffering only two dead themselves.[6] So it was not just the SS and Waffen SS that murdered captured Soviets; consequently, we can safely assume that a very large percentage of the POWs executed by the Germans were shot by regular troops.

Even if they were not summarily executed, the Germans forced these men to walk hundreds of miles to a *Dulag (Durchlager)*, or transit camp, where they were kept in barbaric conditions before being transferred to their final destinations. It was the general policy of the *Wehrmacht* in the East that Russian POWs, who were presumed to be filthy and disease ridden, were not to be transported in the army's trucks or trains. One German officer noted that these soldiers, many of them wounded (and medical assistance was also proscribed by policy) ". . . make an idiotic impression like herds of animals." They were left entirely without shelter, not given food or water on a regular basis, and simply fell by the wayside. They were then executed. The aforementioned German officer thought this unfortunate, as ". . . it was done on the road, even in towns . . ."[7]

One soldier, Nikolai Obrynba, who had been captured at Vitebsk, remembered the horrific details of the march:

> It was the fourth day of our march toward Smolensk. We spent the nights in specially furnished pens, enclosed by barbed wire and guard towers with machine gunners, who illuminated us with flares through the entire night. The tail of the column, which stretched from hill to hill, disappeared into the horizon. Whenever we halted, thousands

of those dying from hunger and cold remained or they collapsed as we marched along. Those still alive were finished off by soldiers wielding submachine guns. A guard would kick a fallen prisoner and, if he could not get up in time, fired his gun. I watched with horror as they reduced healthy people to a state of complete helplessness and death.[8]

Another prisoner, Leonid Volynsky, also remembered these arbitrary shootings:

an exhausted prisoner of war would be sat at the side of the road, an escort would approach on his horse and lash out with his whip. The prisoner would continue sitting, with his head down. Then the escort would take a carbine from his saddle or a pistol from his holster.

At his war crimes trial in Nuremberg, Colonel-General Alfred Jodl, Chief of the Fuehrungsamt (*Wehrmacht* Command Staff) and one of Hitler's closest military advisors, attempted to explain away these atrocities by saying that the only prisoners shot were "... not those that could not, but those that did not want to walk."[9]

Those who survived these death marches and reached the camps found hell on earth:

There were no barracks or permanent housing. The camps were simply open areas fenced off with barbed wire. The prisoners had to lie in the sun, then in mud, and in the fall—with temperatures as low as minus 30 degrees centigrade—faced the possibility of freezing to death.[10]

The commandant of Stalag VIII-F (a large camp in western Poland set up specifically for Soviet prisoners, it was renumbered 318 in 1943), Colonel Falkenberg, noted how "these cursed *Untermenschen* have been observed eating grass, flowers and raw potatoes. Once they can't find anything edible in the camp they turn to cannibalism." Alexander Werth quotes one Hungarian officer's description in his *Russia at War*:

Behind wire there were tens of thousands of prisoners. Many were on the point of expiring. Few could stand on their feet. Their faces were dried up and their eyes sunk deep into their sockets. Hundreds were dying every day, and those who had any strength left dumped them in a vast pit.[11]

That would indeed sometimes be only if their comrades had not consumed their flesh. Cannibalism was fairly common in the camps. Reichsmarshal Hermann Goering joked about this, telling one diplomat that "in the camps for [Soviet] prisoners of war, after having eaten everything possible, including the soles of their boots, they have begun to eat each other, and what is more serious, have also eaten a German sentry."[12] In another camp, a German witness stated that the POWs "whined and groveled before us. They were human beings in whom there was no longer a trace of anything human." When a dead dog was thrown into the compound, "... the Russians would fall on the animal and tear it to pieces with their bare hands ... the intestines they'd stuff in their pockets ..." One guard, Xavier Dorsch, noted that in Minsk, "the problem of feeding the prisoners being unsolvable, they have largely been without nourishment for six to eight days and are almost deranged in their need for sustenance." Another guard, Johannes Gutschmidt, noted in his diary that "there was nothing to eat, not even any water. Many died. Finally, they gave them dry macaroni and they fought over it." A POW named Viktor Yermolayev confirms that the Germans "began throwing us packets of semolina, dehydrated semolina, they threw them to us . . . some caught them . . . and others couldn't. We fell on it like wolves!"[13]

Alexander Solzhenitsyn has given us the best description of the plight of the Soviet POWs in his *The Gulag Archipelago*:

> a multitude of bonfires; and around the bonfires, beings who had once been Russian officers but had now become beastlike creatures who gnawed the bones of dead horses, who baked patties from potato rinds, who smoked manure and were all swarming with lice. Not all these two-legged creatures had died as yet. Not all of them had lost the capacity for intelligible speech, and one could see in the crimson reflections of the bonfires how a belated understanding was dawning on those faces which were descending to the Neanderthal.[14]

According to Alexander Dallin, "German policy had caused, or at the very least had tolerated the degradation of the prisoners—and then held it up to its own people as something to be reviled, as something typical of a sub-human who could never be like Western man."[15]

Daniel Goldhagen probably overstated the excessive mortality rate for Soviet POWs in his *Hitler's Willing Executioners* when he estimated that nearly 3 million "young, healthy Soviet POWs" were murdered "mainly by starvation . . . in less than eight months" before the Germans changed their policy to exploit them as slave laborers.[16] Peter Calvocoressi and Guy Wint have more accurately estimated that 3.5 million out of 5.5 million Soviet POWs were deliberately killed or died as a result of criminal negligence by the middle of 1944.[17] Though the numbers are imprecise, we can state with some degree of certainty that these deaths cannot be explained or rationalized as the result of poor preparation on the part of the Germans during the first months of Operation Barbarossa. In reality, German military planners had anticipated that they would capture a large number of prisoners. In early 1941, the *Wehrmacht* calculated that in the opening months of the war it would capture 2–3 million prisoners, including 1 million in the opening weeks of the campaign. Furthermore, at a conference of German State Secretaries in Berlin in May 1941, it was decided that providing food for the *Wehrmacht* and for Germany had the highest priority; "as a result, millions of people will surely starve."[18]

This callous indifference to the fate of both the Soviet POWs and the civilian population of the USSR points up the difference between Hitler's war in the West and the Nazi *Rassenkampf* (racial struggle) in the East. Before the invasion began the SS briefed German army officers with plans for the outright elimination of prisoners by regular army units and the Waffen SS. The racist nature of the war can also be seen also in the fact that not only were Jewish prisoners simply shot but prisoners from the USSR's Central Asian republics were also often culled from the ranks and executed. Calvocoressi and Wint had it right when they wrote that

> This slaughter of prisoners cannot be accounted for by the peculiar chaos of war in the east … The true cause was the inhuman policy of the Nazis towards the Russians as a people and the acquiescence of army commanders in attitudes and conditions which amounted to a sentence of death on their prisoners.

Alan Bullock, whose *Hitler: A Study in Tyranny*, remains one of the most perceptive studies of the man, has rightly noted that of all Hitler's decisions, the decision to invade Russia "is the one which clearly bears his own personal stamp, the culmination (as he saw it) of his own career."[19]

Hitler's worldview was there for all to see in *Mein Kampf* [My Struggle], where he clearly enunciated his racist, Social Darwinistic policies and talked of invading Russia to achieve the necessary *Lebensraum* (living space) for future colonization by the master Aryan race.[20] If we take Hitler at his word we can then begin to understand why at least 25 million Soviets died in the conflict, a staggering number that simply cannot be explained as being merely the fate of victims of war. Hitler's ravings clearly indicate that he equated "Jewishness" with "Bolshevism" and he believed that as a result of the communist takeover in 1917, the Russians had been irreparably contaminated by Jews and were now inferior beings whose lives were of little value. The historical record is clear on this point, and yet, though often mentioned, this core belief of Hitler's is usually glossed over by scholars in the field. David Crowe, however, points out that Hitler believed that Marxism was a Jewish doctrine that "systematically [planned] to hand the world over to the Jews."[21] Crowe also rightly asserts that Hitler felt the Jews were the cause of all of Germany's misfortunes since 1914 and that he linked them with communism and Bolshevism. He also points out that in Hitler's little known *Second Book* he "married his racial ideas with his foreign policy goals of *Lebensraum* in the East …" and that any "campaign against the Jews was an essential part of the war for Aryan survival and expansion."[22]

Hitler consistently referred to these ideas to explain his policies in government meetings and before party gatherings. For example, at the annual party rally in Nuremberg on 11 September 1935, he declared it was time to take on the Bolsheviks who headed the international Jewish conspiracy.[23] At a cabinet meeting in September 1936 Goering read aloud from a memorandum written by Hitler that declared:

> The essence and goal of Bolshevism is the elimination of those strata of mankind which have hitherto provided the leadership and their replacement by worldwide Jewry … The German Armed Forces must be operational within four years.[24]

Hitler believed that in the coming struggle, a Bolshevik victory would mean "the annihilation of the German people." At the 1937 Party Rally Hitler again demonized Jews as the primary enemy of the Western world, particularly "Jewish Bolshevism in Moscow."[25] It was not a coincidence that the mass killings of Jews began with Operation *Barbarossa* against the Soviet Union. The war against Russia should thus be seen as the "struggle for territorial conquest, a clash of ideologies and the *Rassenkampf* that it undoubtedly was."[26]

On 30 March 1941, Hitler told his senior military commanders that he "wanted to see the impending war against the Soviet Union conducted not according to customary military principles, but as a war of extermination against an ideology and its adherents, whether within the Red Army or in a non-military function."[27] Many *Wehrmacht* leaders saw the war as a struggle between Aryans and Jews which would require unprecedented harshness. General Erich Hoepner, commander of the 4th Panzer Group, wrote:

> The war against Russia is an important chapter in the struggle for existence of the German nation. It is the old battle of the Germanic against the Slav peoples, of the defence of European culture against Moscovite-Asiatic inundation, and the repulse of Jewish Bolshevism. The objective of this battle must be the destruction of present-day Russia and it must therefore be conducted with unprecedented severity. Every military action must be guided in planning and execution by an iron will to exterminate the enemy mercilessly and totally.[28]

The orders and directives issued by the Germans prior to the attack on the Soviet Union show clearly that this was to be a war of annihilation. On 19 May 1941, the OKW, Oberkommando der Wehrmacht (Armed Forces Supreme Command) issued a directive that told army commanders that:

> Bolshevism is the deadly enemy of the National Socialist German people. Germany's struggle is directed against this subversive ideology and its functionaries. This struggle requires ruthless and energetic action against Bolshevik agitators, guerillas, saboteurs, and Jews, and the total elimination of all active or passive resistance.[29]

This was followed by the famous 6 June Commissar Order, which freed German soldiers from legal responsibility for their actions against the Soviet political officers assigned to Red Army units. These officers, upon capture, were "as a matter of principle, to be finished with a weapon." Other directives of the same date said that German troops should deal ruthlessly with "restiveness" among Soviet POWs.[30] Bartov, however, notes that the maltreatment and indiscriminate shootings of Russian POWs, which began in the very first weeks of the campaign, were often carried out by soldiers "in spite of their commanders' objections to such 'unmilitary behavior.'" He contends that it was not only the "criminal orders" that caused these behaviors but also the "ceaseless and ruthless propaganda of the regime against the 'Jewish-Bolshevik *Untermenschen*' to which the soldiers had been exposed throughout their youth . . ."[31]

The Nazis treated Soviet POWs with the same contempt they showed toward Jews. They were completely expendable, but when necessary their labor could be utilized. The Nazis had originally thought that perhaps 100,000 prisoners could be used for labor. On 1 March, Heinrich Himmler, the Reichsfuehrer SS, ordered Rudolph Hoess, the new commandant of the Auschwitz concentration camp, which had only 8,000 inmates at the time, to build a new camp at Birkenau for 100,000 POWs. Of this number 10,000 were to be put to work building a huge industrial complex for IG

Farben.[32] Soon it would become the largest extermination camp in Poland. Majdanek (Waffen SS POW camp, Lublin), another sprawling death and forced labor camp on the outskirts of Lublin, was opened in the summer of 1941 to house 150,000 Soviet POWs. Over 60% of the half million people who passed through Majdanek died there from the harsh labor conditions, malnutrition, or disease. Of this number, 100,000 victims were Poles, 80,000 were Jews, and 50,000 were Soviet POWs.[33]

The first experimental gassing of the Final Solution took place at Auschwitz I from 1 to 3 September 1941 in the basement of Block 11. Its victims were hundreds of Soviet POWs, many still in their combat uniforms.[34] According to Hoess, only a few hundred of the 10,000 Soviet POWs used to construct Birkenau survived until the summer of 1942. He wrote that "they were no longer human. They had become animals who looked for only one thing, food."[35] He recounted how this remnant, which had only survived because they were "more ruthless and unscrupulous," tried a mass escape because they feared they were to be gassed. Hoess wrote that "there never was any intention to gas these Russians," suggesting that the prisoners were simply suffering from a mass psychosis.[36] The Germans also conducted medical experiments upon Soviet POWs. Dr. Berning killed 12 Soviet POWs in Stalag 310 while performing experiments on them. In another case, prisoners were used as live dummies and shot using hollow point bullets.

Most scholars have agreed that it was only in the fall of 1941 that Hitler conceded to the economic realities of the war and permitted the use of Soviet prisoners for slave labor.[37] On 5 August 1941, Goering had allowed for the exploitation of "... 20,000 Russian prisoners of war in Norway."[38] Within a few months this had become general policy and Soviet POWs were now to get the same rations as other POWs, but only half rations of meat and fats.[39] The army also began to change its prisoner transportation policies, and no longer forced prisoners to walk to the camps. It was also forbidden to transport POWs in open conveyances. One prisoner recalled his journey to Stalag 304:

> The experience in the wagons can hardly be described in words ... wounds bled and turned everything black. Men died in each wagon. They died of blood loss, tetanus, blood poisoning, or hunger, thirst and suffocation as well as other deprivations. This inhumane ordeal lasted for ten days. The journey came to an end. At noon they unloaded the men. The dead were thrown out onto the platform.[40]

The POW camps, however, were obviously very low on the Germans' list of priorities. All foodstuffs were naturally earmarked for the army and the German civilian population. During the last 10 days of October 1941, nearly 46,000 Soviet POWs died in the Polish camps while 83,000 more died the following month. It was about this time that a meeting took place at the Reich Ministry of Food and Agriculture in Berlin to discuss the composition of so-called Russian bread (50% rye meal, 20% sugar beet mulch, 20% cellulose and 10% straw or leaves) that would be fed only to working prisoners. It was stated that "non-working prisoners of war have to starve. Working POWs can, in individual cases, be fed from army supplies. In view of the general food supply situation, unfortunately that cannot be ordered generally."[41] Field Marshal Goering, who was at the meeting as head of the Four Year Plan, suggested that the prisoners be allowed to supplement their diet by eating cats. The Ministry took this advice seriously but determined that: "Animals not normally consumed will never do much to satisfy the need for meat. Rations for Russians will have to be based on horsemeat and meat stamped by inspectors as unfit for human consumption."[42] Gabriel Temkin, who was taken prisoner in 1942, recalled later that

> all we were getting to eat was watery soup with pieces of rotten meat, a diet that was literally decimating us. It was the flesh of dead horses lying alongside the roads since the German air strikes in the first week of July that was now to become our staple. The horses, their swollen bellies and open wounds full of white maggots and other parasitic worms, were collected by prisoners on adjacent roads.[43]

Alfred Rosenberg, the Reich Minister of Eastern Territories, who had unsuccessfully lobbied for a more humane approach not only toward captured Soviet POWs but toward the Soviet population in general in hopes of enlisting them against the communists, complained to Field Marshal Wilhelm Keitel that "in the majority of cases, the camp commanders have forbidden the civilian population from putting food at the disposal of prisoners and they have rather let them starve to death." Epidemics such as diphtheria, pneumonia, typhus and tuberculosis also afflicted the prisoners. One prisoner recalled how once a typhus epidemic began "up to 500 men died ... each day. The dead were thrown in mass graves, one on top of the other. Misery, cold weather, hunger, disease, death. That was Camp 304 [Stalag IV-B at Muhlburg]." The Red Cross offered to deliver medicines and equipment in the winter of 1941, but Hitler personally rejected the plan. The Germans began to shoot the sick or leave them in the snow to die of exposure. Between 21 and 28 September 1941, Police Battalion 306 shot over 6,000 prisoners at Stalag 359B.[44]

The 2 million Russian POWs who died in the first six months of the war was unprecedented in warfare. One German official calculated that as of 19 February 1942, only 1 million of the 3.9 million Soviet POWs captured since the summer of 1941 were still alive. The stark contrast between the treatment of Soviet prisoners-of-war and Western POWs is proof positive of the racist war prosecuted by Hitler and his henchmen. According to Larry Wolff in his *Inventing Eastern Europe*, Western European disdain for the Eastern European "other" has been present since at least the Enlightenment.[45] There was indeed a huge difference between the policies towards POWs taken in the East and those in the West. Of the 5.7 million Soviet POWs captured by the Germans, 60%, or 3.3 million of them, died in captivity.[46] In stark contrast, only 4% of Western POWs died in captivity. The death rate of those POWs captured by the Japanese was but 27%.[47]

At the same time, approximately 37% of German soldiers captured by the Soviets died in Russian camps between 1942 and 1955 (1.2 million of 3.1 million captured), staggering figures but still nowhere near the number of Soviet dead.[48] In the West, French POWs were permitted supplies from German reserves, but no such privileges were extended to Russians. Allied officers at Colditz were allowed Red Cross parcels but were forbidden to share them with Soviet prisoners. One Russian prisoner, B. V. Veselovskii, remembered how "the English prisoners were held in sufficiently good conditions. During the days the English played soccer, rugby and other strenuous athletics . . . they were fed with foodstuffs from the International Red Cross."[49] OKW orders of 16 June 1941 stressed that Soviet POWs were not to be treated as "fellow soldiers" but as subhuman creatures that had "lost every right to treatment . . . according to the Geneva Convention."[50] Ostensibly this was because the Soviet Union was not a signatory to that agreement, but it was clearly understood by all signatories that they were to be bound by its strictures in combat. This racist attitude was also seen in German policies toward the civilian population of Russia.

This population was to be mercilessly exploited, and, instead of bringing civilians before a military court as provided for in international law, "the troops were to defend themselves ruthlessly against every threat from the hostile civilian population." In contrast, orders sent to German troops fighting in France in June 1940 warned that the French should not be mistreated. In addition, any illegal acts towards the general population, such as robbery or rape, were considered crimes in France and could lead to a sentence of death. Sex offenses such as "rape" in France were considered to be merely "racial offenses" or "fraternization" in Soviet territory. German troops in France were supposed to pay in cash for any purchases and were theoretically forbidden from interfering in the cultural life of the country. Punishments for plundering in Russia were far lighter than in the West. In fact, soldiers in France were prohibited from living off the land though records show that plundering by troops, including the senseless slaughter of livestock, was the normal *modus operandi* of the *Wehrmacht* in Russia.[51] According to Omer Bartov, the troops of the 18th Panzer Division in Russia

> plundered and looted the population wherever they could lay their hands on their possessions. Boots and furs were particularly high on the soldiers' lists of priorities, as also were potatoes, flour and cattle. The men broke into houses and indeed stripped whole villages of their food reserves, shooting down any person who tried to resist them . . .[52]

For half a century after the close of the Second World War, the myth of the "untainted" *Wehrmacht* was sedulously promoted not only by the Germans but also by the West. But official documents prove definitively that the war in the East differed greatly from that in the West. Omer Bartov concludes in his *Hitler's Army: Soldiers, Nazis, and War in the Third Reich* that the German military was not an apolitical, professional fighting force but a highly motivated one which was thoroughly indoctrinated through a carefully planned campaign of propaganda which instilled in the entire *Wehrmacht* a racist ideology that considered Jews and Slavs to be *Untermenschen*.

The success of this incessant brainwashing can also be seen in the following letter by a non-commissioned officer serving in Russia in July 1941: "you read the *Sturmer* in Germany and look at the pictures, and you will get only a small picture of what we see here and what atrocities the Jews have committed."[53] The German treatment of millions of Russian civilian *Ostarbeiter* (East workers) and captured Soviet Red Army soldiers qualitatively differed from the treatment accorded to those from the West. Few of the prisoners survived long in German captivity. When the Red Army finally liberated them there were still thousands of *starozhili* (old-timers) that had been in the camps since the beginning of the war. Overall, there were as many as 2 million Soviet POWs in German hands. There were also several million Russian civilians still alive who had been used as forced laborers.

In August 1941, Stalin declared that any Soviet soldiers who surrendered were to be treated as deserters. Aware of the ramifications of this order, many prisoners actually tried to avoid returning to their homeland but were forcibly repatriated. According to Ilya Ehrenburg

> In March 1945 my daughter Irina went to Odessa on behalf of the *Red Star*. British, French, Belgian war prisoners liberated by the Red Army were being repatriated from there. There she also saw a troop transport arriving from Marseilles with our own war prisoners on board, among them some who had escaped from German camps and some who had fought together with the French maquis. Irina told me that they were met like criminals, that they were isolated, that there was much talk of their being sent to the camps . . .[54]

The Red Army liberated many of these survivors who were then interrogated by a special agency, SMERSH (Smert' shpionam, or Death to Spies), which sent 10% of these POWs to the GULAG. Some of them were actually vetted and cleared by the so-called "filtration" process only to be arrested several years later.

Of course, we recoil at the thought of this injustice, but it must be kept in mind that in all likelihood many of these men may well have collaborated or cooperated with the Nazis for any number of reasons. Some experts have estimated that as many as 1 million Soviet citizens served in German ranks.[55] On 11 May 1945, Stalin ordered that another series of camps be set up to "process" the repatriated prisoners.[56] In effect, another *dulag* system in reverse was implemented! According to Catherine Merridale, forty-five camps were set up along the Belorussian front, each capable of holding up to 10,000 men. By June 1945, there were 69 camps for these "special" prisoners on Soviet territory and another 74 in occupied Eastern Europe. They could process almost 1.5 million people at a time. Most of the former Soviet POWs were classified as "betrayers of the motherland" for having surrendered.[57] Merridale recounts the story of one P. M. Gavrilov, who was severely wounded at the Battle of Brest in 1941 and passed out from loss of blood. His courage so impressed the Germans that they carried him to a first aid station and transported him alone by truck to a POW camp. Soviet authorities sentenced him to 10 years' hard labor in the GULAG for this "surrender." By August 1945 over half a million prisoners had been interrogated and assigned to work in construction, timbering, and coal mining. The camps, which had been slowly emptying during the war, were filled up again.[58]

The conditions there were almost as bad as those under the Nazis. In some instances the former Soviet soldiers were sent to work without outerwear or footwear. Their housing conditions were atrocious, without sanitation and infested with lice. Many of the camps and mines in Siberia were administered by former *kulaks* (arbitrarily defined "rich" peasants who had been used as scapegoats during Stalin's collectivization of agriculture), who mistreated the inmates and said "as soon as the officers' backs are turned we're going to kill you with hunger and hard labor. And you deserve it because in 1929–30 you were the ones who dekulakized us."[59] One foreman of a Siberian mine told an inmate that "a ton of coal is dearer to us than your life."[60] This unbelievable turn of events, which robbed so many veterans of the respect and honor they deserved for defending their country, was quite possibly the cruelest thing ever done by Stalin. Solzhenitsyn wrote:

> It would appear that during the one thousand one hundred years of Russia's existence as a state there have been, ah, how many foul and terrible deeds! But among them was there ever so multimillioned foul a deed as this: to betray one's own soldiers and proclaim them as traitors?[61]

These unfortunates spent up to 10 years or more in the camps. Most were not released until after Stalin's death in 1953 or until after Nikita Khrushchev's "Secret Speech" at the 20th Party Congress in 1956. They would remain marked men for life with annotations in their workbooks (required documentation, along with internal passports and residency permits, carried by all Soviet citizens) and limits on their civic freedoms, including where they could reside. These veterans showed remarkable courage and tenacity in their efforts to rectify these blots on their service records, petitioning the authorities again and again for redress. Some were not officially "rehabilitated" until after Mikhail Gorbachev implemented his policy of glasnost (openness) in the late 1980s. Sometimes this occurred posthumously, while those who were still alive proudly wore their campaign medals and claimed their rightful place at the head of any lines for consumer goods as *vovy* (*veterany otechestvennoi voini*, or veterans of the (Second) Fatherland War). The author was privileged to meet personally with some of these veterans on many occasions over a four-year period in the western Siberian city of Omsk while supervising student exchanges and teaching at the state university there.

In the winter of 2002, while standing in line at the newly opened Western-style supermarket *Omich* (resident of Omsk), an aged, beribboned veteran stepped in front of me with his purchases. He turned to explain to me his right to do so but I preempted him by noting that I had read the sign posted at the cashier's which read "Veterans of the Fatherland War need not stand in line but may go directly to its head." I thanked him for his sacrifice and service in our common struggle against fascism, and from this serendipitous encounter came a series of teas, invitations to dinner, and meetings with other veterans, several of whom had been captured by the Germans. After their "liberation" by their comrades in arms, they had been forced to undergo the "filtration" process and ultimately ended up working as forced laborers in Omsk where they built oil factories. Some of them had even written their memoirs and told me that these materials, along with other brief autobiographies, personal recollections, etc., had been deposited for posterity's sake with the Muzei i Obshchestvennyi Tsentr "Mir, Progress, Prava Cheloveka" imeni Andreia Sakharova (Andrei Sakharov Museum and Social Center for Peace, Progress and Human Rights) in Moscow.[62] These reminiscences are harrowing accounts of the lost years of their lives.

Anatolii Efimovich Bakanichev was born in a small town near Mozhaisk in 1920. He matriculated at Moscow State University as a biology student in the summer of 1939 and was drafted into the Red Army in November. He was stationed in Belorussia in 1941 and took part in the first battles of the war. Wounded, he surrendered along with thousands of other soldiers.[63] He had a good knowledge of German and served both as an interpreter in the camps and as a manual laborer. He was sent to a camp in Dzerzhinsk (outside of Minsk) and then to Stalag Luft 7 in Poland. After a few months there he was transferred to Germany, first to Stalag 10 and then to a concentration camp outside of Hanover. He remained there until he escaped in 1945 and was picked up by American soldiers. Suffering from typhus, he was turned over to the Soviet authorities. He was not overly concerned when he was repatriated since he had "been wounded in the service of the Motherland" and had proven himself blameless by escaping from captivity.[64]

Passing successfully through "filtration," he was sent back to Moscow in November 1945 and, after signing the usual non-disclosure forms, he received his passport.[65] He started a program of studies to prepare for eventual admittance into the Petroleum Institute. But on 19 February 1948 he was arrested as a "collaborator" and imprisoned in a basement jail at the Belorusskii station. He stayed there for three months, and was ultimately sentenced to 15 years' hard labor and moved to Butyrka Prison in Moscow. He spent another three months in isolation before he began his journey into the whirlwind. The similarities in the modes of conveyance and the parallel conditions in German and Soviet camps did not escape his notice:

> We were transported in railroad cars similar to those used to send us to fascist Germany ... we were put on a barge on the Enisei ... as we went along the Enisei for ten days it got colder and colder ... and then I was in a Stalinist concentration camp, it was basically the same as in the fascist camp, differing only in minor details.[66]

His journey ended at the Norilsk *GORLAG* (*Gosudarstvennyi osobyi rezhimnyi lager'* or state special regime camp) where he spent the next seven years before being released in 1955. He tried to escape in 1949 but was captured and sentenced to another 10 years. In addition, he was also sentenced to four months in the dreaded *barak usilennogo rezhima* (heightened regime barracks). "We suffered terribly from hunger and a lack of warm clothing, and there were no proper washing facilities."[67]

Transferred to a brick factory, he participated in the Norilsk strike (a two-month uprising shortly after Stalin's death in 1953 where the prisoners refused to work, went on hunger strikes, and wrote letters to government officials protesting camp conditions) and even wrote a letter to Khrushchev asserting his innocence. These actions convinced Soviet leaders to relax the harsh work regime and reduce the workday from 12 to 8 hours. The prisoners were even paid a salary. Finally released in 1955, Bakanichev returned to Moscow and finished his engineering degree in 1962. He was assigned to work in Omsk, where he married and began a family. In 1965, he was "rehabilitated" and awarded the medal "For the Victory over Germany," which he continued to wear proudly until his death in 2005. He died believing that "my arrest was a mistake, due probably to some kind of misunderstanding as to the nature of my interpreting duties while in German captivity. They wrongly thought I had collaborated with the enemy because they forced me to be their interpreter."[68] Even after his unjust incarceration and mistreatment, Bakanichev remained a loyal citizen, expressing outrage at the proliferation of fascist groups in contemporary Russia which make use of Nazi imagery and symbols. But he also likened his experiences in German captivity to those suffered in the GULAG. "There were only differences of degree, not of kind," he said, "in 1944 the conditions in the Nazi camps actually did improve, and it was possible to live [*zhit' mozhno*], but, of course, many more still died." Like many of his comrades, Bakanichev had rejoined the Communist Party when he was rehabilitated. Before his death he had proudly showed me his KPRF, or Kommunisticheskaia Partiia Rossiiskoi Federatsii (Communist Party of the Russian Federation) party card, with all dues paid up to date. One cannot blame him or the other *vovy* for not making the logical connection between the two regimes and drawing the conclusion that both were evil, repressive systems.

One who did was Nikolai Aleksandrovich Troitskii. Born in Ussuriisk in 1913, he was educated first at the Tomsk Chemical-Technological Institute and then transferred over to the Medical Institute. He worked as a rural doctor until he was drafted into the army in 1940. On 12 October 1941 he

> went from being a Red Army fighter to being a prisoner of war, but at that time we were not considered as such, we were simply listed as being missing [*propal bez vesti*]. I don't know what is better for the relatives, news of the death of a husband, father or son or that somehow they had gone missing ... neither alive nor dead, just missing. My mother's grief was unimaginable ... she died a few months later.[69]

Herded along the Minsk highway, Troitskii estimated that 75% of those captured with him would die within the next few years; "for those unable to walk, 'transport' was arranged. They were loaded onto wagons and taken away, never to be seen again." Troitskii knew captivity would be hard, since, he wrote: "we knew that being captured by the Germans wouldn't, as they say, be like going to one's mother-in-law for pancakes." But he was unprepared for the sheer viciousness of the German soldiers and the dehumanizing conditions in the camps. "I quickly came to understand that the Germans' attitude toward Russians was based on extreme cruelty and merciless extermination [*istrebleniie*]."[70]

Troitskii could only watch as hundreds died each day during the westward march to a camp near Smolensk. He witnessed arbitrary shootings and the bayoneting of those prisoners that could not continue.

> I remembered all this in hopes that someday a future historian would take note of it. All over Russia there are monuments to those that perished fighting for the Motherland, but who remembers the millions who died without glory in German captivity? Why has it taken so long to recognize the heroism of these people?[71]

In January 1942, Troitskii was loaded onto a truck, where "they packed us so tightly it was impossible to sit or lie down ... it was possible only to stand, like on a Moscow trolley during peak hours." After several days they arrived at a camp run by the *Wehrmacht* near Dvinsk. Since he had medical training, Troitskii was assigned to the hospital as an orderly.[72]

The senior doctor was a man named Belentsev; Troitskii "was surprised to see him, as he was a Jew and I knew the Germans usually shot them outright." A week after his arrival, Troitskii and several other medical personnel were called out into the court-yard. All of them were Jewish except for Troitskii. He was there "undoubtedly because of my surname, which was similar to Trotskii." They were marched off to Gestapo headquarters. Called in one by one, Troitskii finally entered the office and saw two men sitting there, one German and the other a Russian. Troitskii could only wonder

> what had caused this man to serve Satan? Maybe his village had been destroyed in the revolution or his father had been killed. It must have been something huge on the part of Soviet power to have compelled him to help the enemies of his own kind.[73]

The interrogation began with the Russian asking the questions:

> Name and patronymic? Year of birth? You're a doctor? Then, "you're a Jew? Look me straight in the eyes! Are you a Jew?" "No, I'm a Russian," Troitskii answered. "Where were you born?" continued his interlocutor, "Name and patronymic of your mother? Of your father?"[74]

All of this was written down. Troitskii was asked the name of his aunts and uncles, where his mother and father were born, and finally, "Are you circumcised?" After answering no, an SS officer whom he had not previously noticed stepped forward with a large chart in his hands. "He scrutinized my ears, nose, and head, and then consulted the chart," Troitskii recalled. Satisfied, the SS officer pronounced Troitskii a "Dinarskii type."[75] Troitskii found out later that

> according to their racial theories this was an Aryan of the third degree, one mixed with Slavic and other blood. This meant I would remain in the ranks of the living for the time being. The others weren't so lucky. They had been born under an unlucky star. 1942 was especially hard for prisoners of war, and especially for Jews. People died like flies.[76]

In the fall of 1942, Troitskii was moved to a camp in Riga, and later sent to one of the small work camps outside of Berlin. In 1943, he was moved to Bavaria to a camp named Hammelburg, and then from there to Nuremberg. Along with the other prisoners, he built the barracks he would be housed in, and was then transferred to the hospital. He had never before seen

> such a concentration of people suffering from tuberculosis ... the standard medicine for these living skeletons was chlorine calcite, which was completely useless. True, the sick were now [only] dying by the hundreds instead of by the thousands ... since by the end of 1943 the conditions in the camps improved somewhat.[77]

Still, camp life for the Russian prisoners was harsh and the guards occasionally brutal. Troitskii noted that "We Russians lived worse than anyone else in the camps, including the Poles. Of course, that doesn't include the Jews, who didn't even have the right to breathe German air." Troitskii recalled the old Russian song "Mother, mother of mine, why did you give birth to me? It would have been better if you'd drowned me in the river." Some tried to commit suicide; others "would throw themselves on the wire in hopes of being shot."[78]

In the spring of 1944, Troitskii was moved again. As he noted laconically in his memoirs, this "would be my last camp ... well, at least, my last German camp!" He always told himself "You will survive. You will return to the Motherland and to your family."[79] He says he never doubted that the Soviet Union would win the war, and refused the opportunity to join Lt. General Andrei Vlasov's Russkaia Osvobidi-tel'naia Armiia (Russian Liberation Army), which was formed from Soviet volunteers in the POW camps. During an address to Soviet prisoners in Troitskii's camp, an officer from the ROA told them that Stalin did not recognize POWs, and considered them to be betrayers of the Motherland. If the Soviet leader won the war, he would send them to the Urals and Siberia. Troitskii drolly noted that even though this later proved to be true, no one stepped forward to join the ROA. On 14 April 1945, Troitskii was liberated by American troops and transferred to the Soviet zone of occupation. He was sent to Prague where he passed through filtration and was sentenced to eight years' imprisonment at hard labor. Sent to Nakhodka in the Soviet Far East, he worked again as a camp doctor and was then transferred to one of the Arctic penal camps at Kolyma, first by steamer and then on foot, where there was "mass death among the prisoners on the journey from frostbite and hunger." The conditions there were horrific, and "there was really no difference between Hitler's camps and Stalin's ..." Conditions eased somewhat after Stalin's death, and he fondly writes of his illegal fishing and hunting trips with some of the native Iakuts. Released almost immediately after Stalin's death in 1953, he lived in Semipalatinsk in the Kazakh SSR for a half dozen years, married and divorced without children, and then moved to Krasnoiarsk, where he died in 1995.[80]

Another former POW who came to understand the intrinsic evil of both the Nazi and Soviet regimes was Sergei Aleksandrovich Vladimirov. He considered himself fortunate to have been captured in the summer of 1942, because "hundreds of thousands of us had perished the winter of 1941–1942 in camps on our native soil from hunger, cold and disease." When he was first captured, he was forced to march to a holding camp and "it was there that we were sorted by nationality."[81] According to Vladimirov, it was a *Wehrmacht* officer who asked each man their names and nationality; he selected several men and shot them that night. "The Germans were looking for Jews and Red Army commissars, they also promised to reward any prisoners that helped point them out."[82] Of special interest here is the fact that once again we see *Wehrmacht* officers doing the selection and ordering the shooting of Soviet POWs. Many Germans wanted to believe that the atrocities committed on the Eastern front, as well as the implementation of the Final Solution itself, was solely the work of fanatical Nazis and the SS. They wanted to believe that regular soldiers had merely been doing their duty. This myth was shattered in 1995, the 50th anniversary of the end of the war, when the Hamburg Institute for Social Research put on a controversial exhibition of over 1,000 photographs and numerous official army documents that made it quite clear that it was not just the Nazis that committed atrocities and mass murder. Most of the veterans I interviewed specifically recalled incidents where the *Wehrmacht* either cooperated with the SS or its subordinate organizations such as the Reichssicherheitshauptamt, or RSHA (Reich Security Main Office), Sicherheitsdienst or SD (Security Service), etc. in numerous war crimes or perpetrated the atrocities themselves.

Vladimirov was marched westward with his comrades to another holding camp, where he was barely fed for over three weeks. On 14 November 1942, the prisoners "were forced to take off their boots and given back wooden shoes … I had very good boots, but was compelled to part with them." The prisoners were transferred from camp to camp, ultimately ending up in Stalag XVIII-C in Austria. Thousands died en route. According to Vladimirov, "every time we stopped they removed the corpses of those dead prisoners who had perished from the cold or hunger. They fed us soup and bread once a day." In April 1943, he was transferred to another work camp where he and his fellow captives worked at a concrete form factory. In April 1944, he was sent to Schneiderau (a sub-camp of the Bernau POW camp outside Berlin) to remove silt from cesspools, "a filthy and difficult job."[83] The labor of Soviet POWs and Russian civilians was crucial to German industry. The total value of this forced labor has been estimated to have been as high as thirty billion Reichsmarks.[84] In January 1945, Vladimirov and the other prisoners were transferred to another camp that held a large number of Russian prisoners. There was no work for them to do, and the camp's food supplies were exhausted. Fortunately, Vladimirov noted, "the Austrian police gave us dead horses, which we cut into meat and boiled. This saved us from starvation."[85]

Vladimirov recounted how there were some traitors in their midst "who collaborated with the Germans and informed them of everything that went on among the prisoners." At the end of April, these men were seized by the other prisoners and brutally murdered for their disloyalty.[86] Vladimirov was overjoyed when the Red Army arrived. His happiness was short lived, however, since he did not successfully pass the "filtration" process. Instead, he was sentenced to 10 years' hard labor and a five-year loss of political rights. He was completely dismayed by this turn of events, because "we were loyal sons of the Motherland, we had fought, bled and suffered for her and then we were treated as if we had betrayed her."[87] Sent to the Karaganda labor camp in the Kazakh SSR, he worked at the machine-building complex for several years. He was then transferred to Omsk in western Siberia where he worked in an oil refinery. It was there that he learned of Stalin's death, though he was not released until after the 1956 20th Party Congress as part of a general amnesty. He remained in Omsk, married and raised several children, but he was not officially rehabilitated until 1982. Vladimirov died in May 2007 at the age of 85. It was my great honor to attend his funeral along with several other former *zeki* (*zakliuchennye*, prisoners of the GULAG).

These men all suffered terribly at the hands of both their German and Soviet captors. In both instances, they were considered completely expendable. The Soviets considered them politically unreliable, while the Germans viewed them as racially worthless. Nazi policy toward Soviet POWs ranged from outright extermination to callous exploitation and complete disregard for their lives. Himmler made it clear that the Slavic population in the East would be left uneducated and available for Germany's labor needs. Yes, the treatment accorded Soviet prisoners evidently improved by the summer of 1944, but this was simply to make it possible to exploit them further as forced laborers. Hitler's future plans for Russia were made clear in his first ravings in *Mein Kampf*. In July 1941, Goebbels noted in his diary that "what we have been fighting against our whole lives is now about to be eradicated."[88]

The plans for a racist war of annihilation were outlined in the "General Plan for the East." Drawn up by Himmler, it called for the "removal" of 80 million people from Russia in order to allow for its colonization by Germans. This document was to have been presented to Hitler on the occasion of the final defeat of the Soviet Union. It is well known that Hitler intended for Leningrad, the cradle of Bolshevism, to be completely eradicated from the face of the earth; numerous other cities such as Kiev, Moscow and Stalingrad were also to be razed. And case studies of the German response to partisan activity in Belorussia show that the Germans used this struggle as an excuse to implement their plans to annihilate the local population.[89] The fate of the 5 million Soviet civilians who were taken to Germany and used as forced labor there has yet to be fully documented, but it was part of the "General Plan" to turn all of Russia into a colony to furnish raw materials and slave labor for Germany while also providing the necessary *Lebensraum* for German colonization.

Thankfully, final victory eluded the German invaders and the Soviet Union's tenacious resistance forestalled the Nazi plans for the enslavement and exploitation of Russia. The plans for colonization and economic exploitation were "temporarily" shelved as the fortunes of war turned against the Germans. Desperate for the delivery of vital raw materials and labor for the German war machine, alternative plans were put forward by various Nazi ministries that called for the implementation of less draconian measures in order to meet Germany's economic needs.[90] Of course, this did not mean that the Nazi *Weltanschauung*, which considered Slavs to be *Untermenschen*, was called into question. It was simply that Nazi policies toward the Soviets occasionally fell prey to the vicissitudes of the ongoing power struggles among Hitler's minions. Himmler and the other top Nazis were clearly "working toward the Fuhrer" and these plans would not have simply remained on paper. Final victory for Germany would have resulted ultimately in the destruction of the Russian people and their historical culture. In the final analysis, Hitler's lunatic, incoherent ravings first set down on paper in *Mein Kampf* were indeed a blueprint for his future actions; the true horror of Hitler and Nazism was that he meant every word that he wrote.

NOTES

1. Ueberschar, "The Military Campaign," 143.
2. *Velikaia Otechestvennaia Voina, 1941–1945 gg*, vol. 4, 289.
3. Ellman and Maksudov, "Soviet Deaths in the Great Patriotic War," 674.
4. It is highly unlikely that Stalin actually uttered these words; in his biography of Truman published in 1992, David McCullough asserts that Stalin made the remark *en passant* to Churchill while discussing the opening of the second front. He cites as evidence Anton Antonov-Ovseyenko's *The Time of Stalin: Portrait of a Tyranny*, which was published in 1983, but scholars are generally agreed that the remark comes from Erich Maria Remarque's *Die Schwarze Obelisk* which was published in 1956.
5. Churchill, *A Little Matter of Genocide*, 48.
6. Forster, "The German Army and the Ideological War against the Soviet Union," 26.
7. Hamburg Institute for Social Research, *The German Army and Genocide*, 100.
8. North, "Soviet Prisoners of War," 38.
9. Ibid., 39.
10. Hamburg Institute for Social Research, *The German Army and Genocide*, 142.
11. Werth, *Russia at War*, 635.
12. Dallin, *German Rule in Russia*, 415.
13. Werth, *Russia at War*, 636.
14. Solzhenitsyn, *The Gulag Archipelago*, 218.
15. Dallin, *German Rule in Russia*, 416.
16. Goldhagen, *Hitler's Willing Executioners*, 290.
17. Calvocoressi and Wint, *Total War*, 456.
18. Hamburg Institute for Social Research, *The German Army and Genocide*, 142.
19. Stern, *Hitler*, 216.
20. Hitler, *Mein Kampf*, 654–55.
21. Quoted in Crowe, *The Holocaust*, 94.
22. Ibid., 103.
23. Evans, *The Third Reich in Power*, 543.
24. Ibid., 357.
25. Quoted in Fritzsche, *Life and Death in the Third Reich*, 131.
26. Forster, "The German Army and the Ideological War," 15.
27. Ibid., 17. See also Noakes and Pridham, *Nazism 1919–1945*, 1086.

28. Ibid., 18.
29. Quoted in Crowe, *The Holocaust*, 197.
30. Ibid.
31. Bartov, *The Eastern Front, 1941–1945*, 114–15.
32. Streit, "The German Army and the Policies of Genocide," 11. See also Czech, *Auschwitz*, 50.
33. Crowe, *The Holocaust*, 263–64.
34. Ibid., 232.
35. Hoess, *Death Dealer*, 134.
36. Ibid.
37. Ulrich, *Hitler's Foreign Workers*, 140. As late as April 1941 the *Wehrmacht* asserted that it had no interest in preserving the lives of Soviet POWs for forced labor.
38. Bohn, *Reichskommissariat Norwegen*, 377.
39. Megargee, *War of Annihilation*, 117.
40. North, "Soviet Prisoners of War," 39.
41. Megargee, *War of Annihilation*, 118.
42. North, "Soviet Prisoners of War," 40.
43. Ibid.
44. Ibid.
45. Wolff, *Inventing Eastern Europe*, 4–5.
46. Bartov, *The Eastern Front*, 153.
47. Ibid., 154.
48. Klaus, *Durch die Holle des Krieges*, 453.
49. Veselovskii, *Skrytaia biografiia*, 76.
50. Clark, *Barbarossa*, 206.
51. Bartov, *The Eastern Front*, 110–16.
52. Ibid., 135.
53. Fritzsche, *Life and Death*, 148–49.
54. Werth, *Russia at War*, 709.
55. Crowe, *The Holocaust*, 425.
56. These were called *Proverochno-fil'tratsionnyi punkty*, or Verification Filtration Points.
57. Merridale, *Ivan's War*, 351.
58. Glavatskii, *Rossiia, kotoruiu my ne znali*, 1939–1993: khrestomatiia. According to a memo from the head of the GULAG, by 1944 the number of prisoners had fallen from 2.3 million to 1.2 million.
59. Ibid., 353.
60. Ibid.
61. Solzhenitsyn, *The Gulag Archipelago*, 240.
62. If you cannot personally visit this resource at its Moscow location (57/6 *Zemlianoi*) you can access part of their database under "Vospominaniia o Gulage i ikh avtory" at <http://www.sakharov-center.ru>.
63. The testimonies of the great majority of Soviet soldiers taken captive by the Germans indicate that they usually asserted that they were wounded at the time of capture (and often unconscious as well); this evidently was what they had told their interrogators during the filtration process in a vain attempt to avoid the unwarranted stigma attached to their surrender.
64. Personal interview with the author, 22 December 2003.
65. All returning soldiers had to sign this form, in which they promised not to discuss anything they had seen in the West, such as the general level of prosperity, the neat and orderly farmsteads, etc. Even the prisoners who were released from the GULAG a decade or more after the end of the war were required to sign this document.

66. Bakanichev, *Zapiski katorzhanina*, 2–3.

67. Personal interview with the author, 22 December 2003.

68. Personal interview with the author, 22 December 2003.

69. Troitskii, *Tiazhelye sny*, 103. There is evidence to suggest that the relatives of those soldiers who had "betrayed the Motherland" were also liable to have some kind of punitive administrative action taken against them.

70. Ibid., 105.

71. Ibid., 110.

72. Ibid., 111.

73. Ibid., 113–14.

74. Ibid., 115.

75. This meant that there was an admixture of Russian and "Nordic" blood.

76. Ibid., 115–16.

77. Ibid., 120.

78. Ibid., 121.

79. Ibid., 122.

80. Ibid., 123–30.

81. Personal interview with the author, 15 November 2004.

82. Personal interview with the author, 21 November 2004.

83. Personal interview with the author, 3 December 2004.

84. Mueller, *Die deutsche Wirtschaftpolitik in den besetzen sowjetischen Gebieten 1941–1943*, 391.

85. Personal interview with the author, 3 December 2004.

86. Personal interview with the author, 3 December 2004.

87. Personal interview with the author, 4 December 2004.

88. Goebbels, *Die Tagebucher von Joseph Goebbels*, 497.

89. See Mulligan, "Reckoning the Cost of the People's War," 27–48; and especially *Vsenarodnoe partizanskoe dvizhenie v Belorussii v gody Velikoi Otechestvennoi Voiny 1941–1944*.

90. See Mueller, *Hitlers Ostkrieg und die deutsche Siedlungspolitik*.

REFERENCES

Bakanichev, A. E. *Zapiski katorzhanina*. Moscow: Vozvrashchenie, 2004.

Bartov, O. *The Eastern Front, 1941–1945: German Troops and the Barbarisation of Warfare*. London: Palgrave Macmillan, 1985.

Bohn, Robert. *Reichskommissariat Norwegen*. Munich: Oldenbourg, 2000.

Calvocoressi, Peter, and Guy Wint. *Total War*. New York: Penguin, 1979.

Churchill, Ward. *A Little Matter of Genocide*. San Francisco: City Lights Books, 1997.

Clark, Alan. *Barbarossa: The Russian–German Conflict, 1941–1945*. New York: Quill, 1965.

Crowe, David. *The Holocaust: Roots, History and Aftermath*. Boulder: Westview, 2008.

Czech, Danuta. *Auschwitz Chronicle, 1939–1945*. New York: Henry Holt, 1990.

Dallin, Alexander. *German Rule in Russia*. London: Palgrave Macmillan, 1981.

Ellman, M., and S. Maksudov. "Soviet Deaths in the Great Patriotic War: A Note." *Europe-Asia Studies* 46, no. 4 (1994): 647–74.

Evans, Richard. *The Third Reich in Power*. London: Penguin, 2005.

Forster, Jurgen. "The German Army and the Ideological War against the Soviet Union." In *The Policies of Genocide: Jews and Soviet Prisoners of War*, edited by Gerhard Hirschfeld. London: Allen & Unwin, 1986.

Fritzsche, Peter. *Life and Death in the Third Reich*. Cambridge, MA: Harvard University Press, 2008.

Glavatskii, M. E. *Rossiia, kotoruiu my ne znali 1939–1993: khrestomatiia*. Cheliabinsk: Iuzhno-uralskoe knizhnoe izdatel'stvo, 1995.

Goebbels, Joseph. *Die Tagebucher von Joseph Goebbels*, edited by Elke Frohlich. Munich: KG Saur, 1997.

Goldhagen, Daniel. *Hitler's Willing Executioners: Ordinary Germans and the Holocaust*. New York: Alfred A. Knopf, 1996.

Hamburg Institute for Social Research. *The German Army and Genocide: Crimes against War Prisoners, Jews, and other Civilians, 1939–1944*. New York: New Press, 1999.

Hitler, Adolph. *Mein Kampf*. Boston: Houghton Mifflin, 1971.

Hoess, Rudolph. *Death Dealer: The Memoirs of the SS Kommandant at Auschwitz*. New York: Da Capo Press, 1992.

Klaus, Edgar. *Durch die Holle des Krieges*. Berlin: Frieling, 1991.

Megargee, Geoffrey. *War of Annihilation: Combat and Genocide on the Eastern Front*. Lanham, MD: Rowman & Littlefield, 2006.

Merridale, Catherine. *Ivan's War: Life and Death in the Red Army, 1939–1945*. New York: Picador, 2006.

Mueller, Rolf-Dieter. *Die deutsche Wirtschaftspolitik in den besetzen sowjetischen Gebieten 1941–1943*. Boppard am Rhine: Harald Boldt, 1991.

———. *Hitlers Ostkrieg und die deutsche Siedlungspolitik. Die Zusammenarbeit von Wehrmacht, Wirtschaft und SS*. Frankfurt am Main: Fischer Taschenbuch, 1991.

Mulligan, Timothy P. "Reckoning the Cost of the People's War: The German Experience in the Central USSR." *Russian History*, 9 (1982): 27–47.

Noakes, Jeremy, and Geoffrey Pridham. *Nazism 1919–1945*. Vol. 3, *Foreign Policy, War and Racial Extermination. A Documentary Reader*. Exeter: University of Exeter Press, 2001.

North, Jonathan. "Soviet Prisoners of War: Forgotten Nazi Victims of World War II." *World War II*, January–February 2006, 37–41.

Solzhenitsyn, A. *The Gulag Archipelago*. New York: Harper & Row, 1973.

Stern, J. P. *Hitler: The Fuhrer and the People*. Berkeley: University of California Press, 1975.

Streit, Christian. "The German Army and the Policies of Genocide." In *The Policies of Genocide: Jews and Soviet Prisoners of War*, edited by Gerhard Hirschfeld. London: Allen & Unwin, 1986.

Troitskii, N. A. *Tiazhelye sny*. Krasnoiarsk: Kn. Izdatel'stvo, 1998.

Ueberschar, Gerd R. "The Military Campaign." In *Hitler's War in the East: A Critical* Assessment, edited by Rolf-Dieter Muller and Gerd R. Ueberschar. New York and Oxford: Berghahn, 2002.

Ulrich, Herbert. *Hitler's Foreign Workers: Enforced Foreign Labor in Germany under the Third Reich*. Translated by William Templer. Cambridge: Cambridge University Press, 1997.

Velikaia Otechestvennaia Voina, 1941–1945 gg: voenno-istoricheskie ocherki. Moscow: Voenizdat, 1998.

Veselovskii, B. V. *Skrytaia biografiia*. Moscow: Voenizdat, 1996.

Vsenarodnoe partizanskoe dvizhenie v Belorussii v gody Velikoi Otechestvennoi Voiny, 1941–1944. Dokumenty i materialy v trekh tomakh. Minsk: Belarus Gosizdat, 1982.

Werth, A. *Russia at War*. London: Barrie & Rockliff, 1964.

Wolff, Larry. *Inventing Eastern Europe: The Map of Civilization on the Mind of the Enlightenment*. Palo Alto: Stanford University Press, 1994.

"Only the National Socialist": Postwar US and West German Approaches to Nazi "Euthanasia" Crimes, 1946–1953

Michael Bryant

> More than 100,000 euthanized. Men over the age of 70 are to receive no medical treatment. Who is still worthy of life? Only the National Socialist.
>
> Bishop Ludvig Sebastian, 19 August 1942

In Western historical consciousness, National Socialist mass murder has become permanently identified with the Jewish Holocaust, Adolf Hitler's maniacal project to annihilate European Jewry. From its earliest days, the Nazi Party sought to exclude Jews from German public life, and when the Nazis came to power in January 1933, their anti-Jewish animus became official policy. What followed was legal disemancipation of German Jews, physical attacks on their persons, ghettoization, deportation, and physical extermination in the East. The story of the Holocaust is well known and generally accepted. Yet two years before German Jewish policy swerved from persecution and harassment to genocide, the Nazis were already involved in state-organized killing of another disfavored minority. Unlike the destruction of European Jews, the murder of this group—the mentally disabled—occurred within the Reich's own borders. Launched with the signing of a "Hitler decree" in October 1939 (backdated to 1 September), the centrally organized program targeted so-called "incurable" patients, whose lives were to be ended by a doctor-administered "mercy death" (*Gnadentod*). The Nazis attached the term "euthanasia" to their program of destruction, bolstering their rationale for it with humanitarian arguments and cost-based justifications, the latter legitimizing euthanasia as a means to free up scarce resources for use by "valuable" Germans. Over time, the restrictive use of euthanasia just for incurable patients ended; thereafter, the Nazis extended the killing program to healthier patients, sick concentration camp inmates, Jewish patients, and a variety of "asocials" (juvenile delinquents, beggars, tramps, prostitutes). The technology of murder developed in the "euthanasia" program—carbon monoxide asphyxiation in gas chambers camouflaged as shower rooms—would become the model for the first death camps in Poland. Many of the "euthanasia" personnel were likewise transferred to the Polish extermination centers, where they applied the techniques of mass death—refined in murdering the disabled—to the murder of the European Jews.[1]

After the war, both the Americans and the Germans prosecuted medical staff accused of participating in the Nazis' murderous campaign against the disabled. Comparison of these two national groups elicits important differences in their judicial approach to Nazi "euthanasia." The present essay argues that these differences, while grounded in disparate sources of law and criminological conceptions of Nazi violence, nonetheless share a common emphasis: the preservation (in the case of the US) or recovery (in the case of West Germany) of political power. For the Americans, the legal theory of conspiracy became the cornerstone of their understanding of Nazi atrocities against Jews and the disabled. Not only did conspiracy enable the Americans to convict "euthanasia" personnel as perpetrators but it also empowered them to do so without diminishing the principle of national sovereignty. The Americans achieved this dual feat by making the charge of "crimes against humanity" (acts typically inflicted on civilian victims) legally dependent on Nazi warmaking. For the US, this equation of crimes against humanity with war crimes was critical, because the "euthanasia" program, in contrast with the Final Solution, largely targeted German nationals. Were the Americans to prosecute such crimes as free-standing offenses unrelated to the war, they would be setting dangerous precedents that might later be invoked to infringe on American national sovereignty. The West Germans, on the other hand, tended to charge their "euthanasia" defendants under the German law of homicide, rather than conspiracy. Over time, this tended to minimize the culpability of the killers and enable their reintegration into the new Federal Republic. In both the American and German cases, as we will see, legal approaches to Nazi "euthanasia" open a revealing perspective on power as the dynamic force underlying and impelling the trials.

The Americans' most significant encounter with Nazi "euthanasia" occurred in the "successor" trials to the International Military Tribunal (IMT) at Nuremberg. The first of these successor trials, *U.S. v. Karl Brandt et al.* (often referred to as "The Doctors' Trial"),[2] charged 4 of its 23 medical defendants with complicity in the murders of the disabled. For purposes of convenience, this essay will focus on two of the four defendants implicated in "euthanasia," namely Karl Brandt and Viktor Brack. The roots of the Doctors' Trial, however, can be traced back to the first American judicial confrontation with the leading architects of Nazi criminality—the IMT trial held at Nuremberg between 18 October 1945 and 1 October 1946. The American National Military Tribunal that presided over the Doctors' Trial used the legal norms of the IMT trial and added new, revolutionary legal precedents.

The International Military Tribunal as Precursor and Model for the American Medical Case

The first and best-known trial of top Nazis, the International Military Tribunal at Nuremberg, established the essential legal guidelines for the four charges in the Doctors' Trial. The most important legal precedent, at least for the Doctors' Trial, was the doctrine of conspiracy, described by Telford Taylor, the US Deputy Chief of Counsel at the IMT and thereafter the US Chief of Counsel for War Crimes, as "the unifying element of the entire [IMT] case."[3] According to the traditional doctrine of conspiracy, all members of a criminal enterprise were responsible for the crimes perpetrated in connection with it, provided such crimes were related to the conspiracy and promoted its goals. The 24 defendants in the IMT trial were charged with conspiracy in developing a "master plan" to wage aggressive war against other countries. Robert Jackson, the US Chief of Counsel for the prosecution at the IMT trial, discussed the philosophy behind the American case in a report to Harry Truman in June 1945: "Our case against the major defendants is concerned with the Nazi master plan, not with individual barbarities and perversions which occurred independently of a central plan." For the Americans at Nuremberg, all of the crimes charged against the Nazi defendants flowed from a single charge—"a grand, concerted pattern to incite and commit aggressions . . . which have shocked the world."[4] The corollary to this theory was that no act of inhumanity, no matter how extreme, could be prosecuted unless proven to be linked with the Nazis' overarching "master plan" to invade and subjugate other countries. Accordingly, when the Allies drafted the IMT Charter in the summer of 1945, conspiracy was the cornerstone of their legal edifice. It stated that "leaders, organizers, instigators, and accomplices participating in the formulation or execution of a Common Plan or Conspiracy to commit any of the foregoing crimes are responsible for all acts performed by any persons in execution of such plan."[5]

What were the "foregoing crimes?" They were crimes against peace, war crimes, and crimes against humanity. Article 6(a) of the Charter described crimes against peace as "planning, preparation, initiation, or waging of a war of aggression, or a war in violation of international treaties." Article 6(b) identified war crimes as "violations of the laws or customs of war," including, inter alia, murder, abuse, or deportation to slave labor of civilians in occupied territory and murder or abuse of POWs. Finally, Article 6(c) defined crimes against humanity as mistreatment, through acts of murder, deportation, etc., of civilians "before or during the war," as well as political, racial or religious persecution, provided they stood "in connection with any crime within the jurisdiction of the Tribunal." This latter clause is crucial, because it effectively bound crimes against humanity to war crimes—meaning that the Allies could only charge the major war criminals with crimes against humanity linked to the Nazis' aggressive warmaking.[6]

From the Allies' perspective at the IMT, then, the major war criminals were the leading figures in a conspiracy to plan, initiate, and wage unprovoked wars by means of crimes against peace, war crimes, and crimes against humanity. Hence, the defendants faced not only charges of war crimes and crimes against humanity but also conspiracy to commit these crimes. While the IMT judges would ultimately reject the Charter's charge of conspiracy to commit war crimes and crimes against humanity, it affirmed the prosecution's conspiracy count when it came to the charge of planning aggressive war. Moreover, the judges refused to exercise jurisdiction over crimes against humanity that took place before the outbreak of the war (such as the persecution of the Jews). The IMT's final judgment stated that

> to constitute Crimes against Humanity, the acts relied on before the outbreak of war must have been in execution of, or in connection with, any crime within the jurisdiction of the Tribunal. The Tribunal is of the opinion that . . . it has not been satisfactorily proved that [these crimes] were done in execution of, or in connection with, any such crime.

The so-called "war nexus" of Article 6(c) doomed the IMT's efforts to prosecute Nazi persecution of the Jews before September 1939 as crimes against humanity. The judges did, however, convict many of the defendants of crimes against humanity that took place after the war had started, because such atrocities "were all committed in execution of . . . the aggressive war."[7]

The US Doctors' Trial

Whereas the London Charter provided jurisdiction for the IMT, the 12 "successor" American trials at Nuremberg were based on a separate document, Allied Control Council Law No. 10 (ACCL No. 10), which the Allied Control Council published in December 1945. It gave each of the four occupying powers (the US, Great Britain, the USSR, and France) authority to conduct its own national trials of Nazi war criminals within their zones of occupation, in a more or less uniform manner. The substantive portions of the IMT Charter and ACCL No. 10 were very similar. Like the Charter, ACCL No. 10 cited as substantive offenses crimes against peace, war crimes, and crimes against humanity, as well as conspiracy to commit each of these crimes. ACCL No. 10 added another charge—membership in an organization declared criminal by the IMT. ACCL No. 10 also expanded the definition of "crimes against peace" to include both "invasions" and "wars."[8] Its definition of crimes against humanity omitted the "war nexus" clause of the IMT Charter's Article 6(c), in an effort to establish crimes against humanity as a self-contained, independently chargeable offense separate from crimes against peace or war crimes. This change had a dramatic impact on the US Doctors' Trial, since it allowed the American prosecutors to charge 4 of the 23 defendants with participation in the Nazis' "euthanasia" program. Most of the victims were German, and because the IMT Charter required that victims be non-German nationals, the defendants would have slipped through the net of its definition of crimes against humanity.[9]

The history of the American decision to make the crimes of German medical professionals their first ACCL No. 10 trial is too complex to discuss in detail in this essay.[10] When the war ended in Europe, the Allies had no policy for dealing with the crimes of German scientists. Instead, they were more interested in gleaning intelligence about Nazi Germany's weapons programs. This changed in August 1945, when the Allies adopted a policy to begin investigating medical crimes. But the principal thrust—Allied interest in German science—centered on seizure of scientific "assets," and not medical atrocities. Allied investigative bodies were initially tasked with identifying the location of secret weapons and other information deemed vital to national security. While gathering intelligence on German wartime science, the Allied investigators stumbled across medical crimes. Significantly, some of the leading figures accused in the Doctors' Trial, such as Karl Brandt, were first interned on suspicion of involvement in germ warfare research. The testimonies of former concentration camp prisoners in May 1945 helped shift Allied policy away from strategic evaluation of German science to the investigation of its criminality.

In November 1945, a British unit under John Thompson formed to provide the Allies with the results of investigations into German scientific crimes. After a meeting with Thompson's unit in May 1946, US officials assigned top priority to investigating medical crimes, and in August the British Foreign Office turned over its evidence on medical defendants to US negotiators. Ultimately, the US would indict 23 defendants in the "Doctors' Trial," including Karl Brandt, Hitler's escort physician and from 1943 the chief of the Reich's Health Services; chief military medical officers of the Luftwaffe medical services Siegfried Handloser and Oskar Schröder; and SS medical officers Karl Genzken and Joachim Mrugowsky, among others. The defendants were charged with a variety of atrocities, including forced sterilization, human experimentation on concentration camp prisoners, and euthanasia. Karl Brandt, regarded as the linchpin of Nazi medical crimes because of his illustrious rank and closeness to Hitler, lent his name to the Doctors' Trial (*U.S.* v. *Karl Brandt et al.*).[11]

The indictment against the defendants charged them with: (1) conspiring to commit war crimes and crimes against humanity ("common design or conspiracy"); (2) war crimes; (3) crimes against humanity; and (4) membership in a criminal organization. The gravamen of the indictment was the war crimes charge, which accused the defendants of barbarous medical experiments on concentration camp inmates and prisoners of war (POWs). The grisly experiments dominated the transcripts of the medical case, and proved to be its most important and enduring topic. Paragraph 9 of Count 2 and paragraph 14 of Count 3 charged four of the defendants with complicity in the Nazi "euthanasia" program: Karl Brandt, Kurt Blome, Viktor Brack, and Waldemar Hoven.[12] Alone among the 23 defendants on trial, these four were charged with the crime of "euthanasia."

Although the "war nexus" of the IMT Charter was eliminated in the text of Control Council Law No. 10, there is little doubt that the American prosecutors viewed Nazi "euthanasia" as an outgrowth of the Germans' imperialistic warmaking. This conception is explicit in the language of Count 2, which describes euthanasia as a program to exterminate "hundreds of thousands of human beings, including nationals of German-occupied countries" as well as "the aged, insane, incurably ill, ... deformed children, and other persons, by gas, lethal injections, and diverse other means in nursing homes, hospitals, and asylums" because "such persons were regarded as 'useless eaters' and a burden to the German war machine." Consequently, they viewed "euthanasia" as a byproduct of German militarism. The Germans murdered the mentally ill to send the resources that would have been spent to keep them alive to the German army, which was involved in criminal attacks on other countries.[13] This theory of Nazi euthanasia also resonated in Telford Taylor's opening statement to the Tribunal, which the Tribunal ultimately endorsed in its verdict.

"Euthanasia" at the American Doctors' Trial

Karl Brandt and his Defense at Trial

Karl Brandt occupied a central role in the creation of the Nazi "euthanasia" program. In 1939, Hitler ordered Brandt, along with Philipp Bouhler of the Führer's Chancellery, to establish a program that authorized physicians to "euthanize" patients deemed "incurable." This order, which Hitler signed in October 1939 but backdated to 1 September 1939 (so as to coincide with the outbreak of the war), reads as follows:

> Berlin, 1 September 1939
> Reich Leader Bouhler and Dr. med. Brandt are charged with responsibility of enlarging the competence of certain physicians, designated by name, so that patients who, on the basis of human judgement, are considered incurable can be granted mercy death after a critical evaluation of their state of health
>
> (signed) A. Hitler[14]

In January 1940, Brandt took part in a carbon monoxide gassing experiment held at a former jailhouse in the city of Brandenburg with Bouhler's deputy, Viktor Brack. Eighteen to twenty people were murdered in a gas chamber disguised as a shower room. During this same period, Brandt gave lethal injections to six mentally ill patients to determine the lethality of carbon monoxide. Brack and Brandt concluded that carbon monoxide asphyxiation was the best way to "euthanize" patients, and thus became the preferred method of exterminating the disabled in Germany until August 1941.[15] After the German invasion of the Soviet Union, Hitler ordered Brandt to coordinate the military and civilian health care systems, which led to his promotion in July 1942 to Commissioner for the Health Care System. As Commissioner, Brandt became further ensnared in the Nazi mass extermination projects, since it was now his responsibility to coordinate hospital space for wounded soldiers and bombed out civilians. Brandt solved this problem by evacuating mental patients from German psychiatric hospitals to sites where many of them were murdered. Promoted to Reich Commissioner for the Health System in August 1944, Brandt became a member of the Reich Research Council, where, with Paul Rostock, he co-directed Nazi medical research during the final year of the war. This involved him in concentration camp medical experiments involving hepatitis and biological weapons research.[16] Brandt was later charged with war crimes and crimes against humanity when the Doctors'

Trial opened before Military Tribunal I of the National Military Tribunal (NMT) at Nuremberg in late November 1946.[17]

Paul Weindling, a prominent historian of German medicine, has noted that "the strategy of the Medical Trial prosecution was to reconstruct vertical chains of command."[18] According to the prosecutors, the Nazi "euthanasia" program was a centrally planned initiative of a vicious totalitarian state, designed to rid Germany of "useless eaters" in order to transfer valuable resources to the German military and strengthen its conquests. Weindling notes that the American prosecutors interpreted the date of Hitler's secret decree authorizing Brandt and Bouhler to organize the "euthanasia" program—1 September 1939—as confirmation of their view that "euthanasia" was driven by Nazi militarism, and thus chargeable as a war crime.[19] In his opening statement at the NMT, US prosecutor Telford Taylor explicitly identified the Nazis' desire to eliminate those who had become "useless to the German war machine" as a driving motive of the euthanasia program.[20]

During his pre-trial interrogations by the Americans and his testimony before the NMT, Brandt consistently claimed that the euthanasia program was motivated by the highest ideals. Brandt said the program was benignly seeking to "deliver" terminally ill patients from their suffering, at least in its opening stages; by the time it was linked more and more to the "Final Solution" in the fall of 1941, Brandt asserted he had nothing more to do with it, and should not be held responsible for its genocidal crimes. When charged with war crimes because of his involvement in concentration camp experiments, Brandt, like many of his co-defendants, advanced a defense based on a utilitarian rationale: in times of national emergency all citizens, including prisoners, had to renounce their individual interests and contribute to the defense of the country. He thought that experimental medicine was justified if it promoted the welfare of the German people. In the state emergency of total war there was no time to wait for the results of animal experiments; rather, the state had the right and duty to wrest life-giving knowledge from coerced subjects, even if these experiments harmed them. Brandt suggested a similar justification for "euthanizing" the chronically disabled to provide needed hospital space and medical resources for society's productive elements.[21]

Viktor Brack and his Defense at Trial

In October 1939, Hitler ordered Brandt to work alongside Philipp Bouhler in organizing Nazi "euthanasia." Several years earlier, Bouhler had created the Führer's personal chancellery (Kanzlei des Führers, or KdF), serving Hitler as its chief until the end of the war. By 1939, Hitler had selected the KdF as the executory organ of the "euthanasia" program. Bouhler's deputy and head of Section II of the KdF was Viktor Brack. Many of the daily administrative and organizational responsibilities of the "euthanasia" program fell on Brack's shoulders. For this reason, he became a major figure not only in the operational history of the program but also in the Final Solution in late 1941.[22]

In the months preceding the Doctors' Trial, the American prosecutors were interested in the connections between the "euthanasia" program and the larger Nazi assault on other groups. Brack's pre-trial interrogators confronted him with their theory that "euthanasia" was extended in late 1943 to the extermination program targeting the European Jews, rather than ending, as Brack had claimed, in 1941. For Brack's interrogators, Nazi "euthanasia" was a "general test" for the expanded killing program in the last four years of the war. Brack denied linkage between the two events, expressing his view that Hitler did not have the murder of European Jews in mind when he set "euthanasia" in motion. The Americans pursued the "general test" theory of "euthanasia" in their case-in-chief at the Doctors' Trial.[23]

Brack took the stand to address the two most damning charges against him: his involvement in the plan to murder European Jews and his proposal to sterilize a remnant of the surviving Jewish population with X-rays. Because the evidence against Brack was overwhelmingly incriminating, he resorted to a necessity-based defense, arguing that, when he first learned of the Final Solution, he tried to make "the effort if possible to help," to "do anything I could to prevent [the destruction off the Jews]." Brack continued:

> If I had raised the least objection to [the Final Solution] openly I would have aroused great suspicion of myself and would have aroused an all together [*sic*] and false reaction in Himmler. Therefore, I had to make the best of a bad matter and had to pretend that I agreed with Himmler. Therefore, I pretended to be willing to clarify the question of mass sterilization through X-ray methods.[24]

Brack was referring to a matter broached in a letter he sent to Himmler, dated 23 June 1942, regarding "using European Jews as laborers." The letter reads in part:

> Among 10 million Jews in Europe are . . . at least 2 to 3 million men and women who are fit enough for work. Considering the extraordinary difficulties the labor problem presents us with, I hold the view that these 2 or 3 million should be specially selected and preserved. This can be done, if at the same time they are rendered incapable of propagating. About a year ago I reported to you that agents of mine have completed the experiments necessary for this purpose.[25]

Brack's argument at trial was that his reference in the letter to sterilizing the Jewish remnant was a diversion meant to preserve the Jews until the war ended. By getting Himmler to delay exterminating the Jews so as to allow X-ray experiments on Jewish experimental subjects and to evaluate the results, Brack claimed he had saved hundreds of thousands of Jewish lives.[26]

The Judgment of the Military Tribunal I of the NMT

In its judgment of 20 August 1947, the National Military Tribunal left little doubt that it shared the prosecution's hierarchical model of Nazi medical criminality, linking the defendants with the SS, the High Command, the Luftwaffe, and the Nazi Party. "These experiments were not the isolated and casual acts of individual doctors and scientists working solely on their own responsibility, but were the product of coordinated policy-making and planning at high governmental, military, and Nazi Party levels," the Tribunal declared. The concentration camp experiments, it continued, "were conducted as an integral part of the total war effort." Similarly, the Tribunal confirmed the prosecution's theory that "euthanasia" was intended to blot out the lives of economically unproductive people in order to transfer resources to the German military.[27] Although the judges rejected the prosecution's efforts to claim that there was a conspiracy to commit euthanasia, they did acknowledge the existence of multiple, organized "euthanasia" programs. Despite the tenuous evidence of Brandt's role in the variegated spectrum of the "euthanasia" program—he had little or nothing to do with the second phase of it after it was formally stopped in August 1941, nor was he involved in the transfer of euthanasia personnel to the extermination camps of *Aktion Reinhard* in the fall of 1941—the Tribunal nonetheless convicted him of this crime, apparently on the grounds that he failed as a high-ranking medical leader to perform his obligation to supervise the program:

> Karl Brandt admits that . . . he did not follow the program further but left the administrative details of execution to [Philipp] Bouhler. A discharge of that duty would have easily revealed what now is so manifestly evident from the record; that whatever may have been the original aim of the program, its purposes were prostituted by men for whom Brandt was responsible, and great numbers of non-Germans were exterminated under its authority.[28]

It did not matter to the Tribunal that Brandt was motivated by high ideals; what was decisive was his "dereliction" in preventing the murderous nature of the "euthanasia" program. Two factors were key in Brandt's conviction: his negligent failure of supervision and the fact that non-German nationals, especially Jews and the inmates of concentration camps, were victims of the "euthanasia" program. The Tribunal's emphasis on the nationality of the victims is based on the idea that Nazi euthanasia was an excrescence of aggressive war, waged without mercy on non-Germans whom the Nazis regarded as subhuman.

The Tribunal adopted a similar stance toward Viktor Brack. The American judges were less troubled by the "euthanasia" of chronically ill Germans than the expansion of the killing program to non-German nationals in concentration camps. For the Tribunal, the connection between the "euthanasia" program and aggressive warmaking was a crucial factor in convicting Brack:

> One of the prime motives behind the program was to eliminate "useless eaters" from the scene, in order to conserve food, hospital facilities, doctors and nurses for the more important use of the German Armed Forces. Many nationals of countries other than Germany were killed.[29]

Weighing heavily against Brack was his assignment of "euthanasia" personnel to the SS Police Leader for the Lublin district in Poland, Odilo Globocnik, to whom Himmler had entrusted the liquidation of Polish Jewry. The staff members that Brack assigned to Globocnik helped organize and administer the Final Solution in Poland. It was proven that Brack also provided other forms of logistical support for the genocide of the Jews in the East. At the Doctors' Trial, the American prosecutors offered into evidence a notorious document, the so-called "gassing letter" dated 25 October 1941, from the Reich Ministry for the Occupied Territories to the Reich Commissar for the Ostland. The letter mentions that Brack had volunteered to supply both "accommodations as well as the gassing equipment" for use in killing Jews incapable of work. The hardier Jews would be used as slave labor, while those unfit for work would be disposed of with the "Brackian devices." These "devices" were gas vans, deployed since late 1939 to murder mentally ill patients in the annexed portions of Poland (the Wartheland).[30]

Unpersuaded by Brandt and Brack's defenses, Military Tribunal I sentenced them to death on 19 August 1947. After Lucius Clay (head of the Military Government of the US Zone in Germany) and the US Supreme Court refused their appeals, Brandt and Brack were hanged at Landsberg prison on 2 June 1948.

West German Euthanasia Trials: Treading between National and International Law

The Origins of West German Euthanasia Trials

Before the German surrender in the spring of 1945, the Allies had drawn up their plans to purge German society of National Socialist elements and prevent Germany from waging future wars. At the Yalta Conference in February 1945, they decided to partition the country and its capital into four separate zones of occupation. In April, the US Joint Chiefs of Staff (JCS) issued JCS Directive 1067, which reasserted the US's intention to demilitarize, de-Nazify, de-centralize, and democratize the country. JCS 1067 also announced the closure of all German courts and the disbanding of all Nazi "extraordinary" and party courts. Once the war was over, the Allies suspended the operation of all German courts until the judiciary could be purged of National Socialist influences. They would be reopened once they had been scoured of former Nazi officials and "brown" ideology. At Potsdam in July 1945, the Allies declared the German court system would be "reorganized in accordance with the principles of democracy, of justice under law, and of equal rights for all citizens without distinction of race, nationality, or religion."[31]

On 30 August 1945, Allied Control Council Law No. 1 repealed discriminatory legal measures adopted during the Third Reich.[32] Two months later, it promulgated Allied Control Council Law No. 4 on the "Reorganization of the Judicial System," which was designed to create a uniform, reconstituted German court system in each of the three Western zones of occupation. Law No. 4 restored the system of pre-1933 ordinary courts, which consisted of district, state, and appellate courts.[33] Law No. 4 reasserted the traditional pre-1933 criminal jurisdiction of each of these courts: the district courts could impose prison terms up to five years; the state courts had jurisdiction over all cases beyond the competency of the district courts, and presided over appeals from the district courts on both factual and legal grounds; and the appellate courts reviewed appeals from the state courts but on legal grounds alone. Law No. 4, however, denied to the newly reestablished German courts jurisdiction over offenses committed by Germans against the Allied occupation forces or citizens of Allied nations and their property.[34]

The Allied Control Council later modified its denial of German jurisdiction over Nazi crimes with Law No. 10 in December 1945. One of the principal goals of Law No. 10 was to forge a uniform legal basis for national (or "zonal") trials, which each of the four powers would conduct in its own zone of occupation. According to Henry Friedlander, the Allies intended to use Law No. 10 to prosecute Germans in Allied proceedings.[35] For this reason, two of the three crimes cited in Law No. 10—"crimes against peace" and "war crimes"—were clearly outside the jurisdiction of German courts, since these crimes involved acts of violence inflicted by Germans on non-German nationals.[36] ACCL No. 10 left the door open when it came to German jurisdiction over "crimes against humanity," modeling this part of the law on the definition set forth in Article 6(c) of the IMT's Charter. ACCL No. 10 permitted each of the occupying powers to arrest individuals suspected of such crimes and to try them in "an appropriate tribunal." It also indicated that the occupying authority could entrust jurisdiction over crimes against humanity to a German court when the perpetrators and the victims were German nationals or "stateless persons."[37]

ACCL No. 10 denied German court jurisdiction over the crimes of the Final Solution until it became legally unavailable in August 1951. Thereafter, German courts could only apply German criminal law in the trials of accused Nazi perpetrators. ACCL No. 10 allowed the French, British, Americans, and Soviets to permit German courts in their zones to try German defendants for crimes against humanity provided the victims were Germans or stateless persons. In fact, those German courts given such authority had little choice but to prosecute these offenses as crimes against humanity. In some instances, where ACCL No. 10's definition of crimes against humanity did not fully match the alleged offense, the German court could charge a defendant with both a crime against humanity and an additional offense under German law. Consequently, in the British and French Zones, where German courts were required to charge suspected Nazi war criminals with crimes against humanity under ACCL No. 10, criminal indictments issued between 1946 and 1951 reflected a strange mixture of Control Council, international humanitarian, and German domestic law.[38]

Article II of Law No. 10 recognized two types of crimes against humanity: murder (homicide, extermination, enslavement, deportation, etc.) and "persecution" based on "racial, political, or religious grounds." German courts only had jurisdiction over cases where such crimes were committed against German or stateless victims. Furthermore, offenses committed by individual perpetrators acting alone were not crimes against humanity, since the latter required "systematic mass action." The UN War Crimes Commission wrote in its comparison of definitions of crimes against humanity under ACCL No. 10 and the Tokyo Charter (the legal basis for the Tokyo war crimes trials) that the "systematic mass action, particularly if it was authoritative, was necessary to transform a common crime, punishable only under municipal law, into a crime against humanity, which thus became also the concern of international law."[39] Consequently, German courts in the immediate postwar era (1945–1951) prosecuted crimes against humanity either as a form of murder or persecution: the *Kristallnacht* (Night of Broken Glass) pogroms of November 1938, denunciations by "grudge informers," killings of alleged "defeatists" at the end of the war, and political killings from the early years of the Nazi regime. What distinguished these offenses as crimes against humanity was the systematic mass action requirement: when this element was lacking, German courts typically charged their defendants solely with offenses under the German Penal Code. Regarding Nazi mass exterminations, ACCL No. 10 prevented German courts from dealing with the most sensational crimes except one—those of the Nazi euthanasia program. "Euthanasia" readily lent itself to German prosecution under ACCL No. 10 because the victims were mainly German nationals and the murders were carried out on the orders of the Nazi government, which satisfied the systematic mass action requirement.[40]

The case of Dr. Otto Mauthe, the former chief medical officer for the mental health system in the Ministry of the Interior for the State of Württemberg, illustrates the success of such prosecution in West German courts. Mauthe was an example of the modern bureaucratic killer (*Schreibtischtäter*): although there was no evidence to link him to a direct act of violence, he sent thousands of patients to their deaths with the stroke of his pen, making him the classic "desk murderer." His contribution to the Nazi euthanasia program consisted in preparing and signing administrative decrees issued by the Württemberg Ministry of the Interior that sent scores of mentally disabled patients to the "euthanasia" killing centers at Grafeneck and Hadamar. It was later proven at his 1949 trial in Tübingen that Mauthe visited mental hospitals in Württemberg to correct improperly completed registration forms on patients designated for euthanasia. The patients listed on these forms were murdered at one of these centers. In other cases, Mauthe overruled exemptions for patients made by other doctors and ordered their transport to Grafeneck. Finally, the trial record showed that Mauthe had lied to the victims' families about the fates of their relatives.[41]

Unlike earlier German euthanasia trials, which typically charged their defendants with homicide under §211 of the German Penal Code (*Strafgesetzbuch*), the state court of Tübingen chose to apply crimes against humanity under Law No. 10, Article II, 1c, to Mauthe's actions. The court held that, under §211, any crime of homicide involving more than one perpetrator covered "a multiple participation in a single murder," rather than widespread collaboration in the murders of hundreds and thousands of victims. The court argued a point that is rarely encountered in the postwar German trials of Nazi crimes: because German law contained no crime of mass murder, it was legally impossible to charge defendants like Mauthe with such acts under the German Penal Code. The substantive part of German law that defined the elements of criminal offenses was not equipped to cope with Nazi euthanasia. Hence, the court decided to use the charge of crimes against humanity as the best way to assess Mauthe's criminal liability for his role in the murders of 4,000 people. He was convicted of such crimes and sentenced to a five-year prison term.[42]

The German Law of Homicide and Judicial Approaches to "Euthanasia" Crimes

For the most part, German courts in the Western zones charged euthanasia defendants with homicide under §211 of the German Penal Code (*Strafgesetzbuch* of 1871). Prior to 1941, murder under German law was straightforward: anyone who illegally killed another person with premeditation was guilty of murder.[43] The Reich Ministry of Justice revised §211 in 1941, and redefined murder as a killing actuated by certain motives: "joy in killing" (*Mordlust*), sexuality, "covetousness or other base motives," malice, or cruelty. A murderer was also someone who killed using a means dangerous to society, or to facilitate or hide the commission of another crime.[44] Once it had been determined that a murder had been committed under the new version of §211, German law had to determine whether the defendant was guilty of murder as a perpetrator or an accomplice. In the decades preceding World War II, German courts looked at the crime to determine whether the offender controlled the circumstances surrounding the murder (the doctrine of *Tatherrschaft*, literally, "controlling the crime") and whether the killer was subjectively associated with the crime by assisting the main perpetrator commit it (the doctrine of subjectivity, which is often expressed in German law with the formula *als eigene gewollt*, "desiring the crime as one's own"). The first doctrine emphasizes the objective features of how the offender committed the act, while the second probes the mental state of the offender for evidence of subjective approval of the murder. In the years after the war, German courts sometimes applied one aspect, sometimes the other, depending on the case before the court. However, if the court applied the subjective theory in a euthanasia case, the defendant often benefited. In the somber annals of Nazi euthanasia trials, the case of Mathilde Weber demonstrates the advantageous nature of the use of the subjective theory for euthanasia defendants.[45]

Mathilde Weber was the managing physician of the Kalmenhof mental hospital when the facility was converted into a transit center to receive patients from other facilities prior to their transport to Hadamar. Kalmenhof also became a small killing center in its own right, where individual patients were murdered with lethal doses of narcotics. In 1942, a children's ward to murder mentally disabled youngsters was opened in Kalmenhof. Weber was its managing doctor until May 1944. During her tenure, a floor nurse killed children by luminal poisoning. These crimes became the basis of the principal charges against Weber at her trial before the Frankfurt state court in early 1947.[46]

Weber denied knowledge of the children's murders, and blamed them solely on the floor nurse. Since she did not live in the hospital and claimed she only worked there in the morning, she claimed she had no knowledge of the floor nurse's lethal work. She also denied that she was a "Reich Committee doctor," i.e., an employee of the Nazi government agency that had administrative control over the euthanasia program. By implication, she was claiming that she was no loyal soldier in the Nazi campaign against the mentally disabled. Weber also adopted a "collision of duties defense,"[47] arguing that she had decided to continue her work at Kalmenhof in order to sabotage the euthanasia program wherever she could.[48]

The state court of Tübingen acquitted her of the charges relating to the transfer of adult patients to Hadamar for lack of evidence, but convicted her of murdering the disabled children. The court's latter decision was based largely on patient mortality data from the children's ward. After it was opened, patient mortality shot upwards dramatically in the children's ward, but went down just as quickly when Weber and the floor nurse were on leaves of absence from the hospital. During her tenure at Kalmenhof, Weber was temporarily replaced by another managing doctor because of health issues. While she was away, not a single child died in the ward. When she and the floor nurse returned, the mortality rate soared. For the court, such evidence showed an arresting linkage between the children's deaths and the presence of Weber and the floor nurse and negated her claim of non-involvement in the children's ward killings. The court went on to characterize Weber as a perpetrator of the murders carried out in the children's ward, holding that she was inwardly linked to the killing program. To support this finding, the judges pointed to an occasion when Weber accused two of her nurses of violating their oath of silence (all euthanasia functionaries were bound by penalty of death to observe strict confidentiality about the program), and threatened to denounce them to the authorities. For the court, this was a gratuitous act committed with no external compulsion, and showed "how very much she had made the 'operation' her own." Based on this, the court sentenced her to death on 30 January 1947.[49]

Yet the case of Mathilde Weber was far from over. After a Frankfurt appellate court overturned her conviction, the case was sent back to the Tübingen state court for retrial in 1949. This time, she received much more sympathetic treatment. The court reversed itself and interpreted the subjective theory of perpetration to her advantage. The judges explicitly reversed themselves on some of the factual issues they had used to convict her in the first trial; they now agreed that her lack of affiliation with the government office in charge of euthanasia meant she did not share its ideological tenets. The court also now agreed that she had tried to distance herself from the "euthanasia" program. It concluded that Weber had not inwardly willed euthanasia "as her own," and thus was guilty only of complicity in murder—being an accomplice, rather than a perpetrator. In deciding on her punishment, the court also accepted that there were extenuating circumstances—her youth at the time of her service at Kalmenhof, which hampered her ability to respond to the extraordinary demands of her situation there, and her educational background ("she had only the common school and career education behind her"), which made her ill-prepared for the agonizing ethical choices she faced in the children's ward. This line of reasoning led the court to sentence Weber to a jail term of $3\frac{1}{2}$ years.[50]

Trifling as her sentence may have been in comparison with her crimes, Weber never served more than a month of her sentence. As a result of ill health, she was released from custody after her second trial, while her sentence was temporarily suspended until October 1954, when she was deemed sufficiently recovered to be sent to prison. She was released the following month for time served prior to her second trial. In the next phase of her career, she worked as a doctor's receptionist for her brother-in-law, Dr. Julius Muthig, a former SS doctor in the Neuengamme, Dachau, and Oranienburg concentration camps. In 1960, remarried with a new name, she resumed her career practicing medicine in the Federal Republic of Germany.[51]

Leading West German Euthanasia Cases in the Postwar Period (1945–1953)

One of the earliest West German euthanasia trials was held in March 1946, when the state court in Berlin indicted Dr. Hilde Wernicke and nurse Helene Wieczorek for the murder of patients at the Obrawalde mental hospital (Pomerania). The two women were sworn to secrecy after they were informed by the hospital's director in 1943 of the plan to euthananize incurably ill mental patients. They then became part of Obrawalde's killing program. Thereafter, transports of patients arrived at Obrawalde along with lists of those designated for killing. Wernicke's job was to examine recently arrived patients and confirm those already diagnosed with incurable mental illnesses. Over the next year, she evaluated four to six patient histories per day, giving special attention to those who suffered from incurable mental illnesses and physical impairments. She spared patients capable of work. From the spring of 1943 to 1944, Wernicke sent the names of 600 patients to three nurses, including Helene Wieczorek, for "euthanasia." The three nurses "euthanized" them with lethal dosages of morphine and scopolamine. The killings stopped in the fall of 1944, and on 29 January 1945 the staff fled the institution in the face of the advance of the Red Army.[52]

The various judicial panels who heard the case before the state court of Berlin found the defendants guilty of murder as perpetrators. Moreover, they also concluded that they had acted "maliciously," since they had exploited the guilelessness and defenselessness of their victims after winning over their trust—an act that "runs counter to every human feeling on the grossest level." The defendants' subordinate status in the euthanasia program did not help them, as it would defendants in later years. On the issue of perpetration versus complicity, the court found that each of the defendants had endorsed the killings "as her own act." Neither had rejected the director's offer;

rather, each had inwardly assented to the project itself and to its reprehensible philosophy of destroying "valueless" life.[53]

The state court authorities also rejected the defendants' arguments about superior orders. On appeal, the appellate court denied that the Hitler order of 1 September 1939 authorizing Bouhler and Brandt to organize the euthanasia program was a law, since it was never published in the Reich Legal Journal (*Reichsgesetzblatt*), which was required for all newly promulgated laws. Furthermore, even if the Hitler order were valid, the German Civil Service Law[54] obligated every official to refuse an order that violated criminal law. The defendants not only did not refuse the order but also "inwardly approved" of it. For this reason, they were guilty of murder as perpetrators. Because German law prior to 1949 required the death penalty in all murder cases (absent extenuating circumstances), Wernicke and Wieczorek were sentenced to death on 25 March 1946. They became the first—and last—euthanasia defendants tried in West German courts to be executed.[55]

Nine months later, the state court of Frankfurt convicted medical personnel from the Eichberg mental hospital of murdering hundreds of disabled patients during the war. The defendants included the director, Dr. Friedrich Mennecke; Dr. Walter Schmidt, the director of Eichberg's "children's ward," where mentally ill children were killed; and two members of the institution's nursing staff. The Frankfurt court convicted Mennecke and Schmidt of murder as perpetrators, while the nurses were convicted as accomplices of "aiding and abetting murder" (*Beihilfe zum Mord*). Mennecke was sentenced to death and the nurses to several years in prison. Schmidt was originally sentenced to death, though, on appeal, the appellate court commuted his death sentence to life imprisonment. He was released in 1953 after serving six years in prison. Mennecke died in his cell in early 1947.[56]

A similar fate befell the medical staff at the Hadamar killing center in Hessen-Nassau. In October 1945, the US Army conducted the first criminal prosecution of Hadamar medical staff involved in the murders of consumptive eastern workers. Nearly two years later, the Germans held their own Hadamar trial, charging two staff physicians and a mixed group of nurses and office personnel with murdering thousands of mental patients with lethal injections and poison gas. Hadamar's chief doctor, Adolf Wahlmann, had been convicted in the US Army trial in October 1945 for his role in the killings of eastern workers at Hadamar and sentenced to life in prison. In the German Hadamar trial, Wahlmann was indicted for authorizing nurses to administer lethal overdoses of narcotics to disabled German patients. Another Hadamar doctor, Hans-Bodo Gorgass, faced a murder charge for overseeing the asphyxiation of newly arrived mental patients in gas chambers disguised as shower rooms. The court convicted Wahlmann and Gorgass of murder under the German Penal Code and sentenced them to death, although, like their counterparts at Eichberg, the court later commuted their sentences to life imprisonment. Wahlmann was released in 1953 and Gorgass in 1958. The nursing and office staff were convicted as accomplices to murder on the grounds that their "primitive nature," among other factors, impaired their ability to resist taking part in mass murder. The nurses received prison terms between three and eight years, while the office staff were all acquitted because of insufficient evidence of criminal intent.[57]

By the late 1940s, West German courts began to move away from convicting "euthanasia" medical personnel of perpetration of homicide under §211. West German courts had two basic legal tools to support this new, lenient approach to Nazi euthanasia: the subjective theory of perpetration and an innovative defense in German criminal law—the defense of necessity (*Notstand*). The idea that homicide could be justified on a theory of necessity was a latecomer in the history of German criminal law. The German Criminal Code of 1871 made no mention of it as grounds for exculpation, nor did case law acknowledge it. Until 1927, when the German Supreme Court (Reichsgericht) endorsed a new theory of justification in the law of homicide, German law did not permit an actor to justify his killing by arguing that it avoided a greater harm. The case on appeal to the Supreme Court involved a German physician convicted of murder for ordering an abortion for a woman he thought would commit suicide if she was forced to carry the fetus to term. The doctor's actions were objectively illegal, since German law had an absolute prohibition on abortion (no special circumstances, including the health of the mother, were recognized). The German Supreme Court issued a new theory of "extrastatutory necessity" that said that a physician who performed an abortion was not guilty of homicide if the physician carefully weighed the legal interests at stake and found that the mother's life outweighed that of her fetus. In other words, the court held that acting to prevent a greater harm or to serve a higher legal interest absolved the actor of criminal liability, even where the conduct fulfilled all the elements of the statutory offense.[58]

A variant of this extrastatutory necessity doctrine began to emerge in West German euthanasia trials in the late 1940s. Its effect on former German health care personnel charged with murdering their patients was dramatic and exculpatory. A breakthrough was the 1948 trial of Karl Todt, doctor of pedagogy and director of the Scheuern mental hospital, and his medical assistant, Adolf Thiel, in the state court of Koblenz. In March 1941, the facility was converted into a "transit center" for patients who had been identified for extermination. Scheuern received shipments of doomed patients from their home institution; after a brief stay, Todt forwarded them to Hadamar and death. The German authorities charged Todt and Thiel with complicity in the murders of 1,000 patients, since they had transferred them to Hadamar by filling out "registration forms" for them. These forms recorded the nature of a patient's disabilities, and became the nominal basis by which patients were sent to their deaths at Hadamar. The indictment alleged that the defendants had completed the forms with full knowledge of their fate.[59]

The court found that Todt's and Thiel's actions were both unjustified and illegal, but it acquitted them on a theory of a "collision of duties." According to the court, the defendants faced a quandary in their work at Scheuern: they could have resigned their posts and been replaced by Nazi idealogues, or take part in the "euthanasia" program in an effort to save whomever they could. From the court's perspective, Todt and Thiel had opted to keep their jobs to sabotage the euthanasia program from within. They did this by discharging patients who might otherwise have been transported to Hadamar, exaggerating patients' capacity for work, and hiding severely ill patients from the Berlin investigative teams that occasionally visited the facility. The state court determined that Todt and Thiel saved 250 patients from transport while transferring 1,000 patients to Hadamar and death. The court ruled that given the "horribly constraining circumstances" the defendants faced, their 20% success rate was a significant achievement.[60]

This trial was the first in which euthanasia defendants were acquitted based on the idea of a necessity defense ("conflict of duties"). Thereafter, West German courts increasingly found means of exonerating euthanasia medical personnel. In some of these trials, such as the prosecution of Dr. Walter Creutz and other Rhineland physicians in November 1948, it was questionable whether the defendants really tried to subvert the "euthanasia" program.[61] Much of the testimony was offered by medical colleagues of the defendants, and thus liable to impeachment for bias. In other euthanasia trials, evidence of sabotage was at best scant, and in any event heavily outweighed by substantial indication of criminal wrongdoing. This was certainly the case in the trial of Dr. Alfred Leu in Cologne in December 1953. A physician at the Sachsenberg psychiatric hospital near Schwerin, Leu was first prosecuted in October 1951 for his role in the murder of his patients. His defense was the "sabotage" argument: he collaborated in the killings only to minimize the damage and save as many as possible. Had he resigned his post, a more zealous doctor would have replaced him, resulting in the deaths of even more patients. The state court of Cologne accepted this argument, holding that it would be a miscarriage of justice to convict a defendant ensnared like Leu in a "tragic predicament." Leu was acquitted, although the prosecutors appealed his case to the German Supreme Court (Bundesgerichtshof), which reversed the decision and remanded the case for retrial.[62]

Leu was charged with filling out registration forms on his patients as part of the Nazis' program to identify the "life unworthy of life" for extermination. He was also under indictment for his involvement in the murder of disabled children while chief of Sachsenberg's "children's ward." Leu handpicked four experienced nurses to assist in its operation and swore them to silence. The children were murdered with excessive dosages of veronal and luminal. When the first transport list arrived from Berlin, it was made up of 180 children. The court found that Leu exempted 110 children from euthanasia, while the remaining 70, who one witness testified were in a "horrible" physical state, were killed in the ward.[63]

Leu's attorney again raised the "collision of duties" defense, arguing that by participating in the euthanasia program he could rescue some of the children from death. The state court agreed with Leu, holding that his dilemma was a prototypical collision of duties: "The defendant stood before a choice: either to distance himself from the killing and refuse the order given by Berlin, thereby abandoning two-thirds of his department to destruction, or to carry out the extermination orders, thereby participating in the deaths of some children in order to rescue a considerable number of other patients who would otherwise be killed." Leu's conscience forced him to "sabotage the goals of the Reich Committee and the euthanasia program it sponsored." He also believed he had to take part in the destruction of a "limited" number of patients to save others.[64] Since Leu had acted conscientiously to resolve the dilemma facing him, the court acquitted him.

The contrast between Leu's criminal actions and his acquittal is striking. Statements made by Leu during the war supporting the "euthanasia" program were well documented. Several witnesses testified that Leu had told them of his unwavering commitment to the euthanasia program. Others testified that they personally witnessed his supervision of euthanasia deaths in his departments. These witnesses said they believed that Leu had authorized the murder of patients through overdoses of narcotics. They based their testimony on the fact that patients who seemed perfectly healthy on arrival were dead only a few days later. A staff doctor at Sachsenberg, a Dr. Br., described how developments in Leu's stations convinced him that the defendant was murdering his patients with drug overdoses. Dr. Br. had been so upset by these murders that he began to call the Sachsenberg facility a "murder institution." Another witness claimed Leu had killed between 200 and 300 adults at Sachsenberg with overdoses of veronal—a charge initially made in 1941. Leu denied the charge at the time, but characterized euthanasia of incurable patients as a "welcome measure." During a meeting with the authorities in Berlin, Leu denounced this witness and Dr. Br. These authorities, the architects of the murder program against the disabled, praised Leu as a "great guy" who "acted entirely in accordance with the wishes of the Reich Committee."[65] The Leu case marks the terminus of a stormy chapter of German legal history, which began with rigorous convictions and punishment of euthanasia killers and ended with their acquittals.

A Comparative Look at American and German Prosecution of Euthanasia Crimes

In comparing the two legal approaches to such trials, several important points emerge. Each legal group conducted its respective trials using different legal and criminological theories. Legally, the American medical case was based on Control Council Law No. 10's definition of crimes against humanity. As we have seen, Law No. 10 technically dissolved the war nexus affirmed in the London Charter of 1945, which required a connection between conduct charged as a crime against humanity and the war. Nonetheless, it is clear that both the prosecution and the three judges in the American medical case continued to think of euthanasia as part of German military policy. For the Americans at Nuremberg, the Nazis fortified the *Wehrmacht*'s ability to wage wars of aggression by eliminating "useless eaters" and transferring the resources that would have been used to keep them alive to the German military. Criminologically speaking, Nazi euthanasia was, from the American perspective, part of a vast conspiracy by all sectors of the German state to wage wars of aggression and imperial conquest. Conspiracy was enormously useful to the Americans at Nuremberg because it enabled them to disregard common law distinctions between principals and accomplices and find all members of the conspiracy jointly liable for offenses committed by their confederates. In applying the doctrine of conspiracy to euthanasia defendants like Karl Brandt, the Americans enhanced the likelihood that those charged with "euthanasia" would be convicted of heinous crimes and punished to the fullest extent under ACCL No. 10.

This approach tended to presume the defendants' guilt. Brandt was convicted and sentenced to death for his role in human experimentation carried out in Nazi concentration camps and, more importantly, for his role in the euthanasia murders of non-Germans. The euthanasia charge was especially damaging to Brandt because of its connection with the extermination of European Jewry. The factual record, however, does not support the Tribunal's theory about Brandt's involvement. While he did know of experiments in the camps, it was by no means certain that he was involved in the more macabre, destructive Nazi medical experiments: those relating to hypothermia, malaria, seawater, sterilization, typhus, and bone and muscle transplantation. Brandt's responsibility for the expansive nature of the Nazi euthanasia program that began with the severely handicapped and later spread to healthier patients, concentration camp inmates incapable of work, and European Jews, is murkier still. The bulk of his responsibility for euthanasia spanned the two-year period from 1939 to 1941, when euthanasia almost exclusively targeted German patients, and not the non-Germans identified by Military Tribunal I. After August 1941, when the program changed direction, Brandt's direct responsibility was minimal or nonexistent. Military Tribunal I agreed with the prosecution that Brandt was implicated in transferring euthanasia personnel to the death camps of the east, even though there is no evidence that Brandt played any role in the transfer. His rank in the SS, an organization declared criminal by the IMT, coupled with his proximity to Hitler, his visible connections with the early stages of the euthanasia program, and his appointment as chief of the German health care system in the waning years of the war, were all decisive factors in his conviction.[66]

In contrast, the West German euthanasia trials were legally based on the German law of homicide with its substantive definition of murder and its distinctions between perpetration and complicity. German courts' criminological theory of euthanasia—particularly after 1947—emphasized the subjective theory of perpetration, which focused on the actor's mental attitude toward the crime. This contrasted with the Americans' tendency to unite the crimes of euthanasia and conspiracy to wage war in a single, mammoth criminal enterprise, which tended to affirm liability for all members of the conspiracy. The Germans stressed psychology, which tended to

125

reduce liability, even in the face of clear evidence of direct homicidal actions by the defendant. In brief, the Americans presumed guilt under a theory of conspiracy, whereas the Germans presumed innocence under theories of complicity and necessity.

How can we account for the differences in these outcomes? We might adopt a purely formalistic approach and trace them to differences in the law applied by each national trial group. The law of conspiracy—once referred to by Judge Learned Hand as "the darling of the modern prosecutor's nursery"—tends to produce convictions;[67] the German law of homicide, by emphasizing the actor's subjective attitudes toward the criminal act, leans favorably toward the defendant. The formalistic explanation has merit, but it does not adequately explain why the theories of liability were endorsed, nor why cases with substantially similar facts were resolved so differently. The formalistic approach does not, for example, account for the Americans' insistence on tying "euthanasia" to crimes against peace and war crimes, even after ACCL No. 10 had abolished the war nexus between them. Neither does it explain why German courts between 1945 and 1947 routinely convicted euthanasia doctors of murder as perpetrators, but tended, after 1947, to characterize them as accomplices or to acquit them outright. Consequently, one needs to look for other reasons to explain these differences.

I would suggest that the differences between the American and German approaches share a common motivation: concern about political power centered on the turbulent geopolitical events at that time. The US has a long history of zealous regard for its own sovereignty. At the local level, concern for sovereignty was often expressed in xenophobic and nativistic manifestations; within the national government, it was adorned with an exceptionalist ideology that viewed international institutions as potential impediments to the pursuit of alleged national interests. A distrustful attitude toward internationalism, which has been an integral part of the country's DNA since its early history, peaked during and after World War II as the US shifted its national security strategy from fighting Nazi and Japanese militarism to opposing Soviet communism. Although we are prone to mark the beginning of the Cold War by focusing on putative Soviet violations of the Yalta agreement, the Berlin blockade, and the outbreak of the Korean War, America's relationship with the USSR was tense and adversarial well before the end of the 1940s. While the two countries were still allies in the war against Hitler, the US was already looking toward a future in which the Red Army, not Germany's *Wehrmacht*, would be the principal menace to American interests. Much of the impetus behind American intelligence gathering in the final two years of the war flowed from the US's determination to capture German military information (e.g. rocketry and biological-chemical weapons programs) before the Soviets did.[68] US officials' negative experiences with the Soviet delegation during the IMT—Jackson wrote disapprovingly to Taylor that the Soviets regarded the court as "one of the organs of government power, a weapon in the hands of the ruling class for the purpose of safeguarding its interests"—convinced them that a second IMT was not feasible, chiefly because of the risk that the Soviets would insist on holding it in the Russian zone of occupation. They also thought the American public would not tolerate a Soviet judge presiding over a second international tribunal.[69]

In other words, the American Doctors' Trial unfolded as the US was preparing itself for conflict with the Soviet Union. US policy makers who shaped the American war crimes program at Nuremberg, such as Robert Jackson, Secretary of State Cordell Hull, Secretary of War Henry Stimson, and other officials, understood even before the end of the war the direction events would take after Germany and Japan's inevitable defeat. American diplomatic correspondence regarding the future Allied war crimes trial program reflects official concern about the political implications of the trials. In a letter of 27 October 1944, to Hull, Stimson raised the issue of prosecuting Nazi perpetrators for atrocities committed on their co-nationals. Such atrocities committed by an Axis government "would not ordinarily come within the usual legal definition of the term 'war crime.'" Stimson appended an undated and unsigned memorandum to his letter. The author of this memo asserted that many of the Axis atrocities had been committed before war was declared, and that "some of the worst outrages were committed by Axis powers against their own nationals on racial, religious, and political grounds. As to these, the offenders can plead justification under domestic law." For the memo's anonymous author, prosecuting offenders for crimes inflicted on their own nationals "would set the precedent of an international right to sit in judgment on the conduct of the several states toward their own nationals. This would open the door to incalculable consequences and present grave questions of policy." The bind, the author added, was this: the Allied leadership had made "widely publicized statements" threatening Axis war criminals with prosecution for their involvement in such atrocities.[70] The author added: "To let these brutalities go unpunished will leave millions of persons frustrated and disillusioned."[71]

How could the Allies prosecute domestic crimes and thus fulfill their earlier promises without compromising the national sovereignty of the Nazi government and setting "the precedent of an international right" to adjudicate such crimes? The memo's author proposed the solution of linking all of the Nazi government's crimes to a giant conspiracy "to commit murder, terrorism, and the destruction of peaceful populations in violation of the laws of war." In this way, the Allies could prosecute "domestic atrocities" without violating German national sovereignty:

> ... in view of the nature of the charge, everything done in furtherance of the conspiracy from the time of its inception would be admissible, including domestic atrocities against minority groups within Germany, and domestic atrocities induced or procured by the German Government to be committed by other Axis Nations against their respective nationals.[72]

Commenting on this memorandum, Secretary of War Stimson—perhaps the most important architect of the US war crimes trial program in its earliest phases—remarked as follows:

You will observe that the memorandum deals in part with the possible prosecution of enemy nationals for atrocities committed against other enemy nationals, particularly minority groups. The proposal is that these atrocities, whether committed before or after the formal declaration of war, be regarded as steps in the execution of a general conspiracy to which all members of certain enemy organizations were parties.[73]

Stimson advised the State Department to give careful consideration to this proposal when considering how to deal with Axis victims of Axis crimes.[74]

As we have seen, the drafters of the IMT Charter followed Stimson's legal paradigm by basing the American case against Nazi defendants on conspiracy to wage wars of aggression. By refusing to prosecute Nazi crimes unrelated to aggressive war, the Americans ensured that no dangerous precedents in international law would compromise US sovereignty, particularly when it was beginning its struggle against world communism.[75] The doctrine of conspiracy served not only to generate convictions at Nuremberg but also insulated the US against postwar legal challenges to its actions in the midst of American efforts to protect national security against the Soviets.

The new West German state was also preoccupied with sovereignty by the late 1940s. In order to regain it, the Germans believed they had to reinvent themselves as ardent democrats and loyal supporters of *Westpolitik*. A country mired in prosecuting some of its citizens for abominable crimes carried out on behalf of a totalitarian government would find it difficult to vouch for its credentials as a freshly minted, pro-Western ally against the Soviets. The era of Nazi war crimes trials had to be laid to rest. The West German euthanasia trials took place within this broad societal movement to end further punishment of Nazi war criminals. The subjective theory of perpetration and variations on the defense of necessity proved useful instruments for German courts to close the book on the Nazi past. This was the German judiciary's effort to restore Germany's sovereignty after the catastrophes of military defeat, territorial dismemberment, and foreign occupation. Considerations of national sovereignty—for the US, its expansion into a dangerous postwar world; for West Germany, its recovery and preservation—profoundly skewed judicial efforts to deal even-handedly with the crimes of Nazi "euthanasia." The history of these trials reveals the determinative impact of power on efforts, however well intended, to punish extreme forms of criminality committed by the nation-state.

NOTES

1. In the last two decades, a vast literature on the Nazi "euthanasia" program (or "T-4" program, as it is sometimes called, after the Berlin street address of the office responsible for its operation—Tiergartenstrasse No. 4) has accumulated. Some of the leading monographs are: Klee, *"Euthanasie" im NS-Staat*; Friedlander, *The Origins of Nazi Genocide*; Aly and Heim, *Vordenker der Vernichtung*, 1991; Bock, *Zwangssterilization im Nationalsozialismus*; Burleigh, *Death and Deliverance*; Nowak, *"Euthanasie" und Sterilisierung im "Dritten Reich"*; Proctor, *Racial Hygiene*; Schmuhl, *Rassenhygiene, Nationalsozialismus, Euthanasie*. While the scholarly literature on Nazi "euthanasia" trials has lagged in

comparison with scholarship on its evolution, the topic has generated international attention. See, for example, de Mildt, *In the Name of the People*, especially 80–226; Klee, *Was sie taten, Was sie wurden*; Friedrich, *Die kalte Amnestie*; Bryant, *Confronting the "Good Death"*; Weindling, *Nazi Medicine and the Nuremberg Trials*, particularly Chapter 13. Recently, the Dutch scholar Dick de Mildt published a massive compendium of West and East German verdicts in Nazi "euthanasia" cases: see de Mildt, *Tatkomplex*.

2. The trial of Brandt and his co-defendants before the American National Military Tribunal lasted from 9 December 1946 to 20 August 1947.

3. Taylor, *Final Report to the Secretary of the Army*, 200.

4. Quoted in ibid., 70.

5. Charter of the International Military Tribunal, Articles 6, 9, and 10, reproduced in *Trials of War Criminals before the Nuremberg Military Tribunals* ("Green Series"), xi–xii.

6. Ibid., Article 6. In the literature of the Nuremberg War Crimes Trials, the relative clause "in execution of or in connection with any crime within the jurisdiction of the Tribunal" is referred to as the "war nexus."

7. *Trial of the Major War Criminals before the International Military Tribunal, Nuremberg, 14 November 1945—1 October 1946*, vol. 1, 225–26.

8. By adding "invasions" to the definition of crimes against peace, the drafters created a legal ground for prosecuting the *Anschluss* and the annexation of Czechoslovakia, neither of which could be classified as an instance of warmaking.

9. Control Council Law No. 10, *Trials of War Criminals before the Nuremberg Military Tribunals under Control Council Law #10, October 1946–April 1949*, vol. I, xvi.

10. For an exhaustive and foundational account of the history of the medical case, see Weindling, *Nazi Medicine and the Nuremberg Trials*. For a shorter description of the prologue to the medical case, see Bryant, *Confronting the "Good Death*," 90ff.

11. Weindling, *Nazi Medicine, passim*.

12. The reason for the duplication of the euthanasia charge in Counts 2 and 3 likely resides in the nationality of the victims under each count: these were described in Count 2 as "nationals of German-occupied countries" (thus meeting the diversity of citizenship requirement of war crimes), whereas the victims in Count 3 were "German civilians as well as civilians of other nations." As we have seen above, the dissolution by ACCL No. 10 of the war nexus enabled the American authorities in the 12 successor trials to charge the defendants with crimes committed on their own citizens—a practice impossible under the Charter's original definition of crimes against humanity, which had bound them to crimes against peace and war crimes.

13. *Trials of War Criminals*, vol. I, 8–17.

14. Quoted in Bryant, *Confronting the "Good Death*," 38.

15. Ibid., 43–44, 97.

16. This latter engagement accounts for the Americans' interest in Brandt as a source of information on Germany's chemical warfare program.

17. Ebbinghaus and Dörner, *Vernichten und Heilen*, 624–26.

18. Weindling, *Nazi Medicine*, 251ff.

19. The US prosecutors continued to insist on the "war nexus" of crimes against humanity despite its abrogation in Control Council Law No. 10.

20. Bryant, *Confronting*, 97.

21. Dörner, "'Ich darf nicht denken,'" 340, 348–49. Brandt's "state of necessity" argument went so far as to liken the sacrifice of individual patients and prisoners to the excision of cancer cells from the human body. In a conversation with Dr. Leo Alexander, a forensic medical expert at the trial, Brandt described Nazi medicine's conception of individual

well-being vis-à-vis the demands of national health (*Volkskörper*): "We German doctors regard the state as an individual which is the primary object of our medical duty, and we therefore do not shy away from destroying an agglomeration of, for example, a trillion cells ... if we believe they are destructive to the total organism—the state—or if we believe the state will thrive without them." Quoted in Schmidt, "Die Angeklagten Fritz Fischer, Hans W. Romberg und Karl Brandt aus der Sicht des medizinischen Sachverständigen Leo Alexander," 401.

22. Bryant, *Confronting*, 99.
23. Ibid., 101.
24. Ibid., 102.
25. *Trials of War Criminals*, vol. II, 278.
26. Bryant, *Confronting*, 102. Himmler did indeed agree with Brack's recommendation, and ordered two "euthanasia" doctors to begin sterilization experiments with X-rays, a program later abandoned for its impracticality.
27. Judgment of the Military Tribunal I, National Archives Records Administration—College Park (NARA), RG 238, M 887, Roll 1, 61, 11508.
28. *Trials of War Criminals*, vol. II, 197.
29. Ibid., 281.
30. Ibid., 278–79; Bryant, *Confronting*, 103.
31. Loewenstein, "Reconstruction of the Administration of Justice in American-Occupied Germany," 419–20; Friedlander, "The Judiciary and Nazi Crimes in Postwar Germany," 27–28.
32. Control Council Law No. 1 (20 September 1945), cited in Friedlander, "The Judiciary," 28. As Loewenstein notes, both the Potsdam Declaration and JCS 1067 provided for the repeal of "peculiarly Nazi legislation." Loewenstein, "Reconstruction," 420. Control Council Law No. 1 reified the Allied intention to de-Nazify German law, announced as early as April 1945.
33. The Reichsgericht, the German Supreme Court before May 1945, was the fourth type of ordinary court in Germany. Dissolved with Germany's formal surrender in May 1945, it was succeeded by the Bundesgerichtshof when the Federal Republic of Germany came into existence in 1949.
34. Nobleman, "The Administration of Justice in the United States Zone of Germany," 92–94; Loewenstein, "Reconstruction," 422–28; Bryant, "Back into the Unmasterable Past," 199–219; Friedlander, "The Judiciary," 28; Rückerl, *The Investigation of Nazi Crimes 1945–1978*, 34.
35. Friedlander, "The Judiciary," 31.
36. Two sources of law stymied German jurisdiction over crimes against peace and war crimes: (1) the requirement under the Laws of Armed Conflict that jurisdiction over war crimes existed only where there was a diversity of nationality between defendant and victim; and (2) the prohibition in ACCL No. 4, sustained in ACCL No. 10, which forbade German courts from presiding over Nazi crimes perpetrated on the soldiers and civilians of Allied countries. See ACCL No. 10, section 1, paragraph (d), Appendix D to Taylor, *Final Report to the Secretary of the Army*.
37. Bryant, *Confronting*, 109.
38. See Rückerl, *The Investigation of Nazi Crimes*, 40.
39. Excerpted in Bassiouni, *Crimes against Humanity in International Law*, 36–37.
40. Friedlander, "The Judiciary," 32–33.
41. Rüter et al., *Justiz und NS-Verbrechen* (hereafter *JuNSV*), Ltd. Nr. 155a.
42. Ibid. According to Ernst Klee, the German scholar of Nazi euthanasia, Mauthe never served his sentence. In a judicial statement made in 1961, Mauthe said: "I was unjustly

convicted in Tübingen and given five years in prison. I spent one year in pretrial custody, but the rest of the sentence was suspended." He died in 1974. Klee, *Was sie taten, Was sie wurden*, 85; idem, *Das Personenlexicon zum Dritten Reich*, 396.

43. Von Henle and Schierlinger, *Strafgesetzbuch für das Deutsche Reich*, 227.
44. Dombrowski, *Strafgesetzbuch*, 83.
45. Bryant, *Confronting*, 109 ff.
46. *JuNSV*, Lfd. Nr. 014.
47. On the "collision of duties" defense, see below.
48. *JuNSV*, Lfd. Nr. 232–233.
49. Ibid.
50. Ibid.
51. The details of Weber's post-trial career are recounted in Klee, *Was sie taten*, 205–06.
52. *JuNSV*, Lfd. Nr. 003, 33–35.
53. Ibid.
54. The German Civil Service Law of 1937 stipulated in §7, Paragraph 2, Clause 2, that "the civil servant shall not obey an order which would clearly violate the criminal law." Dick de Mildt, ed., *Tatkomplex*, vol. 1, Lfd. Nr.1b: KG 24.8.1946, 13.
55. Ibid., 13–14.
56. *JuNSV*, Lfd. Nr. 011.
57. *JuNSV*, Lfd. Nr. 017.
58. 61 RGSt. 242 (1927).
59. *JuNSV*, Lfd. Nr. 088.
60. Ibid.
61. *JuNSV*, Lfd. Nr. 102 (trial of W. Creutz *et al.*). For other trials that accepted the collision of duties defense to acquit euthanasia defendants, see *JuNSV*, Lfd. Nrs. 155a (trial of Otto Mauthe et al.), 226 (trial of Ludwig Gessner et al.), 225 (trial of Dr. Recktenwald et al.).
62. Bryant, *Confronting*, 198–99.
63. *JuNSV*, Lfd. Nr. 383, 10–13.
64. Ibid.
65. Ibid., 16.
66. On the shortcomings in the Tribunal's judgment on Brandt, see Weindling, *Nazi Medicine*, 299–300.
67. *Harrison* v. *U.S.*, 7 F.2d 259, 263 (CCA 2nd 1925).
68. A former US Army intelligence officer once informed me that his unit's primary interest in Western Europe was seizure of German military intelligence in advance of the Soviets.
69. Jackson, *Report of Robert H. Jackson*, vi; memo from Jackson to Taylor, 5 February 1946, National Archives Records Administration—College Park (NARA), RG 238; Taylor's letter to Howard Petersen, 22 May 1946, NARA, RG 238.
70. NARA, RG 107, Entry 74A, Box 5, German War Crimes, 27 October 1944, attachment, 1f.
71. Ibid., attachment, 3.
72. Ibid., attachment, 6.
73. Ibid., letter of 27 October 1944, 2f.
74. Ibid., attachment, 2.
75. In a September 1944 memorandum to President Roosevelt, Stimson dismissed the idea of prosecuting anything other than war crimes. He implied by analogy that a military commission had no more jurisdiction over a crime unconnected to the war than a foreign court would have over perpetrators of lynching in the American South. See Henry L. Stimson, "Memorandum Opposing the Morgenthau Plan," 9 September 1944, reproduced in Marrus, *The Nuremberg War Crimes Trial 1945–46*, 26–27.

REFERENCES

Aly, Götz, and Susane Heim. *Vordenker der Vernichtung*. Hamburg: Hoffman & Campe, 1991.

Bassiouni, M. Cherif. *Crimes against Humanity in International Law*. The Hague: Kluwer, 1999.

Bock, Gisela. *Zwangssterilization im Nationalsozialismus*. Opladen: Westdeutscher, 1986.

Bryant, Michael S. *Confronting the "Good Death": Nazi Euthanasia on Trial, 1945–53*. Boulder: University Press of Colorado, 2005.

———. "Back into the Unmasterable Past: Southwest Germany and the Judicial Odyssey of Mayor Reinhard Boos, 1947–1949." *Human Rights Review* 8, no. 3 (2007): 199–219.

Burleigh, Michael. *Death and Deliverance: "Euthanasia" in Germany 1900–1945*. Cambridge: Cambridge University Press, 1994.

de Mildt, Dick. *In the Name of the People: Perpetrators of Genocide in the Reflection of their Post-War Prosecution in West Germany*. The Hague: Martinus Nijhof, 1996.

———. *Tatkomplex: NS Euthanasie. Die ost- und westdeutschen Strafurteile seit 1945*. 2 vols. Amsterdam: Amsterdam University Press, 2009.

Dombrowski, Lothar, ed. *Strafgesetzbuch: Textausgabe mit den wichtigsten Nebensgesetzen und Kontrollratsgesetzen*. Stuttgart: W. Kohlhammer, 1948.

Dörner, Klaus. "'Ich darf nicht denken.' Das medizinische Selbstverständnis der Angeklagten." In *Vernichten und Heilen: Der Nürnberger Ärzteprozeß und seine Folgen*, edited by Angelika Ebbinghaus and Klaus Dörner. Berlin: Aufbau Taschenbuch, 2002.

Ebbinghaus, Angelika, and Klaus Dörner, eds. *Vernichten und Heilen: Der Nürnberger Ärzteprozeß und seine Folgen*. Berlin: Aufbau Taschenbuch, 2002.

Friedlander, Henry. "The Judiciary and Nazi Crimes in Postwar Germany." *Simon Wiesenthal Center Annual* 1 (1984): 27–44.

———. *The Origins of Nazi Genocide: From Euthanasia to the Final Solution*. Chapel Hill: University of North Carolina Press, 1995.

Friedrich, Jörg. *Die kalte Amnestie: NS-Täter in der Bundesrepublik*. Munich: Piper, 1994.

Jackson, Robert. *Report of Robert H. Jackson, U.S. Representative to the International Conference on Military Trials, London 1945*. Washington, DC: Department of State, 1949.

Klee, Ernst. *"Euthanasie" im NS-Staat: Die Vernichtung "lebensunwerten Lebens."* Frankfurt am Main: Fischer, 1986.

———. *Was sie taten, Was sie wurden: Ärzte, Juristen, und andere Beteiligte am Kranken- oder Judenmord*. Frankfurt am Main: Fischer, 1998.

———. *Das Personenlexicon zum Dritten Reich: Wer war was vor und nach 1945*. Frankfurt am Main: Fischer, 2003.

Loewenstein, Karl. "Reconstruction of the Administration of Justice in American-Occupied Germany." *Harvard Law Review* 61 (1948): 419–67.

Marrus, Michael. *The Nuremberg War Crimes Trial 1945–46: A Documentary History*. New York: Bedford Books, 1997.

Nobleman, Eli E. "The Administration of Justice in the United States Zone of Germany." *Federal Bar Journal* 8 (1946): 70–97.

Nowak, Kurt. *Euthanasie" und Sterilisierung im "Dritten Reich."* Göttingen: Vandenhoeck & Ruprecht, 1984.

Proctor, Robert N. *Racial Hygiene: Medicine under the Nazis*. Cambridge, MA: Harvard University Press, 1988.

Rückerl, Adalbert. *The Investigation of Nazi Crimes 1945–1978*. Hamden, CT: Archon Books, 1980.

Rüter, Adelheid L., C.F. Rüter, H.H. Fuchs, and Irene Sagel-Grande, eds. *Justiz und NS-Verbrechen: Sammlung deutscher Strafurteile wegen nationalsozialistischer Tötungsverbrechen 1945–1966*. Amsterdam: Amsterdam University Press, 1968–1981.

Schmidt, Ulf. "Die Angeklagten Fritz Fischer, Hans W. Romberg und Karl Brandt aus der Sicht des medizinischen Sachverständigen Leo Alexander." In *Vernichten und Heilen: Der Nürnberger Ärzteprozeß und seine Folgen*, edited by Angelika Ebbinghaus and Klaus Dörner. Berlin: Aufbau Taschenbuch, 2002.

Schmuhl, Hans-Walter. *Rassenhygiene, Nationalsozialismus, Euthanasie: von der Verhütung zur Vernichtung "lebensunwerten Lebens" 1890–1945*. Göttingen: Vandenhoeck & Ruprecht, 1987.

Taylor, Telford. *Final Report to the Secretary of the Army*, CD ROM. Seattle: Aristarchus Knowledge Industries, 1995.

Trial of the Major War Criminals before the International Military Tribunal, Nuremberg, 14 November 1945—1 October 1946. 42 vols. Nuremberg: International Military Tribunal, 1947.

Trials of War Criminals before the Nuremberg Military Tribunals under Control Council Law #10, October 1946–April 1949. 15 vols. Washington, DC: US Government Printing Office, 1946–1949.

von Henle, W., and Franz Schierlinger, eds. *Strafgesetzbuch für das Deutsche Reich*. Munich: C. H. Beck'sche Verlagsbuchhandlung, 1912.

Weindling, Paul J. *Nazi Medicine and the Nuremberg Trials: From Medical War Crimes to Informed Consent*. Basingstoke: Palgrave Macmillan, 2004.

Justice 30 Years Later? The Cambodian Special Tribunal for the Punishment of Crimes against Humanity by the Khmer Rouge

Wolfgang Form

After a two-year tug-of-war between the US, the UN, and Phnom Penh, the Cambodian government, supported by massive international intervention, brought some of those accused of committing Khmer Rouge atrocities to trial before an independent court. The atrocities, which verged on genocide, were perpetrated between 1975 and 1979. The plan was to create a special tribunal consisting of both indigenous and foreign judges to try the perpetrators. Newspapers from 2002 reported that the first indictment would be issued some time during that year. As we know today, this proved to be a rosily optimistic prediction.

The history of Cambodia in the second half of the twentieth century is complexly interwoven with transregional political processes in Indochina. Time played—and continues to play—a unique role. Only after the passage of 20 years was the international community ready to analyze the crimes against humanity inflicted on the Khmer people and Cambodian minorities. Premier Hun Sen, who had himself lost a child during the dictatorship of Pol Pot, had originally been ignored when he demanded that not only the Khmer Rouge's reign of terror between April 1975 and January 1979 be included in the tribunal's investigation but also the period preceding this era. Such insistence was not warmly received by the leading representatives of the UN Security Council, particularly the US. The coup supported by Washington in 1970, which brought to power the corrupt Lon Nol regime, enabled the Khmer Rouge—until that moment a small group of rebels—to develop for the first time into a national force.[1]

The rise of the Khmer Rouge in the 1970s occurred in stages and is intimately involved with the history of Southeast Asia. During World War II, French Indochina (including Cambodia) was occupied by Japan until 1945. Thereafter, the French in Saigon conducted war crimes trials, many of which remain obscure to today.[2] After the French defeat at Dien Bien Phu in 1954, the Geneva Indochina Conference established a provisional peace between Cambodia, Vietnam, and Laos. Cambodia, after 90 years of colonial rule, became independent. The largest ethnic group was the

Khmer, followed by the Chinese, the Vietnamese, and other ethnic minorities (such as the Cham[3] and the primitive mountain tribes). Political power resided in the hands of the Sihanouk royal family. In the 1960s, members of the opposition formed the Khmer People's Revolutionary Party, a diverse group of pro-Vietnamese sympathizers, Marxists, and generic opponents of the royal house. A group led by Ieng Sary and Saloth Sar (who later became notorious under the name "Pol Pot") called for an armed struggle against Sihanouk. This faction recruited heavily from a Cambodian student circle in France. It opposed another, numerically larger group of pro-Vietnamese politicians with close ties to the Communist Party. In the early 1960s, the Pol Pot faction repeatedly retreated into the jungle to plot conspiratorially against Sihanouk.[4]

On the world scene it was a troubled time. The East–West conflict veered increasingly toward armed confrontations or proxy wars. As Vietnam grew in political importance for the government of Prince Sihanouk, the pro-Vietnamese politicians emerged as a formidable internal factor. They were not, however, disposed to support the regime supported by the US, but rather communist North Vietnam. In 1965, Sihanouk cut diplomatic relations with the US and allowed North Vietnam to construct and maintain military bases in Cambodia. The US's entry into the war in Vietnam catalyzed the already clearly discernible developments that led finally to civil war between the Pol Pot regime and the Sihanouk royal house (1967/1968). In 1969, the Nixon administration commenced bombing operations in Cambodia. Internal tensions escalated in March 1970.[5]

Supported by the US, General Lon Nol, a longtime friend of Prince Sihanouk, revolted and seized control of the government. It would appear that the US supported the *coup d'état* for purely strategic reasons, to use Lon Nol as a geopolitical ally. This momentous event unfolded against the backdrop of massive bombing of the country in 1973 by the US, which used B-52s to drop a half-million tons of bombs on Cambodia. Within a few weeks, according to international estimates, more bombs fell on Cambodian territory than on Japan during World War II:

> The extent of the casualties associated with these bombings is one of the most understated statistics of American involvement in international affairs. The Finnish Kampuchea Inquiry Commission estimates that, out of a total population of over seven million, 600,000 Cambodians died and over two million more became refugees as a direct result of the carpet bombing.[6]

Sihanouk, who was briefly placed under house arrest after the coup, soon fled to China, where he was advised to ally with the Khmer Rouge to enhance its chances of gaining power. He followed this recommendation and created a government in exile with the Khmer Rouge: the Royal Government of the National Union of Kampuchea.[7] At this time, the Khmer Rouge was not a homogeneous group. Three main currents battled for political dominance:

1. The national revolutionary Khmer Rouge supporting Pol Pot, essentially composed of French-educated intellectuals. They envisioned formation of a new

agrarian state, one that would transcend every moral concept—especially those of the West.

2. The second faction was oriented toward the Chinese Cultural Revolution, but retained a strong alignment with the Soviet Union. This finally led to its downfall, when China, under the watchword "social imperialism," excoriated Soviet foreign policy. China now supported Pol Pot.

3. The third faction desired to create a second Vietnam, albeit one with the most highly developed industrial infrastructure possible.[8]

Until 1975, Pol Pot's national revolutionary movement dominated the Khmer Rouge. During the civil war from 1968 to 1975, the political opposition increasingly gained traction, although the US provided Lon Nol with lavish supplies of weapons and other *matériel*. Moreover, the US intensified its bombing of Cambodia to destroy the supply lines of the "Ho Chi Minh Trail"[9] in thickly settled regions. Estimates are that between 150,000 and 700,000 people died during this bombing campaign, which also destroyed as much as 40% of the country's roads, as well as numerous settlements and rice fields.[10]

This helped enhance the Khmer Rouge's enormous popularity and support among the population during the civil war. There are persuasive arguments that the policies of Richard Nixon and his advisor, Henry Kissinger, contributed to the rise of Pol Pot. On 17 April 1975, the Khmer Rouge reached the capital city of Phnom Penh. Pol Pot's troops seized control of the government and proclaimed a new state: Democratic Kampuchea (see Figure 1).

At the same time, the entire economy of the country collapsed and all relief supplies were cancelled. Above all, difficulties arose with the food supply. Rice production stagnated and fell to a quarter of the 1969 level. Within a few days, Phnom Penh

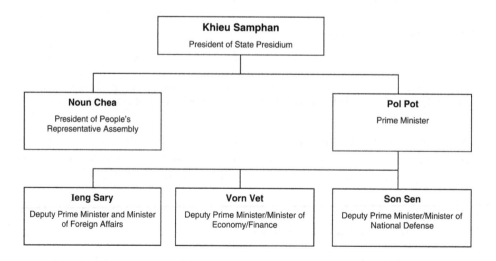

FIGURE 1 Structure of the government of Democratic Kampuchea.

and its provincial cities were evacuated. At the Khmer Rouge Party Day from 20 to 24 May, Pol Pot introduced an eight-point program that *inter alia* called for the expulsion of Vietnamese minorities from the country, the dismissal of all Buddhist monks from their offices, the evacuation of the urban population, and the execution of all functionaries of the former Lon Nol regime.[11]

In 1975, the Khmer Rouge began to enforce a policy of homogenization by "Khmerizing" the population. Some officials demanded there were to be no Muslim Chams, Chinese, or Vietnamese. "Everyone is to join the same, single, Khmer nationality."[12] To eliminate ethnic diversity, the regime banned cultural practices and forced minorities to assimilate into Khmer culture. The terror regime took strict measures to achieve this uniformity. In the case of the Chams, the Khmer Rouge enforced physical uniformity by prohibiting females from using their traditional headdress and by requiring them to cut their hair.[13] According to Ya Mat, a survivor of the genocide of the Cham:

> In 1975 there was a phrase that they used to instruct us: There was a document saying that now, if we did not eat [pork], they would not let us "live in the revolution." They would abolish us … We had come to live in Kampuchea, but there were [to be] no Chams, no Chinese, no nothing.[14]

In the fall of 1975, the "Sentabel" (security police) erected torture and extermination camps.[15] Historian Craig Etcheson notes that "The Khmer Rouge invented their own communism. They modeled their party along Lenin's rules, planned their revolution using Mao's techniques, and ruled according to Stalin's policies of repression. And they pushed everything much further than their predecessors could have imagined."[16] There were a large number of extermination camps and mass graves throughout Cambodia; we know of 189 registered Khmer Rouge prisons, divided into five categories.[17] Most of the prisoners in the first three categories (regional, district, and sub-district levels) were soldiers from the Lon Nol regime. In 1976, many of these soldiers were dismissed or interned in labor camps for deployment in agricultural projects. Nonetheless, this strategic course of action was subsequently altered, insofar as precious few people survived the security centers (which comprised prisons and labor camps). The prison camps of the fourth category (zone level) were erected for prisoners from the ranks of the Khmer Rouge as well as their family members. The final category is the infamous torture prison, S-21 (Security Prison S-21),[18] which was located in the middle of Phnom Penh. It was built on the grounds of a former French school (Tuol Svay Prey) at 103 Street.[19] This prison soon developed into the largest internment and torture station in Cambodia. Sources indicate that between 1975 and 1978, between 14,000 and 30,000 prisoners from all parts of the country were interned here. In S-21, members of the Ankar, an organization declared an "enemy" opponent of the revolution, were interrogated and tortured. The same fate befell the officers, politicians, and sympathizers of the Lon Nol government. In 1999, the warden of S-21, Kaing Guek Ieu (called "Duch"), was arrested; 10 years later, the Extraordinary Chambers in the Courts of Cambodia (ECCC) began court proceedings against him.[20]

Only seven of the prisoners interned in S-21 survived their ordeal. These individuals were primarily sculptors and painters who were given commissions to produce portraits or busts of Pol Pot.

> S-21 was the highest level security office of the Khmer Rouge regime (1975–1979). It was a security office that functioned in reality like a brutal prison. The "S" in S-21 stands for santebal, a Khmer word roughly translating to "security police." The few who survived the prison are still haunted by what took place inside its walls. Yet, one need not be a survivor to be appalled, terrified, and even moved to tears when standing outside the compound's fence; many survivors of Democratic Kampuchea become emotional as they approach the gates of the former prison.[21]

Approximately 1,720 persons worked for the torture center.[22] The prison was used primarily for the systematic torture of its inmates. The building was surrounded with electrified barbed wire; the former French classrooms were converted into prison cells and torture chambers. A network of barbed wire in front of the exits of the individual parts of the building was designed to prevent the distraught prisoners from committing suicide.

After arrival in S-21, the guards photographed the prisoners and forced them to reveal information about themselves. The prisoners were typically chained. Each one had to observe strict rules, and could be punished for violations with beatings or electric shock. Contact with the outside world was virtually impossible; writing to one's relatives was forbidden. Every action required the permission of the guards. Torturers induced the prisoners to admit to everything and confess to all charges against them. As a result, the torturers extracted bizarre confessions. In the eyes of the tormentors, however, these confessions confirmed their belief that the entire country was being overrun by counterrevolutionaries, which in turn led to harsher investigative methods. A cycle of violence ensued, which grew in frightful intensity. Methods of torture included:

- electric shocks;
- submergence in tubs of water;
- waterboarding;
- hanging from a gallows until the victims became unconscious, whereby the victim's hands were bound together behind the back with a rope and the victim suspended from it.

While the instruments of torture were surprisingly primitive, they caused their victims unspeakable agony. The poor hygienic conditions led to lice infestation and fatal illnesses. Foreigners from Australia, France, and the US were among the ranks of those who perished in S-21. In the final year in which the government was unleashed from all restraints, even the utensils of homicide—guns, knives, and other tools of killing—became scarce. Visitors to Cambodian's places of commemoration today are shocked to learn that serrated palm leaf stalks were used as a type of saw to sever the throats of prisoners.[23]

The paranoia of the Pol Pot regime focused increasingly on its own followers. Torturers and executioners were in turn killed by people who took over their jobs. In early 1977, 100 victims were killed in S-21 each day. Whoever survived the torture was brutally murdered in the killing fields of Choeung Ek outside the gates of Phnom Penh. The victims were subsequently buried in mass graves at the scene of their murder. Duch fled S-21 after the Vietnamese invasion (1979), after he had ordered the liquidation of all inmates of the prison. He could not remove all of the documents before his flight—meaning that copious documentation, much of it in photos, was left behind.[24]

These contemporary documents are found today in Tuol Sleng Museum (Phnom Penh). The museum S-21 was constructed after the Vietnamese invasion in 1979. Partition screens with more than 6,000 photos of the victims, taken by prison personnel, are on display. Thousands more are missing or were destroyed. Like the Nazis, the Khmer Rouge kept extraordinarily detailed records and photographed all of the internees. The year of the photo can be read from the number pictured on the chest of the internee; photos of the gruesome torture deaths of the last 14 inmates are exhibited in the room where their decaying corpses were discovered (their graves are now in the nearby courtyard). They form the foundation of the commemorative, didactic effort here to open through visual images individual ports of memory for the bereaved. The pathways of reflection deliberately focus on known persons, enabling history to overcome repression. To viewers not personally affected by the atrocities, an unavoidable confrontation with the photographic documents is conveyed that brings to life the victims and the atrocities they suffered.

Vann Nath is one of seven survivors of the Tuol Sleng torture prison. Today, he operates, with his relatives, a small restaurant in Phnom Penh, and still suffers the aftereffects of torture; his tormentors tortured him with electric shocks. He owes his survival to his talent as a painter. Based on photos, he painted portraits of Pol Pot. In an interview he related the reasons for his arrest:

> I can't tell you even today. I lived in a village community where people were arrested every day. Day and night they were arrested and compelled to hard labor. When I was delivered to the Tuol Sleng prison, the Khmer Rouge accused me of not following the revolutionary policy and not supporting the Ankar party.[25]

These horrors did not end until Vietnam occupied Phnom Penh on 7 January 1979. The Khmer Rouge, driven not only by radical communism but also powerful nationalism, instigated war with Vietnam in 1978 in the Mekong Delta, an area formerly occupied by Cambodians. The Vietnamese troops met with little resistance because Pol Pot's soldiers were weak and emaciated. This did not mean, however, that the Khmer Rouge chapter of Cambodian history was over.[26]

The members of the terror regime fled into the Cambodian jungle, to Thailand, and finally to China. From 1979 to 1991, a bloody civil war raged between four mutually antagonistic groups, who battled each other remorselessly for more than 13 years.[27] The fact that there were no attempts by the international community to examine the horrors of the Pol Pot era during this period centered primarily on the Vietnamese presence in Cambodia.[28]

> The onset of the Cold War greatly diminished the feasibility of putting alleged human rights violators on trial, however. Perceived strategic imperatives generally outweighed concerns for international justice, and even the most heinous regimes often secured political and military protection by aligning with one of the superpowers. The United Nations often found itself crippled by a divided Security Council, and international criminal law lost much of its post war momentum.[29]

Evidence suggests that Asia's central global players—the US and China—were anxious to maintain the political viability of the Khmer Rouge to destabilize the country, rather than deal with a Vietnamese-backed Cambodian government. Between 1979 and 1991, the Cambodian government was considered illegal, a view that made it almost impossible for the UN to provide humanitarian relief.[30] To complicate matters further, the Western powers imposed an embargo on Cambodia in 1983.[31]

The Khmer Rouge was formally shut out of domestic politics. Nonetheless, it remained active as a regional power supported by foreign countries. The Khmer Rouge's crimes against humanity were subordinated to a blind Cold War discipline. The East–West conflict showed its inhumane side in this region of the globe, subordinating the wellbeing of the civilian population. Hegemonic strategies were considered more important in geopolitical calculations than urgently needed humanitarian aid. This affected both spheres of power. The Khmer Rouge represented the side of the devil incarnate; to others, they were anti-Soviet freedom fighters.[32] It is impossible to avoid the conclusion that the Khmer Rouge was still a foreign political presence to be reckoned with, since, as late as 1993, Cambodia's UN delegate was considered the representative of the "Coalition Government of Democratic Kampuchea" (CGDK), which was newly established by the Khmer Rouge.[33] According to Scott Luftglass:

> During the entire period of its rule the Khmer Rouge occupied the Cambodian seat in the UN, without even a single Western country voting against its retention. Perhaps more alarmingly, no country has invoked the Genocide Convention on behalf of the victims, brought a claim against Cambodia before the International Court of Justice, or extradited Khmer Rouge leaders for trial via universal jurisdiction.[34]

There was no abatement of tension in Cambodian domestic or foreign politics during this period. Cambodia was trapped in an international clash of conflict-laden geopolitics. Efforts to study Cambodia's history between 1975 and 1979 within the framework of transitional justice were neglected because of persistent conflict and the expansion of the international involvement in the civil war. Worldwide standards for punishing crimes against humanity, genocide, and war crimes were incompatible with the doctrines of the Cold War. To a large extent, the victims of organized state criminality perished in the midst of Cold War politics. Regardless, shortly after the end of the Khmer Rouge period, the new government instituted measures which could be characterized as transitional justice.

With the passage of Decree Law No. 1 on 15 July 1979 (see Table 1), only a half year after the fall of Pol Pot, the government established the basis for trials of representative figures from the Khmer Rouge regime.[35] Pol Pot and Ieng Sary (*in absentia*) were charged with genocide against the Cambodian population before a People's Revolutionary Tribunal.[36] It was the second time in the history of international criminal law (after the trial against Eichmann in Jerusalem)[37] that genocide was adjudicated by a court. William Schabas summarizes the discussion about the element of the offense as follows:

> Pol Pot and Ieng Sary were convicted by the Cambodian tribunal not for genocide as it is defined in the 1948 Convention on the Prevention and Punishment of the Crime of Genocide, but under a totally idiosyncratic definition closer in substance to what we call "crimes against humanity." According to Article 1 of the "Decree Law No. 1" . . . establishing the tribunal, it was to have jurisdiction over "the acts of genocide committed by the Pol Pot–Ieng Sary clique . . . The 1979 proceedings in Phnom Penh make perfunctory mention of the Convention, but the substance of the indictment does not even purport to demonstrate that genocide—as defined in the Convention—was committed. Indeed, in recent years it has become rather common to discard the argument that the mass killing of Khmers by Pol Pot's supporters constituted genocide . . . Even Professor John Quigley . . . describes the thesis that genocide was committed against the Khmers themselves as only a "possible rationale" for applying the Convention, explaining almost apologetically that his 1979 expert opinion to the Phnom Penh tribunal that genocide had been committed was based on "what I knew at the time . . ."[38]

The conviction of Ieng Sary *in absentia* was criticized by the international community, as was the procedural framework of the trial, which some suggested was similar to a show trial.[39] Sidney Jones, Executive Director of the Asia Division of Human

TABLE 1 Decree Law No. 1

The People's Revolutionary Council of Kampuchea, in light of the tasks of the People's Revolutionary Council of Kampuchea as stated in the Declaration of January 8, 1979 . . .

Article 1
To set up a People's Revolutionary Tribunal at Phnom Penh to try the acts of genocide committed by the Pol Pot–Ieng Sary clique, namely, planned massacres of groups of innocent people; expulsion of inhabitants of cities and villages in order to concentrate them and force them to do hard labor in conditions leading to their physical and mental destruction; wiping out religion; destroying political, cultural and social structures and family and social relations.

Rights Watch, said in 1999: "Any tribunal should be held under strict U.N. control [. . .] The Cambodian people deserve justice, not a show trial. Cambodia has already had one of those, after the Khmer Rouge fell from power in 1979."[40] That only two Khmer Rouge leaders had to answer for their crimes before the court is the strongest argument against its legitimacy. Certainly, important war crimes trials should always prosecute the leading officials of a regime, but reducing the scope of prosecution to only two persons appears even today overly minimal.

The criticism that the trials against Pol Pot and Ieng Sary were not conducted according to principles consistent with the rule of law, which, among other things, require there to be adequate international representatives on hand, applies only conditionally. Cambodia had invited more than 24 international observers to the trial. But since most of these observers failed to appear—meaning that Cambodia was offered little or no assistance with the trial—then the results cannot fairly be laid solely at Cambodia's feet.[41]

In the ensuing years, there were further transitional justice initiatives in Cambodia (see Figure 2). A Commission for the Analysis of Khmer Rouge Crimes was created— without apparent success—in 1982.[42] Four years later (1986/1987), the government of Hun Sen proposed an initiative for Peace and Reconciliation to Cambodian exiles to persuade them to return to their homeland. Simultaneously, Khmer Rouge soldiers were offered an amnesty in exchange for laying down their weapons.[43]

The peace treaty of 1991 marked the first clear break in the violence and terror that had engulfed Cambodia for decades. It included a ceasefire and, above all, a general demobilization. With the help of the UN, the government organized the first democratic elections in several decades and a constituent assembly was prepared. Voter turnout was unexpectedly high (90%), which was a clear signal that Cambodians were looking for a new social orientation. Most of the votes were cast for the royal party Front Uni National pour un Cambodge Indépendant, Neutre, Pacifique et Coopératif (FUNCIPEC), which received 45.5% of the vote.[44] The coalition of the Cambodian People's Revolutionary Party that had governed since 1979, and the Cambodian People's Party, which had been in power since 1991, was in second place with 38% of the vote. The coalition parties discredited themselves primarily through uncoordinated and corruptly executed attempts economically to liberalize the country. Following the collapse of the USSR, which had supplied the Cambodian government with substantial commercial support, withdrawal of its support meant that Cambodia drifted toward the brink of financial ruin. The currency collapsed and the rising cost of living led to growing social tensions. The patent technical incompetence of leading politicians, the lack of strategic planning, a thickly woven net of "amigo networks" or "rope teams" that worked at cross purposes with each other, and a distinctive abuse of authority increasingly paralyzed the already ponderous machinery of state. In the meantime, the Kampuchean People's Party, in search of a new identity, changed its name shortly before the election to the Cambodian People's Party (CPP). The CPP, however, could not wrench itself free from the undertow of its past.[45]

PEOPLE'S REVOLUTIONARY TRIBUNAL HELD IN PHNOM PENH
FOR THE TRIAL OF THE GENOCIDE CRIME OF THE
POL POT-IENG SARY CLIQUE

August 1979

PEOPLE'S REPUBLIC OF KAMPUCHEA
Independence Peace Happiness

JUDGEMENT OF THE REVOLUTIONARY PEOPLE'S TRIBUNAL
HELD IN PHNOM PENH FROM 15 TO 19 AUGUST 1979

THE REVOLUTIONARY PEOPLE'S TRIBUNAL

Created by Decree-Law No. 1, dated 15 July 1979, of the Revolutionary People's
Council of Kampuchea, held its public sittings at the capital city of Phnom Penh
from 15 to 19 August 1979. It is composed of:

Mr. Keo Chanda   President of the Revolutionary
                                   People's Tribunal, Chairman of the
                                   Council of Judges.

Messrs. Chhour Leang Hourt   People's Assessor
        Pen Navuth   "
Mrs. Chea Samy   "
Messrs. Hoa Savatha   "
        Month Savocun   "
        Nouch Than   "
Mrs. Chnouh Chhim   "
Messrs. Kim Kun   "
        Kim Kameth   "
        Luk Sarat   "

The court sessions have taken place

In the presence of Messrs. Mat Ly, Prosecutor, acting as public Minister at the
Tribunal, and Lun Nay

With a secretariat composed of Messrs. Houl Sans Ol and Duh Chandara

For the purpose of pronouncing first and last instance verdicts against:

    1. Pol Pot alias Saloth Sar, born in 1925 at Phum Prek Seau, Kompong Thom
province, with secondary school education, former Prime Minister of the overthrown
Democratic Kampuchea, married to Khieu Ponnary, now in hiding and the object of a
warrant of arrest;

                                                                       /...

FIGURE 2 Judgment: People's Revolutionary Tribunal against Pol Pot and Ieng Sary (Phnom Penh, 1979). *Source*: International Committee of the Red Cross (<http://www.icrc.org/ihl-nat.nsf/39a82e2ca42b52974125673e00508144/1661ad6f34fa77a6c125708b004c2710/$FILE/Case%20Law%20-%20Pol%20Pot%20-%20Cambodia.pdf>; accessed March 2009).

In spite of their defeat in the election, the old elite still controlled political, administrative, and financial power. Without their participation in the government, Cambodia would have likely been ungovernable. Another civil war loomed in the provinces along the border with Vietnam. Prolonged international pressure and intensive diplomatic efforts of the royal house produced a breakthrough in 1993: a national transitional government, composed equally of all four represented in the new parliament, laid the cornerstone for a new constitution. Cambodia became a constitutional monarchy. With strong international support, the new government began to reorganize the infrastructure of the country. However, the missing link between the hope for a basically peaceful society and the realistic political measures necessary to achieve it—a common founding myth, a collective potential for meaning and identity creation—could not be found. Political infighting broke out again, culminating in a two-day struggle in July 1997 between the CPP and FUNCIPEC that resembled a civil war. FUNCIPEC, at one time the strongest parliamentary group, was militarily shattered and the minister president, Prince Ranariddh, politically marginalized. The CPP emerged as the most powerful group in Cambodia. Sympathetic to Vietnam and widely believed to have already been defeated, both political parties no longer faced domestic political opponents; they were thus in a position to control the parliamentary election in 1998.[46]

In the midst of all this, the Khmer Rouge stoked the fires of another conflict. Although the turmoil around Pol Pot had subsided, the guerrilla army of the Khmer Rouge terrorized the country with attacks until 1996. Its primary aim was to weaken the government and intimidate international actors. It murdered civilians and UN peacekeepers who assisted with the reconstruction of the country. The armed attacks of the Khmer Rouge ended, in effect, with the death of Pol Pot on 15 April 1998. Toward the end of that year, the last of the guerrilla units laid down their weapons, and the remaining members of their leadership corps turned themselves in to the authorities.[47]

We can tentatively conclude that the social preconditions for a far-reaching, criminal legal concept based on transitional justice were nonexistent until 1998, or 20 years after the end of the Pol Pot regime. In order to achieve such preconditions, the parties of the first government of a free Cambodia under UN observation would have had to adopt a collective policy of détente. We ought not lose sight of the role played by the diplomatically incendiary relations of Thailand, China, and Singapore with the Khmer Rouge well into the 1990s. These connections reached into the highest circles of the Phnom Penh government until the end of the decade.

The Path to Justice

By 1998, these events had created the basis for a new tribunal to judge the crimes of the Pol Pot Regime. The Khmer Rouge Tribunal, the Extraordinary Chambers in the Courts of Cambodia (ECCC), is the result of decades-long, complex negotiations between the UN and the Cambodian government. Craig Etcheson rightly points out:

> The many unique aspects of the Khmer Rouge Tribunal—its unusual mix of local and international staff at every level, including co-prosecutors and co-investigating judges, and a majority of Cambodian judges, as well as its "supermajority" decision-making mechanism—can only be understood through its political history.[48]

In 1998, national and international efforts were initiated to create a tribunal to punish the crimes of the Khmer Rouge. Without question, the altered international political landscape played a decisive role here. The conflict in the Balkans and the Rwandan genocide had energized international criminal law. Figuratively, efforts were again made to rediscover a path abandoned at the end of World War II—i.e. the development of a common, worldwide strategy to punish violations of international humanitarian law beyond the reach of purely national law.[49]

The agreement concerning a Khmer Rouge Tribunal was the result of a process that stretched over several decades. In the course of dogged negotiations, efforts were repeatedly made to scuttle the entire project. The difficult situation was complicated by the UN's moderate stance. We can declare with some certainty that—until the end of 1999—UN members arrogantly opposed participation of Cambodian judges because they were considered too corrupt and politicized. No mention was made of the fact that there were hardly any educated jurists left in the country,[50] a situation similar to the statement in Shakespeare's *Henry VI*, Part II, 4.2—"The first thing we do, let's kill all the lawyers"—Pol Pot had eliminated all of the country's elite, and had most of the academics murdered.[51]

The dispute over this matter became a "test case for America's doctrine of limited national sovereignty."[52] Like many other Third World countries, Cambodia rejected the idea that its sovereignty was dependent on its human rights record. An angry Prime Minister Hun Sen reminded the UN and the US that both had recognized Pol Pot's phantom state—Democratic Kampuchea—12 years after its disappearance, simply to justify their castigation of socialist Vietnam as an aggressor, a country whose intervention in 1979 had ended the mass murders. These are harsh words, but they aptly describe the difficult situation in crisis-wracked Cambodia. It is all the more astounding that ultimately a compromise was reached. In 2000, nearly all political obstacles to a tribunal appeared to have been surmounted. The UN agreed to officially support the proceedings only after its experts had examined an official translation of the draft law creating the tribunal. The central point of contention in the 48 article basic laws was the idea of prosecuting *the high ranking leaders* of the Khmer Rouge, as well as persons who bore special responsibility for the cruelties.[53]

Until 2000, only two of the worst criminals were behind bars. The first was Oung Choeun, alias Ta Mok, the former head of the Southwest Zone of Democratic Kampuchea and later successor to Pol Pot as "Brother No. 1." He was responsible for the radical party purges that cost tens of thousands of lives. In March 1998, the "butcher," as he was called—a man who had gone from being a Buddhist monk to a Maoist mass murderer—crossed over the border from Thailand accompanied by four of his loyalists and turned himself into the authorities.[54] The second was Kaing Kien or Duch, the former commandant of the Tuol Sleng torture and extermination camp (S-21) in Phnom Penh. He is the only defendant who has so far expressed any regret for his actions. After the retreat of Vietnamese troops in 1989, Duch worked undetected for the UN, and converted to Christianity.[55]

Two months before Ta Mok's arrest, two of the last paladins of Pol Pot, Khieu Samphan, alias "Hern," and Nuon Chea, "the head ideologue," gave themselves up. In Phnom Penh, Hun Sen, who can be credited with ending the internecine guerrilla war, received them like state guests: "We should find a deep hole in which to bury the past," he announced, "and enter the 21st century with the slate wiped clean."[56] He then sent the erstwhile businessman Khieu, who had received his doctorate from the Paris Sorbonne and later served as secretary of the infamous "Office 870," and Nuon Chea to the town of Pailin on the Thai border. They enjoyed a kind of autonomy in this region. These one-time puritanical "revolutionaries" bent on enforcing a macabre "utopia" without money or cities now operated a gambling casino, restaurants, hotels, and trafficked in emeralds and exotic wood.[57]

By 1998/1999, Hun Sen appeared to have had a change of heart about completely burying the past. In his view, an international tribunal could indict Khieu Samphan and Nuon Chea, but he feared massive unrest if Ieng Sary, Pol Pot's friend during his student days in Paris, was placed in the prisoners' dock. In 1979, Ieng Sary was tried and sentenced to death *in absentia* by a People's Court in Phnom Penh for genocide; in 1997—King Sihanouk pardoned him, along with his 1,000 guerrilla fighters, after they had laid down their weapons.

> Cambodians often refer to the Democratic Kampuchea regime, which was responsible for the deaths of nearly a quarter of the population between 1975 and 1979, as the "Pol Pot–Ieng Sary clique." Although few people knew the identities of the secretive leaders of Democratic Kampuchea until after the regime fell, Ieng Sary's was known by the mid-1970s. By placing his name next to Pol Pot's (the two were also brothers-in-law), Cambodians clearly recognize him as one of the masterminds of the genocide.[58]

Ieng Sary, now infirm, still held enough influence among demobilized Khmer Rouge soldiers successfully to follow through with repeated threats to rekindle the war were he not left in peace.[59]

At the end of 1999, progress was made in the protracted negotiations about a Khmer Rouge Tribunal. Everything turned on the question of whether the court would be modeled on the ad hoc tribunals for the former Yugoslavia and Rwanda, or on a hybrid version like that created for East Timor or Sierra Leone. After the arrest in 1999 of leading figures in the Khmer Rouge, no further delay was brooked. At the end of 1999, negotiations entered their—for the time being—final phase. A common proposal for a tribunal was within their grasp. The UN presented a memorandum consisting of 12 points that envisaged a hybrid tribunal. The UN Security Council supported the breakthrough and circulated it through its diplomatic channels. At the same time, the Cambodian government developed its own concept.[60]

> In August 1999, both parties[61] circulated hybrid,[62] but incompatible, proposals. Hun Sen supported a national court with external financing, supported by a small staff of international personal. The UN also accepted a mechanism set up under Cambodian Law, but proposed a Nuremberg-style joint trial of all suspects together, under which proceedings would be dominated by a majority of international personal.[63]

This time, both sides drew closer and agreed on a Memorandum of Understanding (see Table 2).[64] After negotiations that had lasted more than a year, the UN was taken by surprise, because the Cambodian government brought its own set of rules into the national parliamentary debate. These rules consisted of a modified version of the Memorandum of Understanding, which the Cambodians believed would give them greater influence over the shape of the future tribunal (i.e. composition of the court, application of domestic law). At the beginning of 2001, the Law on the Extraordinary Chambers made it through the Cambodian legislature and on 10 August 2001 it was signed by King Sihanouk. Shocked that the Cambodians had not consulted with it, the UN under Kofi Annan suspended negotiations until the beginning of 2002.[65]

In January 2003, new talks failed because the UN and the Cambodian government could not agree on the composition of the court. International pressure helped move the negotiations along, and this time they succeeded. In March 2003 an agreement was reached. At the same time, the UN General Assembly endorsed the results of these talks. Finally, on 6 June 2003, the "Agreement between the UN and the Royal Government of Cambodia concerning the Prosecution under Cambodian Law of Crimes committed during the Period of Democratic Kampuchea" was signed as a bilateral treaty. The UN Legal Counsel, Hans Corell, said: "With this step, the quest of the Cambodian people for justice, national reconciliation, stability, peace and security is brought closer to realization."[66]

The first hurdle was surmounted, though many months passed before the statute finally came into effect. The Cambodian government waited until 19 October 2004 to ratify the agreement, and it reached the UN in November 2004. Kofi Annan, however, because of insufficient financial backing for the tribunal, refrained from publicizing the operative starting date of the agreement, and the struggle over the Khmer Rouge Tribunals raged on. The tribunal's financing proved to be the most formidable obstacle. The Cambodians promised to allocate $13.3 million for the tribunal if the UN

TABLE 2 Tribunal Memorandum of Understanding between the United Nations and the Royal Government of Cambodia

---

Article 8

Crimes falling within the jurisdiction of the chambers

The subject-matter jurisdiction of the chambers shall include the crime of genocide, crimes against humanity and war crimes as defined in international instruments, and such other crimes as defined in the Law on the Establishment of Extraordinary Chambers.

. . .

Article 28

Entry into force

The present Memorandum of Understanding shall enter into force on the day after both parties have notified each other in writing that the legal requirements for entry into force have been complied with.

---

appropriated $43 million for it. Several countries, including the US and Japan, worked through diplomatic channels to come up with the money to fund the trial. All of these efforts bore fruit on 29 April 2005 when the agreement was implemented.[67] Since that time, experts on international law have argued about how Cambodia would transform the agreement into national law, and whether international law potentially violated Cambodian law.[68]

In 2006, the court began its work in a newly constructed military complex several kilometers outside Phnom Penh in the midst of scandals and difficulties that nearly scuttled the tribunal on several occasions. The first defendant, Duch, the former warden of S-21, did not make an appearance in court. The main proceedings against him and other leading figures still alive were to begin in the spring of 2008. The reality, however, was different. Because of procedural complications, Duch's trial did not begin until 17 February 2009. Further indictments are not yet in the offing. Currently, five accused persons are in preventive custody:

Case 1:

- Kang Keck Iev, alias Duch (chief of S-21 prison) (indicted 17 February 2009)[69] Charges of crimes against humanity and grave breaches of the Geneva Conventions of 1949, in addition to the offenses of homicide and torture under Cambodian criminal law. "Following judicial investigations, on 8 August last year, the ECCC's Office of the Co-Investigating Judges issued an indictment against the accused in relation to alleged offences committed in S-21, a security centre also known as Toul Sleng, between 1975 and 1979. Following resolution of an appeal against the indictment, the ECCC's Pre-Trial Chamber remitted the case for trial on 5 December 2008."[70]

Case 2:

- Nuon Chea (member of the Politburo)
- Ieng Sary (member of the Politburo)
- Khieu Samphan (member of the Politburo)
- Ieng Thirith (former social minister)
  Investigations of the four defendants are still ongoing. They are charged with having organized and implemented collective forced evacuations, mass killings, forced labor, torture, arbitrary arrests, and enslavement. The charges of genocide of Buddhist monks, Cham Muslims, and Vietnamese are a component of the Introductory Submission; however, these charges were not included by the co-investigating judges in their arrest warrants. Investigations of sexual violence against women were wholly lacking, although evidence of gender-based violence during the Khmer Rouge regime in the form of war crimes, crimes against humanity, and genocide was available.[71]

Extraordinarily contentious discussion has continued within the confines of the tribunal. The international members of the tribunal favor further investigations of potential defendants. From all appearances, it would seem that the Cambodian court members seek to restrain such efforts.

> The Cambodian, UN and American negotiators never limited the pool of suspects to be charged and brought to trial to five or six individuals, although it was no secret that some Cambodian officials desired a small number, which would exclude current government and military officials . . . In my own many long negotiations with Cambodian and UN authorities, negotiators typically spoke of up to 15 or so individuals ultimately being prosecuted . . . US negotiators at times spoke of 20 to 30 potential defendants.[72]

Structure and Transitional Justice Tasks of the ECCC

What transitional justice approaches are characteristic of the ECCC, and what are the legal bases for the trials? First, we are concerned here with a Cambodian court—that is, chiefly a model of internal transitional justice, a special feature to which the Cambodian government from the very beginning attached the highest priority. Nonetheless, it is accompanied by an international counterpart. Thus, an international court is not strictly involved—a pioneering concept. In contrast to other post-conflict scenarios (such as after World War II, Yugoslavia, and Rwanda), geopolitical conditions have been tilted in favor of national actors. From a strategic view, the government of Hun Sen could prevail against the UN. Only a politically stable state could negotiate such an approach. This may account for why the first negotiations concerning an internationally consequential tribunal lasted until 1998.

In the years following the Paris Peace Treaty of 1991, the domestic political situation seemed too unpredictable to the CPP and the royalists to allow possibilities for influencing future trials. This view, held primarily by the CPP, is fully understandable. Neither the UN nor individual states could intervene directly in Cambodia to install a tribunal to punish Khmer Rouge crimes. There was also no legal reason why the UN Security Council itself, as in the Balkan conflict or Rwanda, could have intervened. This notwithstanding, Cambodian politicians consciously pursued their particular interests. The *New York Times* wrote: "The Cambodian government, critics say, is trying to limit the scope of the trials for its own political reasons, a limit that the critics say would compromise justice and could discredit the entire process."[73]

Does this criticism really impugn transitional justice? To begin with, who defines the limits: is it the world community, which, in a kind of "world law," produces a catalogue of sanctions? Reference to "its own political reasons" is fundamentally lapidary, because each actor has its own political interests and seeks as far as possible to implement them. However, the comments of the *New York Times* highlights the relevant issue: that is, the transnationalization of law versus national legal norms.[74]

We are dealing here primarily with international legal standards that acquire their validity independent of national state interests. In the course of a historical process of transformation, international criminal law increasingly developed into an objective legal order, the validity of which ceased to hinge on the consent of national actors. Rather, it acquired legislative character and is also binding for such states (and other actors) that have not consented to the establishment of certain norms protective of community interests or that simply represent their own interests. Legitimation of such law reposes on its origins in public discourse within international forums (the UN General Assembly, conferences). In order to legitimate international law, however, the participation and collaboration of non-state actors in public discourse about the law to be applied is essential.

Basic complementary constitutional norms are required to guarantee the necessary compliance with this legal order, specifically the fundamental principles of a "rule of law" won through centuries of arduous struggle. The "world law" arising from this conjuncture is characterized by a cooperative, centralized enforcement of law (as seen in the example of the Statute of Rome, which established the International Criminal Court in July 2002[75]). It has strengthened international jurisdiction by creating an international court and applies strategies—on the international side—which seek to promote adherence to law through inducements and effective control of compliance in concert with NGOs. The growing enforcement of adherence to law directly affects the educative character of the legal order based on "world law" for both individuals and victims caught up in conflict.

We have come full circle with the situation in Cambodia. Two distinct aspects are involved: the first deals with the further development of general international criminal law norms independent of the concrete circumstances to which they are connected. This, as already noted, falls within the category of "world law." The critique cited above is aimed primarily at this level. The second aspect confronts us with a situation in which normative international law (the Rome Statute) is inapplicable to the Cambodian case, insofar as the ICC only has jurisdiction for situations that occurred after July 2002. The atrocities of the Khmer Rouge clearly lie outside this timeframe. Nonetheless, the legal bases of the Khmer Rouge Tribunal have been constructed in parallel with discourse about the Rome Statute. The legal bases of the Khmer Rouge Tribunal combine national law and international standards in a unique *mélange*, the product of a complex struggle among Cambodian politicians over state sovereignty. Clearly, financial concerns have also played a considerable role. Both the tribunal and NGOs have received immense sums of money from international donors.

From the perspective of international law, the ECCC may be classified as a hybrid tribunal because, in its approach to legal substance and procedure, it applies both national and international law. In other words, the tribunal is an internationalized domestic tribunal.[76] It is also an independent, functional unit, consisting of a trial court, prosecutors, and an administrative superstructure—although here, in contrast to the ad hoc tribunals (e.g. former Yugoslavia and Rwanda), the individual departments consist of national and international authorities. Five organs form the ECCC, as shown in Figure 3.

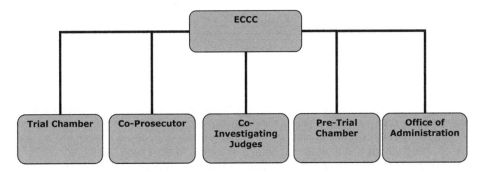

FIGURE 3 The five organs of the ECCC.

The Trial Chamber includes a Supreme Court that functions as an appellate body. Both defendants and civil parties enjoy the right of appeal. The Supreme Trial Chamber may not remand cases to the Trial Chamber—as is customary, for example, in German law—but must itself arrive at a decision. From the beginning, the composition of the court was a problem. The UN and the Cambodian government have argued since 2001 over this issue. The compromise was to appoint five judges to the Trial Chamber. Three judges would be Cambodian nationals and two international judges. The Supreme Court has seven judges, including three international judges. One unique feature of both chambers is the supermajority.[77] This means that the three indigenous judges must receive an additional vote in all decisions. The same applies to the Supreme Court. In effect, this amounts to a right of veto by one of the non-Cambodian judges, and means that without the consent of one of the international judges, no verdict can be reached.[78] Criticisms have also been leveled at the supermajority rule in cases in which, at both the trial and appellate court levels, the Cambodian and international judges produce diametrically opposite votes. In such cases, no legally valid verdict could be issued.

The ECCC has jurisdiction for crimes and grave offenses under (1) Cambodian domestic criminal law, (2) international humanitarian law, (3) international customary law, and (4) international conventions (like the Genocide Convention). These include:

1. *Genocide.* Article 4 of the ECCC Statute (see Table 3) closely follows the 1948 Convention on Genocide. The definition holds that, for an offense to be considered genocide, it must be perpetrated on members of a national, ethnic, religious, or racially defined group, with the intention of wholly or partially destroying it. Individual acts that meet this definition are killing members of the group, causing them severe bodily harm, inflicting on them living conditions designed to effect their physical destruction as a whole or in part, imposition of measures oriented to prevent births within the group as well as violent transfer of children from the group to another. Some forms of genocide do not fall within the jurisdiction of the Khmer Rouge Tribunal, e.g. incitement to genocide (as a form of complicity). There are some

TABLE 3 Article 4

The Extraordinary Chambers shall have the power to bring to trial all Suspects who committed the crimes of genocide as defined in the Convention on the Prevention and Punishment of the Crime of Genocide of 1948, and which were committed during the period from 17 April 1975 to 6 January 1979.

The acts of genocide, which have no statute of limitations, mean any acts committed with the intent to destroy, in whole or in part, a national, ethnical, racial or religious group, such as:

- killing members of the group;
- causing serious bodily or mental harm to members of the group;
- deliberately inflicting on the group conditions of life calculated to bring about its physical destruction in whole or in part;
- imposing measures intended to prevent births within the group;
- forcibly transferring children from one group to another group.

The following acts shall be punishable under this Article:

- attempts to commit acts of genocide;
- conspiracy to commit acts of genocide;
- participation in acts of genocide.

Source: Cambodian government (homepage of the Cambodian government. See <http://www.cambodia.gov.kh/krt/pdfs/KR%20Law%20as%20promulgated%20(Eng%20trans%206%20Sept%202001.pdf)>; accessed March 2009).

who would like to see all the atrocities of the Khmer Rouge defined as genocide. That would mean classifying as genocide the Pol Pot regime's destruction of its own population.[79]

Such an interpretation is beset with significant juridical problems because it is at best problematic to identify an independent group in this case. While the Khmer Rouge murdered entire segments of its population, it is far from clear whether such atrocities fall within the definition of a "group" set forth in the Genocide Convention. However, the Khmer Rouge indisputably wanted to exterminate the Cham and the Chinese, as well as the Vietnamese minority. The crime of genocide can in any case not be extended to all forms of organized mass murder. The requirement of a determinable group is essential to the very definition of genocide. At the same time, other criteria of evaluation can be affirmed beyond those that have thus far been recognized. For example, a group definition could be developed into a material component from the perspective of the prosecutors. In this case, a group would be deemed to exist if it is considered as such by the prosecutors, independently of whether the group would characterize itself (or would be characterized) in this manner. Translating such a notional model into practice would, however, signify a new definition of the Genocide Convention in its current form.[80]

To date, and with good reason, the following principle applies: the genocidal intent has to be to "destroy" a group. That means physically or biologically to destroy the group (or part of it), not just to humiliate or even to make the group suffer physically, but to wipe it off the face of the earth.[81] We may, however, ask whether every mass murder must be regarded as genocide or whether such violations of international humanitarian law may be better and more correctly described as crimes against humanity.

2. *Crimes against Humanity*. The definition of Crimes against Humanity set forth in Article 5 of the ECCC Statute (see Table 4) is intimately related to that of the Rwanda Tribunal. In contrast to the Rome Statute the Cambodian variant rejects as a criminal act the compulsory "disappearance" of persons. To name but a few of the particular elements of the offense under Article 5: (a) the absence of an armed conflict; (b) widespread or systematic attack on a civil population; and (c) discriminatory intent.

3. *War Crimes*. Generally speaking, the atrocities committed by the Khmer Rouge targeted the Cambodian population. However, there were also conflicts with the neighboring states of Vietnam, Laos, and Thailand. For example, prompted by Khmer Rouge incursions into Vietnamese territory in 1978, Vietnam too invaded Cambodia on 7 January 1979. Hence, war crimes might well be charged (see Table 5).

4. *Crimes According to Domestic Law (Article 7)* (see Table 6). This category encompasses in particular manslaughter, torture, and religious persecution.

Who can be charged before the Khmer Rouge Tribunal? Only *senior leaders* and *persons who were most responsible*. Accordingly, former political leaders fall within the personal jurisdiction of the tribunal, as do persons most responsible for the crimes. However, the statute lacks a precise definition. "Only the court can decide who were the senior leaders or the ones most responsible for the crimes committed

TABLE 4 Article 5

The Extraordinary Chambers shall have the power to bring to trial all Suspects who committed crimes against humanity during the period 17 April 1975 to 6 January 1979. Crimes against humanity, which have no statute of limitations, are any acts committed as part of a widespread or systematic attack directed against any civilian population, on national, political, ethnical, racial or religious grounds, such as:

- murder;
- extermination;
- enslavement;
- deportation;
- imprisonment;
- torture;
- rape;
- persecutions on political, racial, and religious grounds;
- other inhumane acts.

Source: Cambodian government.

TABLE 5 Article 6

The Extraordinary Chambers shall have the power to bring to trial all Suspects who committed or ordered the commission of grave breaches of the Geneva Conventions of 12 August 1949, such as the following acts against persons or property protected under provisions of these Conventions, and which were committed during the period 17 April 1975 to 6 January 1979:

- willful killing;
- torture or inhumane treatment;
- willfully causing great suffering or serious injury to body or health;
- destruction and serious damage to property, not justified by military necessity and carried out unlawfully and wantonly;
- compelling a prisoner of war or a civilian to serve in the forces of a hostile power;
- willfully depriving a prisoner of war or civilian the rights of fair and regular trial;
- unlawful deportation or transfer or unlawful confinement of a civilian;
- taking civilians as hostages.

Source: Cambodian government.

TABLE 6 Article 7

The Extraordinary Chambers shall have the power to bring to trial all Suspects most responsible for the destruction of cultural property during armed conflict pursuant to the 1954 Hague Convention for Protection of Cultural Property in the Event of Armed Conflict, and which were committed during the period from 17 April 1975 to 6 January 1979.

Source: Cambodian government.

during Democratic Kampuchea."[82] A limitation of the group of persons to be charged is customary in both international and internationalized tribunals.[83] The circle of persons can be potentially expanded to include all individuals participating in such crimes.[84] The inclusion of a larger group of defendants would not be practicable within the scope of the ECCC if it is considered politically desirable to preserve national jurisdiction.[85]

Victim Participation and the ECCC

A new weapon in the ECCC's international criminal law arsenal was victim participation (as, for example, civil parties, see below) and the outreach work of the court.[86] In many cities and regions of the country, informational meetings were held to inform the population of the ECCC's work. Its mode of operation and definition of its tasks were presented with easily understandable posters.

Like the French legal system, victims are allowed to file a subsidiary charge. A subdivision of the court has been established to handle such charges—the so-called

Victim's Unit. Nevertheless, their legal representation is not regulated by the ECCC Statute, with the exception of the protective measure (Article 23) and the possibility of lodging an appeal of the verdict (Articles 36 and 37). Consequently, the Cambodian Code of Criminal Procedure (CPC) applies, which first became operative in its current form in August 2007.[87] It is the authoritative legal basis for the ECCC and regulates the rights of the victims and their opportunity to appear in court as civil parties. "In the public hearing of the appeal on the pre-trial detention of Nuon Chea on 4 February 2008, victims of the Khmer Rouge regime participated for the first time as civil parties in the proceedings of the ECCC, legally represented by their lawyers."[88]

It is noteworthy that civil parties have the same rights as the prosecutor and defense.[89]

> The Internal Rules of the ECCC provide for the participation of victims of the Khmer Rouge regime in the proceedings as civil parties. They allow victims to play an active role in the trials, including all procedural rights. The rights of Civil Parties are comparable to those of the accused, and include the rights to participate in the investigation, to be represented by a lawyer, to call witnesses and question the accused at trial, and to claim reparations for the harm they suffered.[90]

Along with victim participation in the trials, the "Internal Rules" prepared by the Rules and Procedure Plenary Committee became operational in June 2007.[91] Next to the CPC, they form the basis of the court's daily work. The scope of and possibilities for victim participation in the Khmer Rouge Tribunal are unique in international criminal law:[92]

> The participation of legal representatives of victims of the Khmer Rouge crimes in the ECCC proceedings is considered to be a historic day in international criminal law. To date, no international or hybrid tribunal mandated to investigate war crimes, crimes against humanity or genocide has involved victims as civil parties, giving them full procedural rights.[93]

This was confirmed in various decisions of the court. In March 2008, for example, the Pre-Trial Chamber issued a decision in principle concerning the legal framework of civil parties, granting them complete rights of participation in hearings to consider appeals of arrest warrants.[94]

Civil parties have to be registered with the Victims Unit, which reviews the applications (Victim Participation Forms, or VPFs) before forwarding them to the tribunal. Subsidiary complaints can only be filed by those who are affected by the ongoing investigations as victims. Victims can, of course, participate in the court proceedings as witnesses or report potential perpetrators. In order better to clarify the Internal Rules, the ECCC issued a Practice Directive on Victim Participation enabling victims to: (1) volunteer to be witnesses (by giving testimony about crimes suffered or witnessed); (2) file complaints (by providing the Prosecutors with factual information to aid their case in chief); and (3) apply to become civil parties (by applying to join the proceedings as a party and to claim collective or moral reparation).[95]

On 26–27 November 2008, NGOs and the ECCC Victims Unit in Phnom Penh organized a conference, entitled "Reparations for Victims of the Khmer Rouge Regime," to determine the kinds of reparations that would be given to the victims. During the conference, victims expressed their ideas about reparations. Some emphasized support services for victims such as construction of mental health institutions. A special focus was on court-ordered reparations. According to the Internal Rules, civil parties can be awarded collective and moral reparations (as indicated on VPFs).

> These types of reparations were then discussed within a group from the perspectives of Cambodian youth, Buddhism, gender and the victims' need for trauma healing. According to Youth for Peace (YfP), reparations should address the fundamental need of Cambodian youth to learn about the Khmer Rouge regime … Chounni Synan, YfP Program Officer, therefore suggested creating "safe spaces" for discussions and integrating the history of Democratic Kampuchea within the school curriculum.[96]

Another group tackled the challenge of how best to involve victims in the process of determining reparations. "A third group addressed the technical, legal, financial, and advocacy needs for a successful reparations program going beyond ECCC-ordered reparations."[97]

Unfortunately, by the time this conference was held, the deadline for lodging a claim in the Duch case had passed:

> The Trial Chamber has announced that the Initial Hearing in Case 1 will begin on 17 February 2009. This means that persons who suffered harm as a result of the crimes allegedly committed by Kaing Guek Eav alias Duch at Office S-21 (Tuol Sleng), Office S-24 (Prey Sar) and Choeung Ek should submit their Civil Party applications to the Victims Unit before 4:00 PM on Monday 2 February 2009. Any Civil Party application that is submitted after the deadline will not be considered by the judges of the Trial Chamber. In Case 2, the deadline for the submission of Civil Party applications has not been determined yet. According to the Internal Rules of the ECCC, Civil Party applications must be filed ten working days before the initial hearing.[98]

By the end of 2008, 2,856 VPFs had been submitted.[99] Working in concert with the court, NGOs helped to organize the collection of the forms. In connection with the so-called "victim's participation projects," the Documentation Center of Cambodia (DC-Cam) completed 1,419 VPFs by 1 October 2008 (see Table 7). DC-Cam defines its purpose on his website as "assist[ing] survivors in learning about their participation rights and helping them to register with the ECCC Victims Unit. DC-Cam will not provide legal representation or ongoing assistance throughout the proceedings."[100] However, only a fraction of these 1,419 VPFs appeared as joint plaintiffs—until January 2009 a grand total of 28 for all relevant cases.[101] The instructions published by DC-Cam for completing the ECCC Victim Information Form refer explicitly to the problem of the imbalance of applications and civil parties.

Although the ECCC will select only a small number of survivors to participate, it is very important that survivors complete the Victim Information Form. By completing

TABLE 7 List of Victim Information Forms channeled through DC-Cam as of 1 October 2008

No.		Ethnicity					
		Cham	Chinese	Khmer	Vietnamese	Other	Total
	Cambodia						
1	Banteay Meanchey	0	0	12	0	0	12
2	Battambang	0	0	8	0	0	8
3	Kampong Cham	0	0	9	0	(Stieng) 6	15
4	Kampong Chhnang	11	0	1	0	0	12
5	Kampong Thom	4	0	336	0	0	340
6	Kampot	1	0	41	0	0	42
7	Kandal	0	0	11	0	0	11
8	Kratie	2	0	0	0	(Mil) 4	6
9	Koh Kong	0	0	1	0	0	1
10	Phnom Penh	4	0	5[a]	0	0	9
11	Preah Vihea	0	0	13	0	0	13
12	Prey Veng	0	0	40	0	0	40
13	Pursat	1	0	146	0	(Kampuchea Kraom) 21	168
14	Ratanak Kiri	0	0	3	0	(Preou) 2	5
15	Siem Reap	0	0	155	0	0	155
16	Takeo	0	0	182	0	0	182
17	Svay Rieng	0	0	15	0	0	15
18	Miscellaneous[b]	200	18	118	28	(Chams and Khmers) 18	382
	Overseas						
19	Australia	0	0	1	0	0	1
20	US	0	0	0	0	(US) 2	2
Total		223	18	1,097	28	53	1,419

[a]One of the five is a monk.
[b]The provinces in which the complainants reside have not been identified.
Source: Victim Participation Project, Documentation Center of Cambodia.

this form, survivors will assist the ECCC in its task of trying senior Khmer Rouge leaders. Furthermore, by contributing to the ECCC's archives, survivor testimony will help to create a vast historical record of the crimes of the Democratic Kampuchea era. This will help improve understanding of the period and create a valuable resource for future generations.[102]

Clearly, more is at stake in these initiatives—and for other NGOs as well—than the cooperation of victims as civil parties before the Khmer Rouge Tribunal. Additional transitional justice measures were undertaken based on documentation from victims' reports. Victims were "officially" registered as such for the first time. This was scarcely done in the preceding 30 years. Now legal steps are paired with social and political demands for recognition and some moral reparation. The impetus originates in a juridical context. The result has several national and international implications.

1. Further development of international criminal law (international). The participation of victims before the ECCC exceeds all previous praxis. The experiences gained here can be included as reference points for contemporary and future transitional justice measures in connection with the criminal punishment of the gravest violations of international humanitarian law. Consequently, the ECCC's practices contribute to the development of worldwide international standards of criminal procedure. Should this experimental project succeed, Cambodia will emerge as a pioneer for future internationalized and international tribunals. Even in the event of failure, positive conclusions can be drawn.

2. Searching for the truth (national). The process of coming to terms with the history of the Khmer Rouge regime, as a central theme in transitional justice, is still in its infancy, especially at the local and regional levels. The documentation provided by victims will add important pieces of the puzzle to the still rudimentary picture of repressed Cambodian history.

3. "Case Monitoring" (national). One of the most important tasks of civil parties is vigilantly to follow the proceedings. It is apparent that the influence of victims on the procedural order of events can positively influence acceptance of the tribunal within the population. Even if it is only a small intervening group, it connects the court with the rest of the victim population. This is a new forward-looking aspect of transitional justice.

Acceptance of the Khmer Rouge Tribunal

The meaning of the ECCC for Cambodia is a matter of controversy within the country. Everyone agrees about its economic impact. However, its impact on the structure and further development of Cambodian criminal law and procedure is more complex. In Cambodia, sentiments sway between indifference and relief that now at least a part of the country's past can be juridically confronted. For one of the few witnesses who survived the mass murders, Vann Nath, the state of affairs is completely clear. On the tasks of the court, he opines:

> This belongs to matters that I'm generally unhappy with. It can't be that the perpetrators aren't prosecuted by the court. They're still alive today and they can move about freely within the country. I know them, and I've seen them myself. If these perpetrators aren't prosecuted, they won't even be aware that they committed crimes. Their guilt must be made clear to them.[103]

Victims and relatives hope fervently that the court will not confine itself to political-military leaders. Because the families of victims and perpetrators live in the same neighborhoods (particularly in rural areas), charges leveled against former village and cooperative leaders are common. In view of the court's mandate, we must not assume that the desire of many victims for justice will be disappointed. Moreover, in the world view of many Cambodians, engagement with their own history is also a repressed portion of their history. Fear of rekindling old struggles is pervasive. The court, along with numerous NGOs, seeks to demonstrate to the people the limits of justice and to convey to them the legitimacy of the mandate.

Citizens of Phnom Penh regard potential stimuli to development as overly burdened by political lobbying.[104] Regions distant from urban centers depend significantly on engagement with national and international NGOs (Outreach Measures). The ECCC itself also conducts Outreach programs.[105] As a whole, NGOs play a prominent role in conciliation efforts between the Khmer Rouge Tribunal and the population. One of the leading figures among them is DC-Cam, which has assumed to a significant degree responsibility for supplying the ECCC with evidentiary materials, documents, VPFs, and so forth. Through its involvement in the memorial at S-21, DC-Cam has become very influential nationally. Youk Chhan, founder and director of DC-Cam, has assembled, along with his colleagues, more than 400,000 documents and witness statements pertaining to the crimes of the Khmer Rouge.[106]

In terms of the conciliation efforts between the ECCC and the population, one hears frequent demands for so-called "smooth proceedings," especially at the national level. This demand is based on the assumption that the court can largely rely on already available evidentiary material. Expenditures for investigations, which are yet to be made, are classified as minimal. On the legal side, such demands—which are generally traceable to DC-Cam—are rejected. Without question, it has provided comprehensive assistance in preparing the trials, assembling original documents and witness statements, and expediting the collection of evidence. Hence it is only logical that the prosecutor and investigating judge cooperate closely with DC-Cam. "Private collection activity can not, however, replace national investigation, but only prepare the way."[107] It cannot and ought not supersede the court's decisions and force the court into a role of merely confirming what the interested public or political actors believe they already know.

One potential difficulty is that the parties responsible for organizing the tribunal could create expectations in the population that bear little resemblance to the procedures of an internationalized court procedure. Searching for the truth through a legal process is clearly distinguishable from general strategies of discovering the truth. This is all the more the case for the four defendants in Case 2, against whom the crafting and implementation of criminal policies have to be proven—policies which are not adequately documented to hold up in court, and which to a significant degree are built on circumstantial evidence.

Another issue is the transparency and efficiency of the proceedings as an argument for their acceptance. The proceedings are public, and the visitors' gallery is consistently overcrowded. Bus connections to the court are without charge. Visits to the court are difficult for rural dwellers because travel is time consuming and expensive.

Furthermore, the press has little influence in the countryside.[108] In the eyes of a part of the new political and economic elite, the ECCC is seen as a guarantee that Cambodian politicians cannot avoid respecting international standards—a thoroughly rational concern in view of corruption within the country.

Conclusion

Cambodia did not enjoy peace after the collapse of the Khmer Rouge regime. Vietnamese interventions, international isolation, and a fragmented political landscape prevented the development of an adequate peace process. With the end of the Pol Pot regime, Cambodia for the first time pursued transitional justice measures, which were rejected by the international community. Nothing essentially changed until the Treaty of Paris (1991), though Cambodia remained a country beset by crises. In retrospect, from the end of the 1960s we can discern three significant conflicts relevant to the work of the tribunal today: the rise of Lon Nol (the first civil war—until 1975), the armed struggle of Pol Pot (1975–1979), and the "second civil war" (the People's Republic of Cambodia) from 1979 to 1991.

Hundreds of thousands of human beings perished between 1979 and 1991 from hunger and war. If the victims of US bombing and the civil war during the Lon Nol era are added to these numbers (as many as 200,000 were killed), the scope of destruction is frightfully clear. In the interval between the end of the Khmer Rouge dictatorship and the first free elections, the focus in the first post-1979 years centered chiefly on the consolidation of the political and financial system as well as the infrastructure of the devastated country. Transitional justice in Cambodia was different from transitional justice in postwar Europe, which was supervised by the victors.

Because of the enormous decimation of the population over many years, little social cleansing took place. Like other transitional periods, a "willed amnesia,"[109] coupled with selective memory (killing fields, Tuol Sleng) compromised the confrontation with the past. The interaction of external and internal actors in the struggle to control a criminal court for prosecuting Khmer Rouge crimes only marginally lifts the veil of forgetting. For the first time, the activities of numerous national and international NGOs, in league with the evolving ECCC, enabled the Cambodian people to come to grips with their past as a point of departure for transitional justice. Within the realm of law (Victims Unit, VPFs), results have been created that can serve as a foundation for political action (victim status, debates about compensation, etc.).

Beyond this, the work of the ECCC signifies a momentous step in the direction of professionalizing the rule of legal structures in Cambodia. Judges, prosecutors, and advocates equally profit from new criminal-legal experiences. It remains to be seen how they will deal with the significant challenges facing them. The first growing pains have been overcome, and the tribunal now finds itself in the midst of its work. How—and whether—the final destination, the prosecution of Khmer Rouge perpetrators, will be reached is still unclear. In view of the broad mandate of the court, this is indeed a prodigious challenge. It is for the prosecutors, defense counsel, and civil parties to resolve the formidable legal problems and navigate treacherous political influences. Responsibility for such work has been denied the people of Cambodia. They have waited for nearly 30 years for justice, however modest.

Translated by Michael Bryant

NOTES

1. Luftglass, "Crossroads in Cambodia," 897.
2. Piccigallo, *The Japanese on Trial*, 201.
3. In 1975 about 250,000 Muslim Cham lived in Cambodia. From the beginning, the Cham were singled out as a minority group and subjected to annihilation because they practiced Islam. About 100,000 Cham were murdered at that time, and the survivors were dispersed into small groups. Kiernan, "Orphans of Genocide," 7; idem, "The Demography of Genocide," 585; Liai Duong, *Racial Discrimination*, 11. Not only did the Khmer Rouge take measures to eradicate all cultural identity in the population but they also attempted to prevent the transmission of culture to future generations—essentially attempting to extinguish the Cham culture.
4. Dyrchs, *Das hybride Khmer Rouge-Tribunal*, 28.
5. Kiernan, "Introduction," 485.
6. Barrett, "Holding Individual Leaders," 437; Luftglass, "Crossroads in Cambodia," cited on p. 898, fn. 10.
7. For details, see Vickery, *Cambodia*; Kiernan, *The Pol Pot Regime*; Chandler, *Voices from S-21*.
8. Dyrchs, *Das hybride Khmer Rouge-Tribunal*, 30.
9. The Ho Chi Minh Trail was a logistical system that ran from North to South Vietnam through Laos and Cambodia. The system provided support to the Vietcong, or National Liberation Front, and the North Vietnamese Army, or People's Army of Vietnam (PAVN), during the Vietnam War until 1975. For details see, for example, Prados, *The Blood Road*.
10. *A History of Democratic Campuchea*, 11.
11. Kiernan, *The Pol Pot Regime*, 55; idem, "Historical and Political Background," 178.
12. Kiernan, "Orphans of Genocide," 14.
13. Liai Duong, *Racial Discrimination*, 13; Osman, *Oukoubah*.
14. Kiernan, *The Pol Pot Regime*, 279.
15. For more information about the Pol Pots secret police, see microfilmed records of the Khmer Rouge-era Santebal files (482 reels), located by the Cambodian Genocide Program in 1996, and other Khmer Rouge-related records filmed by Yale's Sterling Memorial Library (SML).
16. *Tagesspiegel*, 27 July 2006.
17. A total of 19,403 mass graves and 80 memorials from the Pol Pot era exist in today's Cambodia.
18. Huy Vannak, *The Khmer Rouge Division 703*, 76. S-21 was given various names. At times, it was called "Ministry S-21" (krasuong S-21). Two reports use the name "M-21" for Office S-21.
19. *A History of Democratic Campuchea*, 41.

20. Ciorciari, *The Khmer Rouge Tribunal*, 12; *Searching for the Truth*, 14–17.
21. Prum, "A Former S-21 Photographer," 12–13.
22. Huy Vannak, *The Khmer Rouge Division 703*, 87.

During 1976, S-21 and its branches employed 1,720 people: an internal force of 141, an external force of 1,377, 148 office cadres, and 54 interrogators. The internal force was divided into combatants in the prisoner guard unit and combatant city messengers (yuthachon nirasa krong). There were 62 city messengers comprising 42 guards for the special prison, 8 prisoner snatchers/arresters, 10 drivers, and 2 medics.

23. For more information see the homepage of the Tuol Sleng Genocide Museum (Phnom Penh) at <http://www.tuolsleng.com/> (accessed March 2009).
24. Huy Vannak, *The Khmer Rouge Division 703*, 74.
25. Deutschlandfunk, 20 March 2007. For more details see Gottesman, *Cambodia after the Khmer Rouge*.
26. Huy Vannak, *The Khmer Rouge Division 703*, 110.

During the last two years of the Democratic Kampuchea regime, Cambodia suffered two large-scale attacks by Vietnamese troops. The first began in September 1977 and ended with the defeat of the Vietnamese on January 6, 1978. The second began on April 7, 1978 with a major Vietnamese assault and ended on January 7, 1979. This time, the Khmer Rouge were defeated.

27. Chhim, *Die Revolutionäre Volkspartei Kampuchea 1979 bis 1989*.
28. Luftglass, "Crossroads in Cambodia," 902–03.
29. Ciorciari, *The Khmer Rouge Tribunal*, 15–16.
30. Germany, for example, did not resume full diplomatic relations with Cambodia until 1993. Dyrchs, *Das hybride Khmer Rouge-Tribunal*, 43.
31. Friedrich Ebert Foundation.
32. Clymer, *The United States and Cambodia*, 141; Fawthrop and Jarvis, *Getting Away with Genocide?*, 54, 56.
33. For more details see Dyrchs, *Das hybride Khmer Rouge-Tribunal*, 44.
34. Luftglass, "Crossroads in Cambodia," 904.
35. For more details see De Nike et al., *Genocide in Cambodia*. The editors composed several documents: the establishment of the tribunal, the indictment, witness statements, forensic reports, other documents introduced into the record, including journalistic accounts, closing statements by the prosecutor and the defense counsel, and the final judgment. Liebermann, "Salvaging the Remains," 181; Quigley, *The Genocide Convention*, 27–31; Schabas, *Genocide in International Law*, 391–92; Starygin, *Amicus Curiae*, 12; Touch, *Searching for the Truth*, 37–38.
36. De Nike et al., *Genocide in Cambodia*; Schabas, "Book Review," 475; "Fair Trial Principles," 3.
37. Arendt, *Eichmann in Jerusalem*; *Eichmann Trial*; Robinson, *And the Crooked Shall Be Made Straight*.
38. Schabas, "Book Review," 473–74.
39. For further information see Dyrchs, *Das hybride Khmer Rouge-Tribunal*, 51.
40. Human Right Watch, Press release, 24 August 1999.
41. Fawthrop and Jarvis, *Getting Away with Genocide?*, 49.
42. Ibid., 72.
43. Ibid., 84.

44. Chhim, *Die Revolutionäre Volkspartei Kampuchea 1979 bis 1989*, 15.
45. Ibid., 19.
46. Ibid., 20.
47. Fawthrop and Jarvis, *Getting Away with Genocide?*, 119.
48. Etcheson, "A 'Fair and Pubic Trial,'" 7.
49. Form, "Planung und Durchführung west-alliierter Kriegsverbrecherprozesse nach dem Zweiten Weltkrieg," 233–53.
50. Neilson, *They Killed All the Lawyers*, 1–2; *Reconciliation after Violent Conflict*, 50.
51. Clark and Wright, *The Works of William Shakespeare*, 156.
52. Wertz, "Fluch der toten Jahre."
53. Dyrchs, *Das hybride Khmer Rouge-Tribunal*, 66–67.
54. Crampton, "Cambodia to Restore Khmer Rouge Sites"; Liebermann, "Salvaging the Remains," 167; Ciorciari, *The Khmer Rouge Tribunal*, 12, 39.
55. Ciorciari, *The Khmer Rouge Tribunal*, 118.
56. Wertz, "Fluch der toten Jahre."
57. Ibid.
58. Youk Chhang, "The Arrests of Ieng Sary," 1.
59. Ibid.
60. Fawthrop and Jarvis, *Getting Away with Genocide?*, 158–60.
61. The CPP and the Royalist Party.
62. A hybrid court like Sierra Leone or East Timor, consisting of national and international judges.
63. Boyle, "Establishing the Responsibility of the Khmer Rouge Leadership," 184. See also Human Right Watch, Press release, 24 August 1999:

> A United Nations team is scheduled to arrive in Cambodia this week to discuss with the Cambodian government a proposed mixed tribunal, which, to date, Cambodian Prime Minister Hun Sen has rejected in public statements. A draft U.N. plan presented to the Security Council on July 30, 1999 calls for a Nuremberg-style joint trial of all defendants together, based on indictments prepared by an international prosecutor and approved by a predominantly non-Cambodian panel of judges [...] The United Nations must avoid giving legitimacy to a process that does not meet international standards. The U.N. and key donors should withhold political and financial support if these standards are not met. The Cambodian government has a history of manipulating the judiciary and disregarding the rule of law.

64. Published in the *Phnom Penh Post*, no. 9/22, 27 October–9 November 2000. Link: <http://www.yale.edu/cgp/mou_v3.html> (accessed March 2009).
65. Dyrchs, *Das hybride Khmer Rouge-Tribunal*, 68–70.
66. UN News Centre:

> The 32-article agreement, endorsed last month by the 191 members of the UN General Assembly, will create Extraordinary Chambers, comprising one trial court and one Supreme Court within the Cambodian legal system to "prosecute those most responsible for crimes and serious violations of Cambodian and international law between 17 April 1975 and 6 January 1979." (<http://www.un.org/apps/news/story.asp?NewsID=7334&Cr=Cambodia&Cr1=>; accessed March 2009).

67. For details see Dyrchs, *Das hybride Khmer Rouge-Tribunal*, 71–79.

68. Meijer, "The Extraordinary Chambers"; Reiger, "Marrying International and Local Justice," 97–108.

69. Case No. 001/18-07-2007/ECCC/TC. "The Trial Chamber orders that the Substantive Hearing concerning the accused Kaing Guek Eav alias Duch will begin on Monday 30 March 2009 at 10:00 hours in the main Courtroom of the ECCC." ECCC press release, 25 February 2009.

70. "First ECCC Trial on Crimes of 1970s Khmer Rouge Regime Officially Opens, February 17, 2009." ECCC press release, 17 February 2009.

71. Studzinsky, "Nebenklage vor den Extraordinary Chambers of the Courts of Cambodia (ECCC)," 44.

72. The *Phnom Penh Post*, 8 January 2009: "How many are too many defendants at the KRT?"

73. *New York Times*, 31 January 2009.

74. Bonacker, "Inklusion und Integration"; Gessner, "Rechtspluralismus und globale soziale Bewegungen."

75. In April 2002 the Rome Statute received its 60th ratification, thereby formally establishing the ICC in July 2002.

76. Liebermann, "Salvaging the Remains," 165.

77. Article 4, paragraph 1 a. ECCC Statute (6.6.2003). Dyrchs, *Das hybride Khmer Rouge-Tribunal*, 132–34. This model is based on a suggestion by US Senator John Kerry (October 1999).

78. The first verdict in accordance with the supermajority principle has already been issued; 24 June 2008: Decision on Admissibility of Civil Parties general Observations (<http://www.eccc.gov.kh/english/cabinet/courtDoc/92/Decision_on_Civil_Party_Observations_C22_I_41_EN.pdf>; accessed March 2009). For more information see Studzinsky, "Nebenklage vor den Extraordinary Chambers of the Courts of Cambodia (ECCC)," 47.

79. Law on the Establishment of Extraordinary Chambers in the Courts of Cambodia for the Prosecution of Crime committed during the period of Democratic Kampuchea, promulgated on 27 October 2004.

80. Dutton, *The Psychology of Genocide*, 100.

81. Wald, "Prosecuting Genocide," 89.

82. "Fair Trial Principles," 6.

83. For example: Nuremberg and Tokyo Tribunals, Special Court for Sierra Leone, International Criminal Tribunal for the Former Yugoslavia or International Criminal Court.

84. For example: US Military Courts in Germany (Dachau Trials), British "Royal" Warrant Courts, German Courts (World War II cases), Dutch Special Courts for War Crimes, etc.

85. Williams, "The Cambodian Extraordinary Chambers," 228–29.

86. Gurd, "Outreach," 117–29.

87. Code of Criminal Procedure of Cambodia (CPC). It appears problematic, however, that only in March 2008 did an unofficial and unpublished English translation come into existence. Studzinsky, "Nebenklage vor den Extraordinary Chambers of the Courts of Cambodia (ECCC)," 45.

88. Statement by the Victims Unit; see <http://www.cambodiatribunal.org/CTM/Victim_Unit_Press_Release.pdf?phpMyAdmin=8319ad34ce0db941ff04d8c788f6365e&phpMyAdmin=ou7lpwtyV9avP1XmRZP6FzDQzg3> (accessed March 2009).

89. The lawyers for the civil parties are equally entitled to cite official documents of the court.

90. Statement by the Victims Unit; see <http://www.cambodiatribunal.org/CTM/Victim_Unit_Press_Release.pdf?phpMyAdmin=8319ad34ce0db941ff04d8c788f6365e&phpMyAdmin=ou7lpwtyV9avP1XmRZP6FzDQzg3> (accessed March 2009).

91. See <http://www.eccc.gov.kh/english/cabinet/fileUpload/27/Internal_Rules_Revision1
_01-02-08_eng.pdf> (accessed March 2009) for the actual version (2 February 2008).
Members: all Judges of the Trial and Pre-Trial Chamber, Supreme Court Chamber,
Co-Investigating Judges and the Co-Prosecutors.

92. According to the Rome Statute (Article 68, paragraph 3), victims can participate in
the ICC trials as civil parties and claim compensation, but by no means do they enjoy
comparable party status.

93. Statement by the Victims Unit; see <http://www.cambodiatribunal.org/CTM/Victim_
Unit_Press_Release.pdf?phpMyAdmin=8319ad34ce0db941ff04d8c788
f6365e&phpMyAdmin=ou7lpwtyV9avP1XmRZP6FzDQzg3> (accessed March 2009).

94. Pre-Trial Chamber (PTC) Decision on Civil Party Participation in Provisional Detention
Appeals (Case No. 002/19-09-2007-ECCC/OCIJ (PTC01), 20 March 2008. See ECCC
homepage (<http://www.eccc.gov.kh/english/court_doc.list.aspx>; accessed March
2009).

95. See ECCC homepage, Victims Unit.

96. Ibid.

97. The Court Report, December 2008 (ECCC homepage), 5.

98. Statement of the Victims Unit; see <http://www.eccc.gov.kh/english/cabinet/press/8
6/Statement_of_VU.pdf> (accessed March 2009).

99. The Court Report, January 2009 (ECCC homepage), 7.

100. See DC-Cam Victim Participation Information Sheet, <http://www.dccam.org/
Projects/Tribunal_Response_Team/Victim_Participation/PDF/Victim_Participation_
Information_Sheet-Eng.pdf> (accessed March 2009).

101. Studzinsky, "Nebenklage vor den Extraordinary Chambers of the Courts of Cambodia
(ECCC)," 46. In less than 1% of the cases, the question about the utility and legitimacy
of such an expenditure has come up. The costs of this undertaking in personnel and logistical terms are considerable, and not only for the ECCC.

102. See DC-Cam homepage (<http://www.dccam.org/Projects/Tribunal_Response_Team/
Victim_Participation/PDF/DC-Cam_Guidance_VPA.pdf>; accessed March 2009).

103. Deutschlandfunk: "Völkermord vor Gericht," 20 March 2007.

104. According to the summary of a workshop co-led by the author in Phnom Penh on 11
December 2008 (Victims' Participation as Transitional Justice).

105. See Outreach Map, ECCC homepage (<http://www.eccc.gov.kh/english/outreach.
map.aspx>; accessed March 2009).

106. See DC-Cam homepage.

107. Assmann, "Khmer-Rouge-Tribunal," 17.

108. See Department of Media and Communications, Royal University of Phnom Penh (RUPP)
(<http://www.culturalprofiles.net/cambodia/units/1081.html>; accessed March 2009).

109. Buckley-Zistel, "Gewählte Amnesie," 132.

REFERENCES

Arendt, Hannah. *Eichmann in Jerusalem: A Report on the Banality of Evil.* Rev. and enlarged
ed. New York: Penguin, 1977.

Assmann, Juergen. "Khmer-Rouge-Tribunal—Besser spät als nie!." *Mitteilungen des Hamburger Richtervereins* 4 (2007): 17–20.

Baker, Iljas. *Bangkok Post,* 3 May 2005.

Barrett, Nicole. "Holding Individual Leaders Responsible for Violations of Customary International Law: The U.S. Bombardment of Cambodia and Laos." *Columbia Human Rights Law Review* 429 (2001): 433–37.

Bonacker, Thorsten. "Inklusion und Integration durch Menschenrechte. Zur Evolution der Weltgesellschaft." *Zeitschrift für Rechtssoziologie* 24 (2003): 121–49.

Boyle, David. "Establishing the Responsibility of the Khmer Rouge Leadership for International Crimes." *Yearbook of International Humanitarian Law* 5 (2002): 167–218.

Buckley-Zistel, Susanne. "Gewählte Amnesie. Die sozialen Dimensionen von Erinnern und Vergessen nach dem Völkermord in Ruanda." *Peripherie* 28 (2008): 131–47.

Chandler, David. *Voices from S-21*. Chiang Mai: Silkworm Books, 2000.

Chhim, Kristina. *Die Revolutionäre Volkspartei Kampuchea 1979 bis 1989*. Frankfurt: Peter Lang, 2000.

Ciorciari. John D. *The Khmer Rouge Tribunal*. Documentation Series no. 10. Phnom Penh: Documentation Center of Cambodia, 2006.

Clark, William George, and William Aldus Wright, eds. *The Works of William Shakespeare*. Vol. 4. New York: A. W. Lovering, 1887.

Clymer, Kenton. *The United States and Cambodia, 1870–1969*. London and New York: RoutledgeCurzon, 2004.

Crampton, Thomas. "Cambodia to Restore Khmer Rouge Sites." *International Herald Tribune*, 21 August 2003.

De Nike, Howard J., John Quigley, and Kenneth J. Robinson, eds. *Genocide in Cambodia: Documents from the Trial of Pol Pot and Ieng Sary*. Philadelphia: University of Pennsylvania Press, 2000.

Dutton, Donald. *The Psychology of Genocide, Massacres, and Extreme Violence*. Westport, CT: Praeger, 2007.

Dyrchs, Susanne. *Das hybride Khmer Rouge-Tribunal. Entstehung, entwicklung und rechtliche Grundlagen*. Frankfurt: Peter Lang, 2008.

Eichmann Trial. The Attorney General of Israel vs. Adolf, Son of Adolf Karl Eichmann. English translation of trial minutes. Jerusalem: Ministry of Justice, 1962.

Etcheson, Craig. "A 'Fair and Public Trial': A Political History of the Extraordinary Chambers." *Open Society Justice Initiative*, Spring 2006, 7–24.

"Fair Trial Principles." Khmer Institute of Democracy, <http://www.khmerrough.com/pdf/FairTrialPrinciples160606.pdf> (accessed March 2009).

Fawthrop, Tom, and Helen Jarvis. *Getting Away with Genocide? Elusive Justice and the Khmer Rouge Tribunal*. London: Pluto Press, 2004.

Form, Wolfgang. "Planung und Durchführung west-alliierter Kriegsverbrecherprozesse nach dem Zweiten Weltkrieg." In *Perspektiven der politischen Soziologie im Wandel von Gesellschaft und Staatlichkeit. Festschrift für Theo Schiller*, edited by Thomas von Winter and Volker Mittendorf. Wiesbaden: VS Verlag für Sozialwissenschaften, 2008.

Friedrich Ebert Foundation. *Kambodscha 1975–2005. Wege durch die Nacht*. Bonn: Friedrich Ebert Foundation, 2005.

Gessner, Volkmar. "Rechtspluralismus und globale soziale Bewegungen." *Zeitschrift für Rechtssoziologie* 23 (2002): 277–305.

Gottesman, Evan. *Cambodia after the Khmer Rouge: Inside the Politics of Nation Building*. New Haven: Yale University Press, 2002.

Gurd, Tracey. "Outreach: A Key to Success." *Open Society Justice Initiative*, Spring 2006, 117–29.

A History of Democratic Campuchea—1975–1979. Phnom Penh: Documentation Center of Cambodia, 2007.

Huy Vannak. *The Khmer Rouge Division 703: From Victory to Self-Destruction*. Phnom Penh: Documentation Center of Cambodia, 2003.

Kiernan, Ben. "Orphans of Genocide: The Cham Muslims of Kampuchea under Pol Pot." *Bulletin of Concerned Asian Scholars* 20 (1988): 2–33.

———. *The Pol Pot Regime*. New Haven: Yale University Press, 1996.

———. "Introduction: Conflict in Cambodia, 1945–2002." *Critical Asian Studies* 34, no. 4 (2002): 483–95.

———. "The Demography of Genocide in Southeast Asia. The Death Tolls in Cambodia, 1975–79 and East Timor, 1975–80." *Critical Asian Studies* 35, no. 4 (2003): 585–97.

———. "Historical and Political Background to the Conflict in Cambodia, 1945–2002." In *New Approaches in International Criminal Justice: Kosovo, East Timor, Sierra Leone and Cambodia*, edited by Kai Ambos and Mohamed Othman. Freiburg: Iuscrim, 2003.

Liai Duong. *Racial Discrimination in the Cambodian Genocide, Genocide Studies Program*. GSP Working Paper no. 34. New Haven: MacMillan Center for International and Area Studies, Yale University, 2006.

Liebermann, Michael. "Salvaging the Remains: The Khmer Rouge Tribunal on Trial." *Military Law Review* 186 (2005): 164–87.

Luftglass, Scott. "Crossroads in Cambodia: The United Nation's Responsibility to Withdraw Involvement from the Establishment of a Cambodian Tribunal to Prosecute the Khmer Rouge." *Virginia Law Review* 90 (May 2004): 893–964.

Meijer, Ernestine. "The Extraordinary Chambers in the Courts of Cambodia for Prosecuting Crimes Committed by the Khmer Rouge: Jurisdiction, Organization, and Procedure of an Internationalized National Tribunal." In *Internationalized Criminal Courts and Tribunals: Sierra Leone, East Timor, Kosovo, and Cambodia*, edited by Cesare P. R. Romano, Andre Nollkaemper and Jann K. Kleffner. Oxford: Oxford University Press, 2004.

Neilson, Kathryn E. *They Killed All the Lawyers: Rebuilding the Judicial System in Cambodia*. Occasional Paper no. 13 (October 1996), <http://www.capi.uvic.ca/pubs/oc_papers/NEILSON.pdf> (accessed March 2009).

Osman, Ysa. *Oukoubah*. Phnom Penh: Documentation Center of Cambodia, 2002.

Piccigallo, Philip R. *The Japanese on Trial: Allied War Crimes Operation in the East, 1945–1951*. Austin and London: University of Texas Press, 1979.

Prados, John. *The Blood Road: The Ho Chi Minh Trail and the Vietnam War*. New York: John Wiley, 1998.

Prum, Phalla. "A Former S-21 Photographer did not Claim he Remembered a New Zealander, a Cuban, a Swiss and their Thai Boat Driver." *Searching for the Truth*, Fourth Quarter 2007, 12–13.

Quigley, John B. *The Genocide Convention: An International Law*. Aldershot: Ashgate, 2006.

Reconciliation after Violent Conflict—A Handbook. Stockholm: International Institute for Democracy and Electoral Assistance, 2003.

Reiger, Caitlin. "Marrying International and Local Justice." *Open Society Justice Initiative*, Spring 2006, 97–108.

Robinson, Jacob. *And the Crooked Shall Be Made Straight: The Eichmann Trial, the Jewish Catastrophe, and Hannah Arendt's Narrative*. New York: Macmillan, 1965.

Schabas, William. *Genocide in International Law: The Crimes of Crimes*. Cambridge: Cambridge University Press, 2000.

———. "Book Review: Genocide in Cambodia, Documents from the Trial of Pol Pot and Ieng Sary. By Howard J. De Nike, John Quigley & Kenneth J. Robinson." *Human Rights Quarterly* 23, no. 2 (2001): 471–77.

Searching for the Truth, Fourth Quarter 2007 (Magazine of the Documentation Center of Cambodia).

Starygin, Stan. *Amicus Curiae in Support of the Detainee. Judicial Investigation Opened Against Kaing Guek Eav (alias Duch)*. Appeal of the Defense to the Pre-Trial Chamber (2007), <http://www.eccc.gov.kh/english/cabinet/files/PTC_amicus_briefs/1-Stan-Starygin-Brief.pdf> (accessed March 2009).

Studzinsky, Silke. "Nebenklage vor den Extraordinary Chambers of the Courts of Cambodia (ECCC)—Herausforderung und Chance oder mission impossible?" *Zeitschrift für internationale Strafrechtsdogmatik* 1 (2009): 44–50.

Touch, Bora. *Searching for the Truth*, no. 14 (February 2001): 37–38.

Vickery, Michael. *Cambodia 1975–1982*. Boston: South End Press, 1984.

Wald, Patricia M. "Prosecuting Genocide." *Open Society Justice Initiative*, Spring 2006, 85–96.

Wertz, Armin. "Fluch der toten Jahre." *Freitag*, 19 January 2001.

Williams, Sarah. "The Cambodian Extraordinary Chambers—A Dangerous Precedent for International Justice?" *International and Comparative Law Quarterly* 53 (2004): 227–45.

Youk, Chhang. "The Arrests of Ieng Sary and Ieng Thirith: A Victory for Cambodia's 'Peasants.'" *Searching for the Truth*, Fourth Quarter 2007, 1–2.

Adjudication Deferred: Command Responsibility for War Crimes and US Military Justice from My Lai to Haditha and Beyond

William C. Peters

The public international law doctrine of command responsibility, like many firmly accepted rules in law, is more clearly stated than consistently applied. Intended to establish a base level of order and responsibility for sustained violence endemic to the inherently ugly nature of war, even state militaries of fully mature Western democracies demonstrate difficulty appreciating its importance and applying its law.

Lessons Unlearned

What follows is not primarily concerned with a military superior's direct culpability for acts amounting to war crimes or illegal orders that, without misunderstanding, compel their commission by subordinates. Instead, our focus is the indirect role of a commander's actions,[1] or a failure to act where duty imposes the obligation, that contributes to crime in a given battle space. Originating from traditional principles of customary international law, development of the doctrine of command responsibility took a significant step forward after World War II with the High Command and Hostages trials sitting at Nuremberg under Allied Control Council Law No. 10, and the verdicts of the International Military Tribunal for the Far East. The US Supreme Court affirmed the legal basis of command responsibility in a 1946 ruling. It has now been codified by international humanitarian and criminal law treaties, incorporated in UN Security Council resolutions as "superior responsibility," and extensively developed in recent years by decisions of international courts, especially the International Criminal Tribunal for the Former Yugoslavia. The gravamen of the rule is that commanders are themselves criminally liable for conduct of their subordinates that amounts to war crimes if the commander either knew or reasonably should have known of violations of the laws of war and did not take adequate measures necessary to repress or prevent the breach. That is, a commander is duty bound by law to take all reasonable measures within his or her power to halt ongoing crimes and to investigate and properly punish those already committed to serve the ends of justice and help deter future violations.

The My Lai massacre in 1968, and its subsequent cover-up by numerous senior Army officers, forced the US defense community to pay attention to war crimes and "reawakened questions concerning the responsibility of a military commander for the unlawful acts of his subordinates."[2] Forty years have passed since that spectral event and the flood of scholarly analyses it produced.[3] Still, the aftermath of more recent tragedies occurring during campaigns of the current global war waged in Afghanistan and Iraq suggests that both the US defense establishment and Congress[4] have failed to learn a central lesson of command responsibility.

The lesson yet mastered is this: rules, and the broader rule of law that they comprise, can only serve their purpose insofar as they are evenly and impartially applied. This is, of course, a very difficult, painful topic to consider for any institution in matters of suspected criminal misconduct. The highly hierarchical nature of military organizations, combined with the essence of command responsibility which applies, by its very definition, to more senior members of the military, makes it doubly so for the armed forces of states which pride themselves with securing the very rule of law that constitutional democracies emphasize.

This article first examines the development of command responsibility as a doctrine of customary international law. It traces the origins and uniquely military contextual footings of the principle. It then depicts the institutional development and acceptance of command responsibility by way of early US municipal law and domestic and international court rulings, its embrace by convention-based international law in Protocol I Additional to the Geneva Conventions of 1949, and its inclusion in UN Security Council resolutions. The section goes on to discuss recent clarification of the doctrine and includes judicial rulings on the requirement for a commander's actual knowledge of subordinate misconduct, case law from the international tribunals for the former Yugoslavia and Rwanda, and the potential role of the International Criminal Court for future application of the doctrine.

This article revisits the My Lai massacre, its investigation, and the principal senior officers who avoided criminal trial. It also discusses the comparable non-judicial dispositions, by administrative measures only, for numerous senior leaders that resulted from the infamous debacle in Iraq at Abu Ghraib in 2004. It concludes with a look at the more recent, puzzling examples of Marine Corps Lieutenant Colonel Jeffrey Chessani and US Army Colonel Michael Steele, where suspicions of both indirect and direct command responsibility for war crimes have gone unresolved because adjudication of criminal liability has been deferred, yet again. This section also discusses a number of recent proposals designed to address the dearth of criminal cases brought to establish a commander's liability for war crimes committed by his unit.

I offer an argument that supports courts-martial in the US under the Uniform Code of Military Justice[5] (UCMJ) for members of the US armed forces when colorable allegations of command responsibility for war crimes are advanced. Indeed, should the US ever join the regime of the Rome Statute of the International Criminal Court,[6] the rule of complementarity will compel such action.[7] To further the likelihood of properly addressing war crime allegations, Congress should create the position of Department of Defense special prosecutor for war crimes and establish it as an office with responsibility as legal advisor to the military's service secretaries. Such an overseer of military justice at the secretariat level would encourage uniformed members of the armed forces that serve as convening authorities to bring cases to trial where appropriate. The special prosecutor would ensure adjudication of alleged war crimes if the military fails to act. In practice, the record shows that senior US military commanders have repeatedly and systemically avoided courts-martial and formal adjudication of serious war crime allegations since My Lai and the reawakening of responsibility for these international crimes that catastrophe supposedly engendered.

The problem of command responsibility for the American military since Vietnam is not that legal advisors in the armed services do not fully grasp the applicable law. Neither is there a lack of genuine concern among some in leadership positions about the importance of adhering to law of war principles, avoiding noncombatant deaths where possible,[8] and inculcating an institutional mindset that reinforces the importance of the rule of law, even amidst the chaos of combat operations. But the institutional experts on military law and the law of war, not surprisingly, remain lawyers. As with other staff officers in military force structures the world over, lawyers are only advisors to those commanders who make policy and implement military justice. Of course, it is also the commanders who are the very ones directly affected when issues of potential command responsibility for war crimes surface. Intersecting this conflict of interest that is built in to UCMJ procedure, US Army judge advocate lawyers are continuously implored to be "soldiers first," a subtle but clear institutional message from above which suggests that doing one's duty in law and the profession of soldiering are somehow incompatible. As a result, US Army lawyers are frequently put in a position of serving their commander's wishes above their constitutional oath and service-client's legal interests or risk the ire of a commander who decides it is simply time to "get some new lawyers."[9]

This article's center of gravity should not be misconstrued. It is not that senior US officers with some responsibility for the war crimes committed at My Lai, Bagram, Abu Ghraib, Haditha, and Samarra have gone unpunished. Rather, it is that the soldiers that commanders led, the US citizenry its armed forces serve, and the broader community of nations will never know whether criminal liability properly attached to the senior uniformed leadership involved in those tragedies. The system of military justice did not operate as designed to bring finality and adjudicate culpability regarding a legal principle of international law, championed by the US since 1945, when pre-trial investigations made clear that courts-martial were warranted.

A Rule of Law Defined

In a speech given years after the American Civil War, Union General William Tecumseh Sherman reportedly observed that war is all hell. Few personally familiar with the experience would disagree and humankind has long attempted to temper the destructive nature of war. Practices observed in war consistently by belligerents over long periods of time led to the creation of rules of war broadly observed as customary. *Opinio juris*, the notion that some state practices follow from a sense of legal obligation, and not out of simple geopolitical self-interest, is the qualifying element that transforms traditional state behavior and brings the practice it touches within the realm of customary international law.[10] From the earliest recorded annals of military history to the Rome Statute of the International Criminal Court, the rule of command responsibility has been at the heart of one subset of public international law, the law of war.[11]

Since at least 500 BCE, sovereigns have recognized the central role of command in the success or failure of a military campaign.[12] Although a rule declaring a leader's culpability for a subordinate's criminality during war had yet to develop, the need for clarity of a leader's instructions and strict discipline over those failing an order's execution was understood from earliest times. In his famous treatise, *The Art of War*, Sun Tzu wrote: "[i]f the words of command are not clear and distinct, if orders are not thoroughly understood, the general is to blame. But if his orders are clear, and the soldiers nevertheless disobey, then it is the fault of their officers."[13]

Given the hierarchical nature of military service and its strictures of obedience and discipline, the concept that a superior may be responsible for the misconduct of those he leads in war is, in large part, a corollary of the rule of combatant immunity.[14] Even states engaged in armed conflict with each other do not hold soldiers criminally responsible for murder in the battlefield deaths of opposing combatants, provided the operational plan and its execution comport with the law of war. If soldiers are not culpable for otherwise criminal conduct because of a condition of war and a superior's orders, the question arises, why should a superior not be accountable when crimes that are made punishable by the same law of war do occur?

An early formulation of today's standard can be found in a 1439 edict of Charles VII of France, which directed that officers would be held responsible for "abuses, ills, and offences committed by members of [their] company"[15] where the immediate offender avoided punishment due to the commander's negligence. In the seventeenth century, King Gustavus Adolphus of Sweden issued his Articles of Military Law that held commanders liable for directly ordering unlawful acts, while the Dutch scholar Hugo Grotius extended the concept to hold superiors "accountable for the Crimes of their Subjects, if they know of them, and do not prevent them, when they can and ought to do so."[16] In US domestic law, the 1775 Massachusetts Articles of War affirmatively required every commanding officer to keep order among his subordinates, whether garrisoned or on the march, and to "redress all such abuses or disorders which may be committed by any Officer or Soldier under his command."[17] In April 1863, during the American Civil War, President Lincoln promulgated his General Orders 100.[18] Often cited as the Lieber Code after its author, Professor Francis Lieber of Columbia University, articles 71 and 156 reflected the continued development of the principle of command responsibility. Article 71 reinforced the rule on direct command responsibility for war crimes where a superior orders or encourages the illegal infliction of wounds on an already wholly disabled enemy. At the same time, article 156 provided that "[c]ommon justice and plain expediency require that *the military commander protect the manifestly loyal citizens, in revolted territories, against the hardships of the war as much as the common misfortune of all war admits*."[19]

By the turn of the twentieth century, the basis for the customary rule of command responsibility appeared in one of the earliest international law of war conventions, the 1907 Hague Convention Respecting the Laws and Customs of War on Land. It expressly established that all laws, rights, and duties of war were premised on the first principle that commanders are responsible for the conduct of their soldiers.[20] Early attempts at judicial enforcement followed from this vague concept and met with mostly uneven results. After the Great War in 1919, the Versailles peace treaty established a Commission on the Responsibility of the Authors of the War and on Enforcement of Penalties. The commission determined that those individuals culpable of "outrages of every description committed on land, at sea, and in the air, against the laws and customs of war and the laws of humanity"[21] should be prosecuted without regard for position or rank. From an initial list of some 3,000 suspected war criminals, the number was culled to less than 900.[22] Although articles 227 through 230 of the treaty called for Allied tribunals to try those deemed responsible for war crimes, including Germany's Kaiser Wilhelm II,[23] only a handful of cases initiated by the Allies ever went to trial, and those that did were adjudicated by Germany's Supreme Court sitting at Leipzig. The results were perhaps predictable. Ultimately, only 12 accused went to trial, and none of the general officers were found guilty. A single conviction for direct command responsibility was meted out to a mid-grade major for passing on an illegal order to execute prisoners of war that was issued by Lieutenant General Karl Stenger. Stenger was found not guilty of ordering the killings.[24]

Mindful of the lessons of Leipzig, the victorious UN conducted war crimes trials in Germany and Japan after World War II that forever altered accepted doctrines of individual criminality and command responsibility. At Nuremberg, US Army lawyers General Telford Taylor, Colonel Murray Bernays, and Benjamin Ferencz, among others, fashioned a workable legal solution to the problem of international crime on a colossal scale. The main problem with determining individual criminal liability under command responsibility has always centered on the question of the senior officer's state of mind. Some theorists, such as Michael Walzer, suggest that where war crimes are to be found the commander should be held strictly liable both morally and criminally:

> [O]fficers are presumptively guilty; the burden of proof, if they would demonstrate their innocence, lies with them. And until we find some way of imposing that burden, we shall not have done all that we can do in defense of the "weak and unarmed" ...[25]

To hold someone culpable using a standard of strict liability for their own misconduct is rare in criminal law. The criminal state of mind of a perpetrator, or *mens rea*, is that element in penal statutes that can separate affirmative misconduct from an unfortunate event. To hold anyone, even the individual military commander, criminally culpable for the acts of another in terms of strict liability offends all notions of justice. The post-World War II judicial record acknowledges this and reflects a slow-to-develop standard of a rebuttable presumption of the commander's responsibility under law when war crimes are committed.

In December 1945, a Canadian military commission convicted the German commander of the 25th SS Panzer Grenadiers Regiment for the murder of 18 prisoners of war at Normandy in June of 1944. The Judge Advocate in the *Abbaye Ardennes* Case argued:

> When may a military commander be held responsible for a war crime committed by men under his command in the sense that he may be punished as a war criminal? [This] is not easily answered ... Regulations do not mean that a military commander is in every case liable to be punished as a war criminal for every war crime committed by his subordinates but once certain facts have been proved by the Prosecution, there is an onus cast upon the accused to adduce evidence to negative or rebut the inference of responsibility which the Court is entitled to make. All the facts and circumstances must then be considered to determine whether the accused was in fact responsible ...[26]

However, this eminently reasonable approach toward a commander's criminal accountability was largely eclipsed by the US Supreme Court's holding in the Yamashita decision,[27] announced just a few months later.

Japanese General Tomoyuki Yamashita took command of the Fourteenth Army Group of the Imperial Japanese Army in the Philippines less than two weeks before US forces landed at Leyte in October 1944. Before his surrender in September 1945, forces under his command committed widespread atrocities. They killed an estimated 25,000 civilians in Batangas Province, murdered another 8,000 civilians over a two-week period in Manila, and raped at least 500 women.[28] Yamashita was subsequently convicted of war crimes on the basis of his command responsibility. Afterwards, in a petition to the US Supreme Court, Yamashita challenged the jurisdiction of the military commission that convicted him. The multiple charges outlining widespread abuses against the civilian population neither claimed the general directed the war crimes nor did they allege that he had specific knowledge of his subordinates' plans for their commission. Yamashita argued, *inter alia*, that absent his order directing the wanton atrocities committed by his troops, the charges preferred against him failed to state that he violated the laws of war.

The court disagreed. Chief Justice Harlan Stone's majority opinion reasoned:

> It is plain that the charge on which petitioner was tried charged him with a breach of his duty to control the operations of the members of his command, by permitting them to commit the specified atrocities. This was enough to require the commission to hear evidence tending to establish the culpable failure of petitioner to perform the duty imposed on him by the law of war and to pass upon its sufficiency to establish guilt.[29]

The Supreme Court's narrow holding only affirmed the jurisdiction of the military commission that tried Yamashita, convicted him, and sentenced him to death. However, Stone's opinion has never been overturned and remains valid constitutional law. It acknowledges criminal liability following the principle of command responsibility under circumstances that the Tribunal ruling in the case could only presume a commander's knowledge of subordinates' war crimes because of their widespread nature and effect.

After the International Military Tribunal's rulings against the 22 principal Nazi leaders in October 1946, a number of subsequent cases were adjudicated concerning more junior participants in the Hitlerite Holocaust and war of aggression. The two most influential decisions for command responsibility by the US Tribunal under Allied Control Council for Germany Law Number 10[30] were the High Command[31] and Hostages[32] Cases. Both prosecutions involved numerous German general officers, among them Wilhelm Von Leeb, a field marshal of various senior command positions culminating in Commander-in-Chief of Army Group North, and Wilhelm List, the Commander-in-Chief of the 12th Army during the German invasion of Yugoslavia and Greece and later the *Wehrmacht* commander for the southeast.

Both courts made clear in their rulings that they applied international law in force at the time of the Control Council's creation. Although the decisions were careful to point out they were not extending "new elements of criminality,"[33] both judgments greatly clarified the limits of a commander's liability for war crimes committed by subordinates. The standard that a commander must have either known of atrocities occurring on his or her watch, or reasonably should have known, before liability could be found, was articulated by the Tribunal's ruling in the High Command Case. Criminality, it concluded, must only attach to a commander for war crimes

> directly traceable to him or where his failure to properly supervise his subordinates constitutes criminal negligence on his part. In the latter case it must be a personal neglect amounting to a wanton, immoral disregard of the action of his subordinates amounting to acquiescence.[34]

The Hostages Case also considered and ruled on the legal issues facing commanders in occupied territory:

> The commanding general of occupied territory having executive authority as well as military command, will not be heard to say that a unit taking unlawful orders from someone other than himself, was responsible for the crime and that he is thereby absolved from responsibility ... [T]his cannot be a defence for the commanding general of occupied territory. The duty and responsibility for maintaining

peace and order, and the prevention of crime rests upon the commanding general. He cannot ignore obvious facts and plead ignorance as a defence. The fact is that the reports of subordinate units almost without exception advised these defendants of the policy of terrorism and intimidation being carried out by units in the field.[35]

As a result of these two rulings, the "knew or should have known" standard of command criminal responsibility, and not a strict standard or "must have known" formulation, which is often attributed to Yamashita jurisprudence, was widely accepted in international law in the last half of the twentieth century. It was incorporated by the US Army in its *Law of Land Warfare* manual in 1956[36] and codified in a protocol to the Geneva Conventions in 1977.[37] The relevant language of this convention for our purposes "is devoted to the special responsibility of a superior who has not taken measures which he was able to take to prevent or repress a breach committed by a subordinate."[38]

Today, the statutes of the International Criminal Tribunals for the Former Yugoslavia (ICTY) and Rwanda (ICTR) use identical language to clarify a military commander's (and also head of state's or responsible civilian government official's), individual criminal liability under the doctrine of command responsibility. UN Security Council resolutions state that culpability attaches where the superior "knew or had reason to know that the subordinate was about to commit such acts or had done so and the superior failed to take the necessary and reasonable measures to prevent such acts or to punish the perpetrators thereof."[39] The penal emphasis is both forward and backward looking. A commander must take all necessary and reasonable measures to halt ongoing war crimes, prevent their future commission where he has reason to know such is likely to happen, and must also investigate and punish those responsible after they have occurred.

In the case of the *Prosecutor* v. *Jean-Paul Akeyesu*,[40] the ICTR applied the doctrine of command responsibility to hold a sitting civilian *bourgmestre* (equivalent to a regional administrative mayor) criminally liable for inciting mass murder. In the Balkans, the ICTY has further clarified the *mens rea* component of command responsibility through rulings in the Delalić (1998)[41] and Blaškić (2000)[42] prosecutions. These judicial developments suggest that the standard of a commander's knowledge is now actual knowledge of the existence of war crimes, which may be proven "through either direct or circumstantial evidence,"[43] as well as an affirmative duty to investigate circumstances of subordinate conduct irrespective of specific reports of atrocities.[44]

More will undoubtedly evolve over the coming decade to develop this strand in international law. The statute of the International Criminal Court applies the "knew or should have known" standard of command culpability owing to the circumstances at the time where a superior fails "to take all necessary and reasonable measures within his or her power to prevent or repress their commission *or to submit the matter to the competent authorities for investigation and prosecution.*"[45]

The Failing of US Courts-Martial in Practice, My Lai to Abu Ghraib

In their classic treatment of the My Lai massacre and its aftermath, *Four Hours in My Lai*, Michael Bilton and Kevin Sim recount how the 1989 documentary of the same name was treated by some reviewers in the US: "[C]ritics complained that it seemed cruel to remind people of such a terrible happening after twenty years,"[46] they noted in their book's introduction—with a fitting response:

> Cruel to whom? To the victims? To the perpetrators? Or cruel to those who would prefer a more comforting view of war? Delusion has always played a big part in war, and the cruelest delusion of all is the tempting idea that war can be something other than it is ..."[47]

War, even when fought in conformance with international law, is tragic. Its results are stark, graphic, ugly, and filled with horrors. The rule of law and the legal doctrine of command responsibility, however, do not pretend otherwise; the law does not delude us when it seeks only to hold accountable those who are responsible for unnecessary and preventable violations of the law of war.

On the morning of 16 March 1968, Task Force Barker of the US Army's Americal Division murdered approximately 500 unarmed and compliant noncombatant civilians in the village of Son My in the Republic of South Vietnam.[48] Victims included numerous women, children, and elderly men. US maps identified the location of the most infamous of these war crimes[49] as My Lai 4. Along with unlawful executions that day, other wanton crimes included "group acts of ... rape, sodomy, [and] killing of detainees. They further included the killing of livestock, destruction of crops, closing of wells, and the burning of dwellings within several subhamlets."[50] Details of this massacre, which at the time of its disclosure to the world was officially called "a tragedy of major proportions,"[51] have been examined exhaustively elsewhere.[52] For our purposes, the following suffices: after painstaking and multiple investigations of the seven cases of officers charged at courts-martial under a theory of indirect command responsibility for war crimes, five would never be adjudicated at trial, including the three most senior accused.

Under the UCMJ, now and during the Vietnam War, commanders at each level in the US military are charged with enforcing standards of discipline and adjudicating allegations of criminal misconduct. They have the ability to file criminal charges against any soldier suspected of an offense when supported by sufficient evidence and the power to convene courts-martial for soldiers assigned to their units. Only officers in command positions may order that a trial be held; when they do so, they act in their capacity as a convening authority. In the land forces, it is usually a commander with a rank of lieutenant colonel and above who convenes a court to dispose of allegations of criminal misconduct. Of the three levels of courts available under the UCMJ, general courts-martial are designed to dispense justice for the most serious of offenses. These cases are almost always convened by a general officer, but the federal statute that created the UCMJ also allows the most senior civilian leadership of the armed services to authorize such trials.[53] However, military justice is above all else a commander's prerogative. Once a criminal complaint is formally filed in a court-martial case, more senior military commanders in the defendant's chain of command may withdraw and dismiss the charge, substitute administrative measures, or take no action at all.[54]

The name most commonly associated with the My Lai massacre is William Calley. His court-martial and convictions were for his direct commission of war crimes; no theory of indirect command responsibility played a role in his prosecution. Other officers were courts-martialed for alleged crimes committed at My Lai, including Captain Ernest Medina, the commander of C Company, 23rd Infantry, to which Calley belonged. Medina was acquitted on involuntary manslaughter charges after the judge instructed the panel of officers hearing his case that the prosecution had to prove Medina's actual knowledge of ongoing war crimes that he had a duty to stop.[55] Captain Medina's jury of five officers, senior in rank to him, took only one hour to deliberate.[56] The brigade commander responsible for the task force, Colonel Oren Henderson, was also tried and found not guilty of all charges.[57] Those avoiding courts-martial that would have determined whether their actions were criminal, however, included the American Division's two general officers, Major General Samuel Koster and Brigadier General George Young, and the unit's chief of staff, Colonel Nels Parson.

Lieutenant General William Peers, who headed the commission that investigated the atrocities at My Lai, later questioned the uneven judicial treatment of the accused. Originally, Koster, Young, and Parson were charged under the UCMJ for dereliction of duty for their failure properly to investigate reports of the massacre and the cover-up of the crimes, as well as their failure to obey orders by not reporting war crimes they knew had been committed. These three most senior officers had all criminal charges filed against them dismissed prior to a trial on the merits. In place of adjudication by a court, they were issued administrative letters of censure and had their service medals revoked. General Peers, a former division commander in Vietnam and a World War II veteran of combat operations in Burma and China with the Office of Strategic Services, could not understand why the cases did not go to trial. "We of the Inquiry," he wrote in 1979, "were intimately familiar with each of the cases, and not only I but all members of the panel felt the commissions and omissions, as listed in the report, were valid and should have been subject to the most rigorous examination."[58]

In early 1968, the American Division had clear orders from multiple higher head-quarters which required that known or suspected war crimes, atrocities, and serious incidents be reported.[59] Division headquarters knew on the day of the massacre that numerous noncombatants were killed during the sweep through My Lai 4. The very afternoon of the killings, General Koster personally countermanded an order from C Company's brigade headquarters that directed Medina to return to the villages to get an accurate account of the number of dead and how they died.[60] General Young and Colonel Parson were similarly told of allegations made by helicopter pilot Warrant Officer Hugh Thompson that large numbers of civilians were dead from indiscriminate US small arms fire in the villages, and not, as initially reported, only the handful killed by artillery strikes on the village's perimeter.

Koster and Young were not the only American Division general officers who avoided courts-martial after being suspected of command responsibility for war crimes. In June 1971, Brigadier General John Donaldson was charged with direct war crimes in the alleged killings of six Vietnamese noncombatants and the unlawful assault on two others.[61] Donaldson had commanded the American Division's 11th Brigade immediately following Colonel Henderson and had even testified at Henderson's court-martial about the location of the report of investigation that Henderson had initially conducted on the March 1968 massacre. Donaldson's charges were also dismissed, again, prior to a court-martial and opportunity for a full trial on the merits.[62] Of course, a bare allegation of misconduct does not mean the alleged acts were actually committed or, if they were, that they amounted to criminal conduct under all attendant circumstances. But the very purpose of a trial is to determine whether there was criminal culpability and, if so, to reach some finality in law. If no culpability exists, one might reasonably think that both the institution and the accused would want to set the record straight, particularly when charges of international war crimes are at issue.

Indicative of the extent of Army senior officers' involvement in war crime investigations during this period in Vietnam, allegations of indirect command responsibility for his unit's misconduct were lodged against yet another Army general officer—by one of the general's own battalion commanders. Several months before Donaldson was charged with war crimes, Lieutenant Colonel Anthony Herbert, a former battalion commander of the 173rd Airborne Brigade, brought courts-martial complaints against its commanding general and deputy commanding officer, Brigadier General John Barnes and Colonel Joseph Ross Franklin. They were charged with violating lawful orders for failing to report to their superiors Herbert's earlier and repeated reports of incidents of detainee abuse within the brigade. Herbert alleged that soldiers under their command had participated in the murder and abuse of detained combatants, including torture by means of electric shock and field-expedient waterboarding.[63] The Army responded by investigating Herbert, attempted to discredit him by portraying him as a serial liar, and suggested the allegations were precipitated by his relief from command. Contemporaneous secret records compiled by the Vietnam War Crimes Working Group, now stored at the National Archives of the US and declassified in 1994, verify the substance of what Herbert insisted he reported at the time. These files indicate that criminal abuses in the brigade were even more widespread than he alleged.[64] Still, the charges against Barnes and Franklin were dismissed in December 1971 without benefit of adjudication by trial.[65]

Thirty-five years later, journalist Seymour Hersh, who helped expose the My Lai atrocities in 1969,[66] brought the name Abu Ghraib to the world's attention as a reporter for *The New Yorker* magazine.[67] The Department of Defense was well aware of allegations of systemic abuse of detainees even before photographs from the Abu Ghraib confinement facility captured attention worldwide. By the summer of 2002, a number of US commanders from company grade to general officer either knew or should have known of law of war violations being committed by their subordinates. They had a legal duty to halt the war crimes and investigate and punish the offenders.[68]

In June and again December 2002, detainees were beaten to death at both the Asadabad[69] and Bagram[70] air bases in Afghanistan. From the summer of 2002 until the spring of 2003, wholesale abuse of detainees at Bagram was rampant. Only one US officer was mildly sanctioned for circumstances surrounding the beating deaths of two Afghan nationals while in the custody of US interrogators. Courts-martial charges were prepared against Army Captain Christopher Beiring for dereliction of his duties,[71] but were later dismissed after a pre-trial hearing into the available evidence; instead, he was administratively reprimanded.[72] Under the UCMJ, a duty may be imposed upon a soldier by "treaty, statute, regulation, lawful order, standard operating procedure, or custom of the service."[73] Still, the pre-trial hearing officer recommended against Beiring's court-martial going forward to trial. No commanders were court-martialed for any part they contributed to the systemic abuses at Bagram. The chief military intelligence interrogator at the air base during the time in question, Captain Carolyn Wood, was redeployed to Abu Ghraib in 2003 and took over interrogations there that August. Despite the recommendation of the Army's Criminal Investigation Command that Wood be court-martialed for dereliction of duty, no charges were ever filed against her.[74]

In 2003, problems of detainee abuse similar to those at US facilities in Afghanistan began occurring more frequently in the Iraqi theater. In February 2004, the International Committee of the Red Cross (ICRC) submitted a report to coalition authorities that outlined numerous allegations of severe mistreatment of detainees in Iraq which constituted "serious violations of International Humanitarian Law. These violations have been documented and sometimes observed while visiting prisoners of war, civilian internees and other protected persons by the Geneva Conventions . . .";[75] the report's executive summary stated:

> In particular they witnessed the practice of keeping persons deprived of their liberty completely naked in totally empty concrete cells and in total darkness, allegedly for several consecutive days. Upon witnessing such cases, the ICRC interrupted its visit and requested an explanation from the authorities. The military intelligence officer in charge of the interrogation explained that this practice was "part of the process."[76]

Of course, any officers in leadership positions who implement such a "process" for a subordinate to execute are creating a *prima facie* case of command responsibility for war crimes. The above example of systemic abuse, regardless of a characterization of the war in Iraq at the time under international law and the status of the detainee in question, is a clear violation of either common article 3 of the Geneva Conventions or a protected person's treatment under the fourth Convention of 1949, which deals with treatment of civilians during time of war.[77]

Before the ICRC report was formally submitted, Army Major General Antonio Taguba was appointed to investigate the detention and internment operations of the 800th Military Police Brigade deployed at forward operating base (FOB) Abu Ghraib. Abu Ghraib, located 20 miles west of Baghdad, had been a notorious execution center under Saddam Hussein's regime where thousands had been systematically tortured and murdered. L. Paul Bremer, the presidential envoy to the Coalition Provisional Authority, ordered it to serve as the Baghdad Central Correctional Facility beginning in July 2003.[78] Two US units were assigned there, the Army's 800th Military Police Brigade commanded by Brigadier General Janice Karpinski and the 205th Military Intelligence Brigade. The 205th commander, Colonel Thomas Pappas, also commanded FOB Abu Ghraib, where the prison itself was located, beginning in November 2003. A command emphasis theater wide in Iraq during the summer of 2003 was the collection of actionable intelligence and the coalition force's "ability to rapidly exploit internees"[79] toward that end. Abu Ghraib's detention operations were a critical component of that emphasis.

Investigation of abuse was already circulating through Department of Defense channels prior to Seymour Hersh publicizing the infamous breaches of international law committed by Army forces at Abu Ghraib. In March 2004, after General Taguba submitted his report on military police practices at the correctional facility, Major General George Fay was appointed to investigate Colonel Pappas's intelligence-gathering activities there. The two reports contained the initial official conclusions and recommendations about abuses at Abu Ghraib.

Since military procedure requires those conducting an investigation to be senior in rank to anyone whose actions may reasonably become the subject of investigation, Fay's inquiry subsequently expanded to include Army Lieutenant General Anthony Jones as a follow-on investigating officer. Jones was tasked to examine "whether organizations or personnel higher than the 205th Military Intelligence (MI) Brigade chain of command, or events and circumstances outside of the 205th MI Brigade, were involved, directly or indirectly in the questionable activities regarding alleged detainee abuse[s] ..."[80] Finally, in August 2004, an Independent Panel to Review DoD Detention Operations submitted its findings—the Schlesinger Report. The panel included two former US secretaries of defense, James Schlesinger and Harold Brown, a former member of Congress, and a retired four-star Air Force general officer. The scope of their inquiry into detainee offenses was even broader than the Jones/Fay investigation.

During her sworn testimony to General Taguba, General Karpinski placed indirect command responsibility for the Abu Ghraib war crimes primarily on three soldiers, two of whom were field-grade military intelligence officers. All were in command positions at the time of the abuses. Karpinski testified that Colonel Thomas Pappas and Lieutenant Colonels Jerry Phillabaum and Steven Jordan bore the brunt of liability.[81]

She seemed vaguely familiar with the standards and conditions under which units of her own brigade were operating, and also complained of inadequate support from her immediate commander, Lieutenant General Ricardo Sanchez.[82] The Taguba Report determined that General Karpinski placed no command emphasis on ensuring her soldiers were trained to standard in detainee operations. Nor were her unit's members basically familiar with the Geneva Conventions and their rules regarding the treatment of prisoners as they related to those interned at Abu Ghraib. General Taguba also concluded that Karpinski had failed to take adequate measures to correct repeated and serious lapses in accountability within her brigade.[83]

As to specific military intelligence personnel at Abu Ghraib, Taguba observed that he "suspect[ed] that COL Thomas M. Pappas, LTC Steve L. Jordan [and two civilian contractors] were either directly or indirectly responsible for the abuses at Abu Ghraib (BCCF) and strongly recommend[ed] immediate disciplinary action . . ."[84] The Jones/Fay investigation concluded that Captain Carolyn Wood, who served at Bagram air base Afghanistan in 2002 and early 2003, also failed in her duties. "Given her knowledge of prior abuses in Afghanistan, as well as the reported sexual assault of a female detainee by three 519 MI BN Soldiers [sic] working in the ICE, CPT Wood should have been aware of the potential for detainee abuse at Abu Ghraib."[85] The investigation added that, "[a]s the Officer-in-Charge (OIC) she was in a position to take steps to prevent further abuse. Her failure to do so allowed the abuse by Soldiers [sic] and civilians to go undetected . . ."[86]

Most importantly, the Schlesinger Report, generated by a panel of the most senior civilian defense experts, applied and found the proper international law standard of command responsibility in its findings concerning Abu Ghraib. "The Panel finds that the . . . commanders of both brigades [the 800th MP and 205th MI] *either knew, or should have known*, abuses were taking place and taken measures to prevent them."[87] Command responsibility for war crimes perpetrated at Abu Ghraib was thus arguably pervasive. Taken together, the findings of the Taguba and Schlesinger inquiries lead to no other reasonable conclusion. If General Karpinski and Colonel Pappas knew or should have known of the abuses committed by their subordinates, and if Karpinski failed to take adequate measures to train her soldiers and correct past known violations of standards for detainee care, and particularly when Colonel Pappas and Lieutenant Colonel Jordan were found "directly or indirectly" responsible for much of the abuse, then the subsequent courts-martial of only those junior enlisted soldiers with direct culpability for the war crimes seems grossly misplaced.[88]

No senior commander ever faced court-martial charges for their role in the Abu Ghraib catastrophe and not a single officer was judicially punished. Despite exhaustive investigations, criminal charges were never brought against General Karpinski, Colonel Pappas, or even the officer in charge of the interrogations, Captain Carolyn Wood. Rather, just as at My Lai 30 years earlier, the Army, through its UCMJ convening authorities, punished those more senior suspects deemed to be responsible with reliefs from command, poor efficiency ratings, unplanned retirements, and administrative reprimands.

Only Lieutenant Colonel Steven Jordan faced a court-martial on eight charges—including the cruelty and maltreatment of those under his care, disobeying orders, dereliction of duty, and lying to investigators.[89] As the case progressed through the military justice system, Colonel Pappas, Jordan's immediate superior, was granted immunity from prosecution in exchange for his testimony against his own military subordinate.[90] If Pappas required immunity to be legally comfortable with his testimony, one must wonder why he, as the senior officer, was not the one charged and subjected to the scrutiny of a trial. Jordan was convicted on a single count of disobeying an order from General Fay not to discuss his case with potential witnesses while the investigation was being conducted. A year later, even that conviction by a jury of Jordan's peers was set aside by the commanding general for the Military District of Washington,[91] during the convening authority's post-trial review. Like William Peers before him, Antonio Taguba thinks that those more senior officers responsible for Abu Ghraib should have been held accountable. During his investigation, while Taguba was trying to impress the seriousness of what happened at Abu Ghraib on the US military's culture of current leaders, one three-star general officer refused to even look at photographs of what American soldiers did there. "I don't want to get involved by looking ...," the unnamed lieutenant general told Taguba.[92] When viewed through the prism of Bagram and Abu Ghraib, the US military's system of justice over the last several years can rightly be called an embarrassment.

Still, a handful of senior military members did speak up. Retired Brigadier General David Irvine wrote in a Human Rights First report that

> [i]t is very clear that cruel treatment of detainees became a common Army practice because generals and colonels and majors allowed it to occur, even encouraged it. What is unquestionably broken is the fundamental principle of command accountability, and that starts at the very top.[93]

That some officers above the rank of mid-grade major found their voice in a crisis of injustice and command irresponsibility was briefly encouraging. Subsequent tragedies at Haditha and Samarra, Iraq, have dampened hope of meaningful change in the military justice system.

Command Responsibility, Haditha and Beyond

More recent developments in US military justice and command responsibility have arisen since the Abu Ghraib scandal. Two new cases of war crimes in Iraq, committed by a few US Marines at Haditha and Army soldiers of the 101st Airborne Division's 3rd Brigade Combat Team near Samarra, provide fresh examples of commanding officers who avoided court adjudication of their actions. To its credit, the Marine Corps initiated prosecutions against both enlisted marines with direct culpability for their crimes and several officers in the chain of command, including a lieutenant colonel. Charges of dereliction of duty against the battalion commander were subsequently dismissed, however, on inapposite legal grounds. Even worse, an Army brigade commander who reportedly issued an illegal order to kill all military-age Iraqi males during the raid outside Samarra was never charged for breach of command responsibility. The colonel received an administrative reprimand; his enlisted subordinates were court-martialed and convicted for their crimes.

On 19 November 2005, elements of Kilo Company, 3rd Battalion, 1st Marines, killed at least 24 civilian noncombatants at Haditha, Iraq.[94] The dead included seven children, three women, and several elderly males. There were a number of combat engagements in and around Haditha that day, including a roadside bomb attack that killed one marine and wounded two others. The marines were also subjected to extensive small arms fire from combatants hiding among civilians throughout neighboring villas. However, the official investigation into the incident conducted by Army Major General Eldon A. Bargewell concluded that some of the marines involved did not follow proper house-clearing techniques—in which they were properly trained—and failed positively to identify targets of fire.[95] As a consequence, a number of innocent women, children, and elderly men were killed, many in their own homes.

Initially, the Marine Corps' command released a press statement that claimed 15 Iraqi civilians had been accidently killed in the roadside bombing and caught up in the crossfire that followed between US and enemy forces. No meaningful military investigation of what occurred that day began until *Time* magazine reporter Tim McGirk presented the results of his inquiry to a US military spokesman in Baghdad three months later.[96] The first Marine Corps investigation into what happened was conducted in mid-February 2006. Colonel Gregory Watt concluded that insurgents had violated the law of armed conflict by engaging the marines with small arms fire from civilian noncombatant houses. His report also found that some marines did not positively identify their targets of fire in two houses, resulting in the deaths of numerous civilian noncombatants.[97] His report recommended that a criminal investigation be launched, although, with the passage of time since the incident, he was skeptical of the likelihood of obtaining evidence suitable for a prosecution.[98]

Since there were indications of command responsibility above the battalion level, Major General Bargewell was appointed to investigate all facets of the Haditha killings. The scope of this inquiry included the marines' training in rules of engagement and house clearing in urban environments, as well as the failure to report the incident and lack of a timely investigation into the civilian casualties. General Bargewell ultimately found that

> house clearing and room clearing techniques were adequately trained by the Marines in accordance with controlling doctrine ... [but] that some of the Marines [*sic*] did not follow proper house and room clearing techniques by failing to PID [positively identify] combatants.[99]

In reference to the command's failure properly to investigate civilian deaths, Barge-well found that "a case of willful dereliction of duty could be made against some individuals"[100] because they refused to inquire more closely into the possibility of war crimes out of concern for protecting their careers and the reputation of their unit. The investigation concluded that this reticence to report war crimes may have been bolstered by a command climate that tended to "discourage the disciplined application of ROE [rules of engagement] and LOAC [law of armed conflict]."[101] A general officer and two colonels received administrative letters of censure for their failure to ensure the killings were adequately investigated in a timely manner.

The most senior officer to be charged under a theory of command responsibility for Haditha and its aftermath was Lieutenant Colonel Jeffery Chessani, Kilo Company's battalion commander. Charged with dereliction of duty for failing to investigate and report the killing of noncombatant civilians, evidence adduced at a pre-trial hearing indicated that some of the Iraqis killed at Haditha were shot in the head at close range, while others may have been shot standing near their car with their hands raised in the air.[102] While the circumstances of the Haditha killings pale in comparison to the scope and intentional nature of the massacre at My Lai, wanton recklessness that results in the death of noncombatants in war is still criminal behavior. Hays Parks, a senior Defense Department lawyer and expert on the law of war, testified that it was clear to him that the killings at Haditha warranted a war crimes investigation. He testified that

> rules were adopted after the My Lai massacre in Vietnam, in which commanders made only cursory inquiries in the days after the mass killing. "The idea is to encourage the commanders to continue the battle but turn over incidents to competent investigators rather than doing it themselves."[103]

Although Chessani's case was referred to a general court-martial, the military judge dismissed the charges before a finding on the merits could be reached in June 2008.[104] The trial judge ruled that decisions by the convening authority for the case, General James Mattis, were subject to the "appearance" of unlawful command influence[105] because a subordinate service lawyer, four pay grades junior to Mattis, had been present on several occasions while he discussed the case with prosecutors.[106] How in the hierarchy of military service a colonel could "appear" unlawfully to influence the decision of a four-star general is less than clear. Both General Mattis and the staff lawyer, Colonel John Ewers, testified that they never discussed the Haditha prosecution, while Mattis testified during the hearing on the motion to dismiss that he was not improperly influenced by anyone.[107] The Marine Corps has appealed the court's ruling and a final decision on the issue remains pending as of this writing.

Less than six months after the tragedy at Haditha, a US Army unit murdered several unarmed Iraqi men at a remote site adjacent to an abandoned chemical plant outside of Samarra, Iraq. Three of the victims' hands were bound with flex-cuffs before they were shot on 9 May 2006, at the site of a suspected insurgent training compound.[108]

Prior to the courts-martial of the four enlisted soldiers charged in the murders, it was revealed that the unit's brigade commander, Colonel Michael Steele, had issued unlawful orders to kill all military-aged males found during the operation. Lawyers for two of the accused soldiers revealed Colonel Steele's illegal guidance just prior to their clients' pre-trial hearing. Colonel Steele subsequently refused to testify at the military hearing, invoking his article 31 UCMJ right to avoid self-incriminating statements.[109]

A subsequent Army investigation conducted by Brigadier General Thomas Maffey concluded only that Steele "issued improper orders to his soldiers that contributed to the deaths of four unarmed Iraqi men during [the] raid."[110] The classified report concluded that Colonel Steele directed his troops shortly before the mission, in specific language that remains undisclosed, that there was no need for his soldiers to distinguish combatants from noncombatants as targets of fire, provided they were military-aged males. This violation of the fundamental law of war principle of distinction by a seasoned US commander arguably reflects a casualness toward enforcing law of war standards similar to those cited in the Bargewell Report about Lieutenant Colonel Chessani's Marine Corps unit at Haditha. "Although the colonel's 'miscommunication' of the rules contributed to the deaths of four unarmed Iraqis, General Maffey wrote, formal charges were not warranted 'in light of his honest belief of the correctness of the mission R.O.E. [rules of engagement].'"[111]

The way ahead for US military justice and the vexing problem of command responsibility remains open. Acknowledging serious deficiencies in the current process is only the first step. A number of former Army lawyers have suggested quite sensible solutions, including law professors Vic Hansen and James W. Smith III. While their proposed remedies hold much promise, the solutions they offer are not without their own shortcomings. Professor Hansen, a former faculty member at the Army's Judge Advocate General's School and now at the New England School of Law, has proposed a specific amendment to the UCMJ that would add a new article 92A to the US military's criminal code that provides additional elements to the existing offense of dereliction of duty. He identifies the new offense as "Criminal Responsibility for Commanders,"[112] and argues that the system currently existing does not provide sufficient incentive for commanders to emphasize compliance with law of war principles.[113] While his observations of the problem are on the mark, and his legislation would clarify the level of knowledge about existing war crimes necessary for a commander to be held criminally liable, the broader problem may be that senior commander derelictions of duty are simply not being prosecuted. A remedy of the statute will add no value if the underlying crimes continue never to be referred for trial in the first instance.

Professor Smith, who teaches at Florida A&M University College of Law, has also proposed a procedural change for processing of courts-martial cases under the UCMJ.[114] He thinks that commanders should be required to receive written advice from their staff lawyer on any issues of command responsibility prior to the initial filing of a criminal charge, known in military practice as a preferral.[115] While this would necessarily build a paper trail that might benefit a commander's subordinates in situations like Samarra, where only junior enlisted soldiers faced prosecution, it could also serve as a further disincentive to bring criminal cases to trial where a superior's responsibility is suspected of playing any meaningful role. Pre-decisional memoranda and the executive branch's deliberative process are routinely excluded from public scrutiny under the Freedom of Information Act,[116] and no court-martial, after all, means no public record of trial proceedings and no attorney discovery.

Stanford University law professor Jenny Martinez seeks a broader solution to problems of command responsibility prosecutions across the spectrum of court systems available to adjudicate them. She suggests a "duty of knowledge" approach is necessary, and argues the time has come to recognize a higher standard that approaches strict liability based on a commander's affirmative duty to discover whether subordinates have committed or are about to commit breaches of the law of war.[117] Although theoretically sound for purposes of criminal prosecution, military commanders simply cannot be expected to assume the role of all-knowing sleuths while conducting combat operations. Anyone who has served in war should acknowledge that commanders have sufficiently robust duties which occupy frenetic days and nights and preclude their being able to know about the conduct of every soldier under their command at all times.

One thoughtful court member has proposed the creation of an independent prosecutor responsible to the judiciary as opposed to the executive branch of government. Writing in the *Thomas Jefferson Law Review*, Missouri Court of Appeals Law Clerk J. Sengheiser has called for an "independent prosecutor, but he or she must be independent of the military, isolated from political pressure and the incident at issue, and must have the authority to initiate proceedings against the highest commanders if there is probable cause to believe they are criminally liable ..."[118] Not persuaded that the history of independent prosecutors in the US reflects an absence of politics, I would go a step further. It is entirely possible that infusing political accountability, through a decidedly political process, into the military justice system is just what it will take to avoid catastrophes like Abu Ghraib in the future. Our institutional military has demonstrated over the past four decades that it is simply not up to the task of adjudicating allegations of command responsibility when senior commanders are involved.

The UCMJ already authorizes politically appointed service secretaries to convene general courts-martial.[119] Congress should create an office of special prosecutor for war crimes to serve as legal advisor to the Secretary of the Army, Navy, and Air Force. Its legal mandate would be strictly limited to advice on war crimes and the special prosecutor would be expected to prefer courts-martial charges against anyone within the scope of the new office's charter, regardless of position, across all branches of service. The service secretaries could then refer cases to trial, if necessary, without institutional restraints of general officers who refuse to get involved in such crucial matters of military justice by "looking." Such a mechanism would serve as a much-needed backstop for existing UCMJ procedure. It would also encourage uniformed convening authorities to let cases go to trial where pre-trial investigations indicate that charges are appropriate and allow the evidence presented there to adjudicate liability, if owing, by revealing what commanders knew and what they did.

Summary

If, as one preeminent law of war scholar has observed, command responsibility in law is "all about dereliction of duty,"[120] and it is applicable where commanders may be held accountable for their omissions to act where duty imposes the requirement, then the US military's failure to prosecute their own senior members for war crimes is a troublesome problem indeed. The application of a legal doctrine grounded in negligence may be turned on itself when left unexercised. When it comes to officers implicated in command responsibility for violations of the law of war, the record suggests that US military justice since the My Lai massacre has proven no more effective in establishing ultimate responsibility for war crimes than the Leipzig trials in the aftermath of World War I. If the institutional armed services cannot be entrusted to police their own ranks, then Congress should pass legislation creating a special prosecutor for war crimes to ensure adjudication of cases by trial on the merits when facts, adduced through investigation of all circumstances, warrant going forward. Honorable men and women of the US armed forces, the citizens of our republic they faithfully serve, and the community of nations deserve nothing less.

NOTES

1. One foremost US law of war scholar identifies this indirect liability with traditional legal analysis as grounded in accomplice theory and *respondeat superior*. See Solis, *The Law of Armed Conflict*, Chapter 10.
2. Parks, "Command Responsibility for War Crimes," 1.
3. For a sampling of the literature see Anderson, *Facing My Lai*; Belknap, *The Vietnam War on Trial*; Bilton and Sim, *Four Hours in My Lai*; Hammer, *The Court-Martial of Lt. Calley*; Hersh, *My Lai 4*; idem, *Cover-Up*; Oliver, *The My Lai Massacre in American History and Memory*; Peers, *The My Lai Inquiry*; Addicott and Hudson, "The Twenty-Fifth Anniversary of My Lai"; Eckhardt, "My Lai"; Paust, "My Lai and Vietnam"; Smidt, "Yamashita, Medina, and Beyond."
4. Congress bears ultimate responsibility for the oversight of US military justice. US Constitution, Art. I, Sect. 8 cl. 14. "Congress shall have Power ... To make Rules for the Government and Regulation of the land and naval Forces."
5. 10 United States Code 801 *et seq.*
6. See Cohen, "A Court for a New America." See also American Society of International Law Task Force Recommendations on US Policy Toward the International Criminal Court.

7. Rome Statute of the International Criminal Court, articles 1 and 20.3.

8. Kahl, "How We Fight," 83.

9. "Get some new lawyers" is a remark attributed to US Secretary of State Madeline Albright in 1999 when told by Foreign Secretary Robin Cook that British legal advisors could not support the air war against Yugoslavia absent a UN Security Council resolution. Byers, *War Law*, 47.

10. Shaw, *International Law*, 70–71.

11. Despite distinctions in convention-based law between international and non-international armed conflicts, this article treats "the law of war" and "the law of armed conflict" as synonymous. "International humanitarian law," an expansive term of more recent development, is integral to the law of war, given its focus on the protection of noncombatant victims of war.

12. Bantekas, *Principles of Direct and Superior Responsibility in International Humanitarian Law*, 67.

13. Sun Tzu, *The Art of War*, 9, qtd. in Parks, "Command Responsibility," 4.

14. Martinez, "Understanding *Mens Rea* in Command Responsibility," 661–62.

15. Green, "Command Responsibility in International Humanitarian Law," 321.

16. Ibid.

17. Articles of War, Provisional Congress of Massachusetts Bay, 5 April 1775, reprinted in Parks, "Command Responsibility," 5. See also Bantekas, *Principles of Direct and Superior Responsibility*, 68. For an early US Supreme Court decision on the legal liability of military commanders for misapplying existing law, regardless of superior orders, see *Little* v. *Barreme* (the *Flying Fish*), 1804.

18. Instructions for the Government of Armies of the United States in the Field, 24 April 1863.

19. Ibid., article 156, emphasis added.

20. Hague Convention No. IV, Annex, article 1.

21. Commission on Responsibility of Authors of War, qtd. in Lippman, "Humanitarian Law," 5.

22. Lippman, ibid., 7.

23. Shaw, *International Law*, 234. The Kaiser avoided trial by taking up residence in the Netherlands, which declined extradition.

24. US Army *Pamphlet, International Law*, 221–22, reprinted in Parks, "Command Responsibility," 13.

25. Walzer, *Just and Unjust Wars*, 322. The quotation regarding the soldier's responsibility to protect the "weak and unarmed" is from General Douglas MacArthur's order affirming the death sentence of Japanese General Tomoyuki Yamashita who was executed by the US Army for war crimes in February 1946. Ibid., 317.

26. *Abbaye Ardenne* Case (1945). Unpublished trial transcript, reproduced in Green, *Essays on the Modern Law of War*, 226–27.

27. *In Re Yamashita* (1946).

28. Landrum, "The Yamashita War Crimes Trial," 294–95, citing Lael, *The Yamashita Precedent*.

29. *In Re Yamashita*, 17. While the Supreme Court highlighted the defendant's breach of duty to control his forces, one law of war scholar finds Yamashita directly culpable for the execution of at least 2,000 suspected Filipino guerillas. See Parks, "Command Responsibility," 27–31.

30. The preamble to Control Council Law No. 10 put forth its purpose to give effect to the Moscow Declaration of 1943, the London Agreement of 1945, and the Charter of the IMT so as "to establish a uniform legal basis in Germany for the prosecution of war

criminals and other similar offenders, other than those dealt with by the International Military Tribunal ..." (The German "High Command Case," 59).

31. *U.S.* v. *Wilhelm von Leeb, et al.* 1948.

32. *U.S.* v. *Wilhelm List, et al.* 1948.

33. *U.S.* v. *Wilhelm von Leeb, et al.*, 67.

34. Ibid., 76.

35. *U.S.* v. *Wilhelm List, et al.*, 69–70.

36. Department of the Army, *Field Manual*, 27-10, 178–79.

37. Additional Protocol I, article 86.2. The United States signed the convention, although the Senate has still to provide its advice and consent. However, as to its binding effect, the command responsibility standards it imposes have been judged to be customary international law. See *Prosecutor* v. *Delalić*, paragraph 343.

38. Sandoz et al., *Commentary to the Additional Protocols*, paragraph 3524.

39. Statute of the ICTY article 7.3, statute of the ICTR article 6.3.

40. *Prosecutor* v. *Jean-Paul Akeyesu*, ICTR No. IT-96-4-T.

41. *Prosecutor* v. *Delalić*, ICTY, No. IT-96-21-T. As to Delalić, it should be noted that the Trial Chamber concluded that he lacked a position of command such that he could be held culpable even if actual knowledge of subordinate criminality were proven. Ibid., paragraphs 718–20.

42. *Prosecutor* v. *Blaškić*, ICTY, No. IT-95-14-T.

43. Ibid., paragraph 307.

44. See *Prosecutor* v. *Blaškić*, paragraph 322.

45. Rome Statute of the International Criminal Court, article 28.1(b), emphasis added.

46. Bilton and Sim, *Four Hours in My Lai*, 9.

47. Ibid., 9–10.

48. Goldstein et al., *Peers Commission Report*, 314, 322.

49. In *Vietnam Studies Law at War Vietnam 1964–1973*, then Judge Advocate General of the US Army Major General George Prugh argued, as an aside, that the atrocities committed by US forces at My Lai did not meet the definition of a "war crime" because the victims were South Vietnamese nationals. South Vietnam being allied with the United States, the victims were not protected persons under the Geneva Conventions and thus no grave breach of the Law of War could be inflicted upon them. Ibid., 102. This view of what constitutes war crimes is an exceedingly narrow one but his point is valid in that, when committed, the crimes were violations of South Vietnamese and US domestic law rather than convention-based international law. His discussion did not assess whether mass murder of civilian noncombatants or insurgents *hors de combat* during a period of non-international armed conflict is a war crime under principles of customary international law.

50. Goldstein et al., *Peers Commission Report*, 315.

51. Peers, *The My Lai Inquiry*, 217. By 1975, the massacre that was a "tragedy" later became in official Department of the Army publications an "occurrence," "aberration," and an "incident." Prugh, *Vietnam Studies Law at War Vietnam 1964–1973*, 113, 114, 158.

52. See, for example, n. 3 above.

53. 10 U.S. Code 822.

54. *Manual for Courts-Martial*, United States, Rules 604, 401, and 407.

55. Goldstein et al., *Peers Commission Report*, 465–68.

56. Bigart, "Medina Found Not Guilty of All Charges on My Lai."

57. Henderson was tried on charges of dereliction of duty for failing to properly investigate the massacre, disobeying lawful regulations which required he report the commission of war crimes of which he had knowledge, and lying under oath to the Board of Inquiry that

investigated the matter. In 1979, General Peers said of the verdict absolving Henderson of criminal accountability, "[i]f his actions are judged as acceptable standards for an officer in his position, the Army is indeed in deep trouble." Peers, *The My Lai Inquiry*, 226.

58. Ibid., 222.

59. Goldstein et al., *Peers Commission Report*, 236, 211–26.

60. Ibid., 258.

61. Beecher, "General, Ex-Aide Accused of Murdering Vietnamese." Lieutenant Colonel William J. McCloskey was charged along with Donaldson for two additional killings. See also *Time Magazine*, "Charge of a General."

62. Robinson, "Army Drops Charges against General Accused of Killing 6 South Vietnamese Civilians."

63. Herbert, *Soldier*, 426. See also *Time Magazine*, "Colonel Herbert v. the Army." Colonel J. Ross Franklin, the deputy commander that Lieutenant Colonel Herbert accused of indirect command responsibility in war crimes, served as a member of Lieutenant General Peers' commission that investigated My Lai. Goldstein et al., *Peers Commission Report*, 366.

64. Nelson and Turse, "A Tortured Past."

65. Herbert, *Soldier*, 434.

66. Hersh, "Lieutenant Accused of Murdering 109 Civilians."

67. Hersh, "Torture at Abu Ghraib," 47.

68. For a compilation of detainee deaths while being held in the custody of US forces, see Shamsi and Pearlstein, *Command's Responsibility*.

69. Schmidt and Priest, "Civilian Charged in Beating Death of Afghan Detainee."

70. Carlson, "The John McCain of Bagram Prison." See also Lasseter, "Day 2."

71. See Department of Defense form 458, Beiring's charge sheet of offenses.

72. Golden, "Years After 2 Afghans Died, Abuse Case Falters"; Lasseter, "Abuse Worse before Guantanamo."

73. *Manual for Courts-Martial*, article 92c(3).

74. Golden, "Years After 2 Afghans Died, Abuse Case Falters."

75. Greenberg and Dratel, *The Torture Papers*, 384.

76. Ibid., 393.

77. Geneva Convention Relative to the Protection of Civilian Persons in Time of War (GC IV), articles 3 and 37.

78. Bremer, *My Year in Iraq*, 133–34.

79. Taguba Report, reprinted in Danner, *Torture and Truth*, 283.

80. Jones/Fay Report, reprinted in ibid., 411.

81. Greenberg and Dratel, *The Torture Papers*, 543–44.

82. Ibid., 529–52.

83. Taguba Report, reprinted in Danner, *Torture and Truth*, 319. Cruel and degrading treatment inflicted upon detainees at Abu Ghraib included:

    [p]unching, slapping, and kicking detainees; jumping on their naked feet; ... [f]orcibly arranging detainees in various sexually explicit positions for photographing; ... [f]orcing naked male detainees to wear women's underwear; ... [f]orcing groups of male detainees to masturbate themselves while being photographed ... [p]ositioning a naked detainee on a MRE Box, with a sandbag on his head, and attaching wires to his fingers, toes, and penis to simulate electric torture; ... [p]lacing a dog chain or strap around a naked detainee's neck and having a female Soldier [*sic*] pose for a picture ... (Ibid., 292)

84. Ibid., 324.

85. Jones/Fay Report, reprinted in Danner, *Torture and Truth*, 559.

86. Ibid.

87. Schlesinger Report, reprinted in Danner, *Torture and Truth*, 351–52 (emphasis added).

88. See Smith, "A Few Good Scapegoats."

89. "Officer to Face Court-Martial on 8 Charges in Abu Ghraib Abuse."

90. Pelton, "Strife at Prison is Shown." So too, Major General Geoffry Miller, a military police officer from Guantanamo, Cuba, who advised the Iraqi theater senior command on how best to obtain "actionable intelligence," invoked his right to remain silent under article 31 of the UCMJ rather than testify in the court-martial of a junior enlisted soldier who was prosecuted for executing Army policies "at the tip of the spear."

91. White, "Army Officer is Cleared in Abu Ghraib Scandal."

92. Hersh, "The General's Report," 58, 59.

93. Shamsi and Pearlstein, *Command's Responsibility*, 3.

94. Bargewell Report, 7.

95. Ibid., 92.

96. Kluger, "How Haditha Came to Light," 29.

97. Watt Report, 6, 5.

98. Ibid., 7.

99. Bargewell Report, 92.

100. Ibid., 23.

101. Ibid., 93.

102. Perry, "Haditha Killings Detailed in Hearing."

103. Ibid.

104. Perry, "Charges against Marine Dropped."

105. Unlawful command influence is prohibited by article 37 of the UCMJ (10 USC 837) which provides in pertinent part:

> No person subject to this chapter may attempt to coerce or, by any unauthorized means, influence the action of a court-martial . . . or any member thereof, in reaching the findings or sentence in any case, or action of any convening authority, approving, or reviewing authority with respect to his judicial acts.

106. Perry, "Charges against Marine Dropped."

107. Ibid.

108. Worth, "Sergeant Tells of Plot to Kill Iraqi Detainees."

109. Ibid. See also Hall, "Accused Soldier Wants Colonel to Testify."

110. von Zielbauer, "Army Says Improper Orders by Colonel Led to 4 Deaths."

111. Ibid.

112. Hansen, "Creating and Improving Legal Incentives for Law of War Compliance," 272; idem, "What's Good for the Goose is Good for the Gander," 412.

113. Hansen, "Creating and Improving Legal Incentives for Law of War Compliance," 248.

114. Smith, "A Few Good Scapegoats," 702.

115. Ibid. See *Manual for Courts-Martial*, United States, Rule 307.

116. 5 U.S. Code 552(b)(5).

117. Martinez, "Understanding *Mens Rea* in Command Responsibility," 660–64.

118. Sengheiser, "Command Responsibility for Omissions and Detainee Abuse in the 'War on Terror,'" 719.

119. 10 U.S. Code 822(4). The Department of Defense Directive on law of war expressly calls for secretaries of the military departments to provide "for disposition, under Reference (g) [the Uniform Code of Military Justice], of cases involving alleged violations of the law of war ...," DOD Directive No. 2311.01E, Subject: DoD Law of War Program at 5.8.4.
120. Dinstein, *The Conduct of Hostilities under the Law of International Armed Conflict*, 238.

REFERENCES

Addicott, Jeffrey F., and William A. Hudson Jr. "The Twenty-Fifth Anniversary of My Lai: A Time to Inculcate the Lessons." *Military Law Review* 139 (1993): 153–185.

Anderson, David L. *Facing My Lai: Moving Beyond the Massacre*. Lawrence: University Press of Kansas, 2000.

Bantekas, Ilias. *Principles of Direct and Superior Responsibility in International Humanitarian Law*. Manchester: Manchester University Press, 2002.

Beecher, William. "General, Ex-Aide Accused of Murdering Vietnamese." *New York Times*, 3 June 1971, 1.

Belknap, Michael R. *The Vietnam War on Trial*. Lawrence: University Press of Kansas, 2002.

Bigart, Homer. "Medina Found Not Guilty of All Charges on My Lai." *New York Times*, 3 September 1971, 1.

Bilton, Michael, and Kevin Sim. *Four Hours in My Lai*. New York: Viking, 1992.

Bremer, L. Paul. *My Year in Iraq*. New York: Simon & Schuster, 2006.

Byers, Michael. *War Law*. New York: Grove Atlantic, 2005.

Carlson, Margaret. "The John McCain of Bagram Prison." *Los Angeles Times*, 2 June 2005, D-11.

Cohen, Roger. "A Court for a New America." *New York Times*, 4 December 2008, op-ed.

Danner, Mark. *Torture and Truth*. New York: New York Review of Books, 2004.

Dinstein, Yoram. *The Conduct of Hostilities under the Law of International Armed Conflict*. New York: Cambridge University Press, 2004.

Eckhardt, William George. "My Lai: An American Tragedy." *University of Missouri-Kansas City Law Review* 68 (2000): 671–703.

Golden, Tim. "Years After 2 Afghans Died, Abuse Case Falters." *New York Times*, 13 February 2006.

Goldstein, Joseph, Burke Marshall, and Jack Schwartz. *The My Lai Massacre and its Cover-up: Beyond the Reach of Law? (Peers Commission Report)*. New York: Macmillan, 1976.

Green, L. C. *Essays on the Modern Law of War*. Dobbs Ferry, NY: Transnational, 1985.

———. "Command Responsibility in International Humanitarian Law." *Transnational Law and Contemporary Problems* 5 (Fall 1995): 319–371.

Greenberg, Karen J., and Joshua L. Dratel, eds. *The Torture Papers—The Road to Abu Ghraib*. New York: Cambridge University Press, 2005.

Hall, Kristen M. "Accused Soldier Wants Colonel to Testify." *Nashville Tennessean*, 6 March 2007, newswire.

Hammer, Richard. *The Court-Martial of Lt. Calley*. New York: Coward, McCann & Geoghegan, 1971.

Hansen, Victor. "What's Good for the Goose is Good for the Gander, Lessons from Abu Ghraib: Time for the United States to Adopt a Standard of Command Responsibility Towards its Own." *Gonzaga Law Review* 42 (2006/2007): 335–414.

———. "Creating and Improving Legal Incentives for Law of War Compliance." *New England Law Review* 42 (2008): 247–273.

Herbert, Anthony. *Soldier*. New York: Holt, Rinehart & Winston, 1973.

Hersh, Seymour M. "Lieutenant Accused of Murdering 109 Civilians." In *St. Louis Post-Dispatch*, 13 November 1969.

———. *My Lai 4: A Report on the Massacre and its Aftermath*. New York: Random House, 1970.

———. *Cover-Up: The Army's Secret Investigation of the Massacre at My Lai 4*. New York: Random House, 1972.

———. "Torture at Abu Ghraib." *The New Yorker*, 10 May 2004, 42–47.

———. "The General's Report." *The New Yorker*, 25 June 2007, 58–69.

Kahl, Colin H. "How We Fight." *Foreign Affairs*, November/December 2006, 83–101.

Kluger, Jeffrey. "How Haditha Came to Light." *Time*, 12 June 2006, 28–29.

Lael, Richard L. *The Yamashita Precedent: War Crimes and Command Responsibility*. Wilmington, DE: Scholarly Resources, 1982.

Landrum, Bruce D. "The Yamashita War Crimes Trial: Command Responsibility Then and Now." *Military Law Review* 149 (Summer 1995): 293–301.

Lasseter, Tom. "Abuse Worse before Guantanamo." *Miami Herald*, 16 June 2008, 1.

———. "Day 2: U.S. Abuse of Detainees was Routine at Afghanistan Bases." *McClatchy Washington Bureau*, 16 June 2008.

Lieber, Francis. (Lieber Code) *Instructions for the Government of Armies of the United States in the Field* (General Order No. 100), 24 April 1863.

Lippman, Mathew. "Humanitarian Law: The Uncertain Contours of Command Responsibility." *Tulsa Journal of Comparative and International Law* 9 (2001): 1–93.

Martinez, Jenny S. "Understanding *Mens Rea* in Command Responsibility." *Journal of International Criminal Justice* 5 (2007): 638–664.

Nelson, Deborah, and Nick Turse. "A Tortured Past." *Los Angeles Times*, 20 August 2006, 1.

"Officer to Face Court-Martial on 8 Charges in Abu Ghraib Abuse." *New York Times*, 27 January 2007, 18, <http://query.nytimes.com/gst/fullpage.html?res=9A0CE1DB173FF934A15752C0A9619C8B63> (accessed 14 September 2009).

Oliver, Kendrick. *The My Lai Massacre in American History and Memory*. Manchester: Manchester University Press, 2006.

Parks, William H. "Command Responsibility for War Crimes." *Military Law Review* 62 (1973): 1–104.

Paust, Jordan J. "My Lai and Vietnam: Norms, Myths and Leader Responsibility." *Military Law Review* 57 (1972): 99–187.

Peers, William R. *The My Lai Inquiry*. New York: W. W. Norton, 1979.

Pelton, Tom. "Strife at Prison is Shown." *Baltimore Sun*, 19 October 2006.

Perry, Tony. "Haditha Killings Detailed at Hearing." *Los Angeles Times*, 1 June 2007, A8.

———. "Charges against Marine Dropped." *Los Angeles Times*, 18 June 2008, 3.

Prugh, George S. *Vietnam Studies Law at War 1964–1973*. Washington, DC: Department of the Army, 1975.

Robinson, Douglas. "Army Drops Charges against General Accused of Killing 6 South Vietnamese Civilians." *New York Times*, 10 December 1971, 18.

Sandoz, Yves, Chrostopher Swinarski, and Bruno Zimmermann, eds. *Commentary on the Additional Protocols of 8 June 1977*. Geneva: Martinus Nijhoff, 1987.

Schmidt, Susan, and Dana Priest. "Civilian Charged in Beating Death of Afghan Detainee." *Washington Post*, 18 June 2004, A1.

Senghelser, Jason. "Command Responsibility for Omissions and Detainee Abuse in the 'War on Terror.'" *Thomas Jefferson Law Review* 30 (2008): 693–721.

Shamsi, Hina, and Deborah Pearlstein. *Command's Responsibility: Detainee Deaths in U.S. Custody in Iraq and Afghanistan.* Report. New York: Human Rights First, 2006.

Shaw, Malcolm N. *International Law.* New York: Cambridge University Press, 2003.

Smidt, Michael L. "Yamashita, Medina, and Beyond: Command Responsibility in Contemporary Military Operations." *Military Law Review* 164 (2000): 155–234.

Smith, James W. III "A Few Good Scapegoats: The Abu Ghraib Courts-Martial and the Failure of the Military Justice System." *Whittier Law Review* 27 (2006): 671–724.

Solis, Gary. *The Law of Armed Conflict: International Humanitarian Law in War.* New York: Cambridge University Press, forthcoming November 2009.

Sun, Tzu. *The Art of War.* Translated by L. Giles. Harrisburg, PA: Military Service Publishing, 1944.

Time Magazine. "Charge of a General." 14 June 1971, <http://www.time.com/time/magazine/article/0,9171,909864,00.html> (accessed 14 September 2009).

———. "Colonel Herbert v. the Army." 22 November 1971, <http://www.time.com/time/magazine/article/0,9171,905528,00.html> (accessed 14 September 2009).

von Zielbauer, Paul. "Army Says Improper Orders by Colonel Led to 4 Deaths." *New York Times*, 21 January 2007, 10.

Walzer, Michael. *Just and Unjust Wars.* New York: Basic Books, 2000.

White, Josh. "Army Officer is Cleared in Abu Ghraib Scandal." *Washington Post*, 10 January 2008, 6.

Worth, Robert F. "Sergeant Tells of Plot to Kill Iraqi Detainees." *New York Times*, 28 July 2006, 8.

CASES, CODES, PROTOCOLS, REPORTS, AND STATUTES

Abbeye Ardennes Case. <http://www.ess.uwe.ac.uk/wcc/meyer.htm#8.%20THE%20 PROSECUTOR'S%20CLOSING%20ADDRESS> (accessed 14 September 2009).

American Society of International Law Task Force Recommendations on US Policy Toward the International Criminal Court, 2 February 2009, <http://www.asil.org/pdfs/pressreleases/pr090202.pdf> (accessed 14 September 2009).

Articles of War, Provisional Congress of Massachusetts Bay, Act of 5 April 1775.

Bargewell Report. On file with the author and available at <http://warchronicle.com/TheyAreNotKillers/DefendOurMarines/TopicIndex/EvidenceRoom.htm> (accessed 14 September 2009).

Constitution of the United States of America.

Department of the Army. *Field Manual 27-10, The Law of Land Warfare*, July 1956.

Department of the Army. *Pamphlet 27-161-2, International Law,* vol. II, October 1962.

Department of Defense Directive, Subject: DoD Law of War Program, Number 2311.01E (2006).

Department of Defense Form 458 (Beiring Charge Sheet). On file with the author and available at <http://media.mcclatchydc.com/smedia/2008/06/03/12/Behring.source.prod_affiliate. 91.pdf> (accessed 14 September 2009).

Geneva Convention Relative to the Protection of Civilian Persons in Time of War (GC IV). 12 August 1949; 6 U.S.T. 3516, 75 U.N.T.S. 287.

Hague Convention No. IV, Respecting the Laws and Customs of War on Land. 18 October 1907; 36 Stat. 2277, 205 Consol. T.S. 539.

ICTR No. 96-4-T. *Prosecutor v. Jean-Paul Akeyesu* (1998).

ICTY No. 96-21-T. *Prosecutor v. Delalić* (1998).

ICTY No. 95-14-T. *Prosecutor v. Blaškić* (2000).

In Re Yamashita, 327 U.S. Supreme Court Reports 1 (1946).

Little v. *Barreme* (the *Flying Fish*), 6 U.S. Supreme Court Reports (2 Cranch) 170 (1804).

Manual for Courts-Martial. United States (2008).

Protocol I Additional to the Geneva Conventions of August 12, 1949. 8 June 1977, 16 I.L.M. 1391.

Rome Statute of the International Criminal Court. 17 July 1998, 37 I.L.M. 999.

Statute of the International Criminal Tribunal for the Former Yugoslavia. <http://www.icty.org/x/file/Legal%20Library/Statute/statute_sept08_en.pdf> (accessed 14 September 2009).

Statute of the International Criminal Tribunal for Rwanda. <http://69.94.11.53/ENGLISH/basicdocs/statute/2007.pdf> (accessed 14 September 2009).

United States v. *Wilhelm von Leeb, et al.* ("The High Command Case"). 1948, Trials of War Criminals before the Nuremberg Military Tribunals under Control Council Law No. 10.

United States v. *Wilhelm List, et al.* ("The Hostages Case"). 1948, Trials of War Criminals before the Nuremberg Military Tribunals under Control Council Law No. 10.

Watt Report. On file with the author and available at <http://warchronicle.com/TheyAreNotKillers/DefendOurMarines/TopicIndex/EvidenceRoom.htm> (accessed 14 September 2009).

5 United States Code 552(b)(5) 2007.

10 United States Code 801 *et seq.* 1994.

10 United States Code 822 2006.

10 United States Code 822 (4) 2006.

10 United States Code 837 1968.

INDEX

Page numbers in *Italics* represent tables.
Page numbers in **Bold** represent figures.

For Product Safety Concerns and Information please contact our EU
representative GPSR@taylorandfrancis.com Taylor & Francis Verlag GmbH,
Kaufingerstraße 24, 80331 München, Germany

Batch number: 08153807

Printed by Printforce, the Netherlands